Customer Worthy:

Total Customer Engineering

Design, Measure, and Optimize Every Customer Interaction with the 90-Cell CxC Matrix and AI

Michael R. Hoffman

Author of Customer Worthy | Creator of the CxC Matrix

Customer Worthy Publishing · www.customerworthy.com

AF720223

Customer Worthy: Total Customer Engineering

First published as Customer Worthy, 2010. This **Total Customer Engineering Design, Measure, and Optimize Every Customer Interaction with the 90-Cell CxC Matrix and AI** represents a comprehensive revision and expansion incorporating artificial intelligence, the Customer Sensor Economy, and the CxC Matrix 2.0 architecture.

For permissions, speaking engagements, and consulting inquiries: mrh@customerworthy.com | 908-542-1134

ISBN: 979-8-9952226-3-7 (Paperback)

For every executive who has ever stared at a phone on hold

and thought: there has to be a better way.

There is.

And for the 500,000+ readers of the first edition — whose questions,

implementations, and challenges made this edition possible.

Table of Contents

Sitting on hold with my own cell phone carrier, I ran the arithmetic: sixty million subscribers, twelve minutes of average hold time, three service calls per customer per year. The product was ninety-nine billion dollars — annihilated not through malice but through indifference. Through sixty million customer journeys that no one had designed.

That napkin became the first edition of Customer Worthy.

The book introduced the CxC Matrix — the Customer by Contact Matrix — which mapped fifteen lifecycle stages against six interaction channels to produce ninety cells. Each cell was a moment where your company meets your customer. Each was either designed with intention or left to improvisation. More than five hundred thousand readers downloaded that edition. Implementations spread across financial services, healthcare, retail, and enterprise technology. And in every engagement, the same pattern appeared: companies that designed all ninety cells outperformed the ones that designed twenty and improvised the rest.

But what those implementations taught me — the thing I had not fully appreciated when I wrote the first edition — is that the framework was most powerful not in the dramatic failures like Dot's, but in the smallest, most overlooked moments.

Consider a grocery store receipt.

Two items. Eight dollars and fifty-eight cents. Handed across a counter in two seconds and forgotten before the customer reaches the parking lot. Most companies treat that slip of paper as a financial record — a legal artifact, nothing more. But look at it through the CxC Matrix and it becomes something else entirely: a container with a dozen open slots. A chance to acknowledge the customer by name. A moment to connect a cashier to a human interaction rather than a transaction. An opportunity to suggest a recipe using what the customer just bought, surface their loyalty progress, share a story about the farm the produce came from, or extend an offer so relevant it feels like a gift rather than a promotion.

None of those improvements require a budget line. They require a decision — a deliberate choice to treat every customer touchpoint as an experience worth designing.

The receipt and Dot's nightmare are not opposites. They are the same problem at different scales. One is a passive moment of zero — an interaction that took nothing and gave nothing, that could have compounded value and instead dissolved into noise. The other is an active moment of catastrophic negative — an interaction that consumed twenty hours, generated one hundred thirty-two thousand dollars in destroyed value, and created permanent, searchable, shareable documentation of organizational failure across fourteen thousand five hundred people who will never know Dot's name but will remember the story.

Both represent the same fundamental failure: *an interaction that was not engineered.*

THE NEW ARITHMETIC

Fifteen years after that napkin, the National Customer Rage Survey puts revenue at risk from poor customer experience at eight hundred eighty-seven billion dollars. Customer rage has tripled since 2020. And yet companies earning one billion dollars annually can add seven hundred million within three years of genuine customer experience investment. The gap has never been wider. The return has never been higher.

What changed is not the framework. It is the stakes on both sides.

While waiting on hold on Dot's behalf, I did what any connected professional does today: I created content. Using AI tools on my phone, I produced LinkedIn posts, two YouTube videos, 3 videos on X, and a detailed public analysis — most of it drafted while the hold music played. Within three days, that content reached fourteen thousand five hundred people. It is still accumulating views. It is indexed permanently. It cannot be recalled.

The total value destroyed by Dot's experience — her time, her suffering, her husband's anger, the company's labor costs, lost lifetime revenue, and that permanent reputational damage — calculated to one hundred thirty-two thousand dollars.

To collect a disputed nine hundred dollar charge where she had video proof.

That could have been resolved in fifteen minutes.

By one empowered employee.

With access to integrated systems.

Now hold that number against the receipt.

Multiply eight dollars and fifty-eight cents by every customer who passed through that store last year. Multiply it by every passively handled moment — every hold queue, every unanswered chat, every automated email that addressed a human being as "Dear Valued Customer," every return process that treated a loyal patron as a suspect, every ninety-cell interaction matrix where sixty of the cells were simply never considered. That is not a napkin number. That is the hidden economy sitting inside your existing customer relationships, untouched, undesigned, and compounding in the wrong direction.

Total Customer Engineering is the discipline of reversing that direction — systematically, measurably, permanently.

WHAT THIS BOOK IS

Customer Worthy: Total Customer Engineering is a field manual for building organizations that do not produce Dots and do not waste receipts. Not because it is the right thing to do — though it is — but because it is now the commercially decisive thing to do.

By the time you finish, you will have a complete map of every interaction your customers have with your organization — the ones you are managing and the ones you are not. You will have a financial model that attaches a dollar value to every cell in that map, turning customer experience from a budget argument you lose into a capital allocation argument you win. You will have a measurement system built on what customers actually do — not what they say on surveys — that sees departures months before they happen.

Specifically, you will leave with:

— A model for the customer who lives simultaneously in physical, digital, hybrid, and synthetic worlds — and a framework for designing every one of those environments with intention.

— The CxC Matrix 2.0: a single visual and economic tool your entire organization can use to find the five to fifteen million dollars in hidden value sitting in the gaps between departments that have never examined each other's work.

— A measurement system built on behavioral data — not survey scores — that identifies at-risk customers months before they leave.

— A practical guide to making AI work for your customers rather than at their expense — where every automation compounds trust instead of quietly eroding it.

— A repeatable method to transform every interaction — the eight-dollar receipt, the thirty-minute hold queue, the enterprise renewal conversation — into a platform that builds value instead of consuming cost.

The examples are drawn from live deployments and real organizations. The frameworks have been used in boardrooms, war rooms, and project rooms across industries. This is not a memoir of interesting projects or a forecast of distant futures. It is a practical engineering system built for the world as it exists right now.

Dot eventually got her refund.

It took one letter from an attorney and twenty minutes for the charges to vanish. Twenty minutes. After twenty hours, six months, and one hundred thirty-two thousand dollars in destroyed value that no marketing budget will ever fully restore.

Somewhere today, a customer is standing at a register being handed an eight-dollar receipt. She will glance at it and drop it in her bag. The company will record the transaction and move on. No one will ask what else that moment could have been. No one will calculate what it costs, multiplied across a year of customers, to treat every small interaction as a financial record rather than a relationship event.

Consider two numbers. The first: 74% of American consumers experienced a product or service problem in the past year—the highest level ever recorded. The second: a customer paying your company $45,000 a year, retained for an average of 6.5 years, who refers 1.8 additional customers over that period, is worth $857,000 in total customer value. Lose that customer at the negotiation stage and you don't lose a $45,000 contract. You lose $857,000—and transfer it directly to a competitor.

Most organizations cannot calculate that number. They cannot tell you the economic value of a single customer interaction at a specific lifecycle stage in a specific channel. They cannot tell you which of their ninety possible customer touchpoints are generating value and which are quietly destroying it. They cannot tell you where customers are silently departing—not because they complained, but because they stopped expecting things to change.

This book gives you the system to see all of that. And then to fix it.

• • •

The CxC Matrix maps fifteen lifecycle stages—from the moment a customer becomes aware of a need through the moment they become an advocate who recruits the next customer—against six interaction channels. The result is ninety cells, each one a specific moment of truth, an economic event, and a competitive decision point. Most companies consciously manage about twenty of their ninety cells. The other seventy are happening anyway—without design, without measurement, and without anyone accountable for the experience the customer is having there.

The Nine Objectives framework ensures that every customer interaction—every call, every email, every website visit, every delivery—achieves not one business purpose but up to nine. The average organization captures two or three objectives per interaction. The ones that capture seven or eight transform their customer contact infrastructure from their largest expense line into one of their most productive revenue platforms.

The Customer Experience Algorithm moves beyond backward-looking satisfaction scores to real-time behavioral measurement that predicts what customers will do next—with enough lead time to change the outcome. The customer who stopped logging in, stopped contacting support, stopped responding to outreach isn't satisfied. They're leaving. The behavioral signals are visible months before the departure—if your measurement system is built to see them.

AI transforms every layer. Not as an abstraction about the future—as operational capability available now. AI that scores customer propensity in real time and activates the right response at the right moment. AI that simulates the impact of a price change or a service reduction across your entire customer base before you implement it. AI that identifies the $14 million in hidden value sitting in the gaps between departments that have never examined each other's work simultaneously.

And underneath all of it—the question that every chapter, every framework, every calculation in this book is designed to make answerable:

Is this Customer Worthy?

Not in the abstract. For this customer, at this stage, in this channel, right now—is this interaction creating certainty, building memory, and winning the next stage of the relationship? Or is it creating the gap that a competitor will fill?

Begin with Chapter One. By the time you finish the book, you will never look at a receipt, a hold message, a delivery notification, or a renewal email the same way again. Every one of them is a cell in the Matrix. Every one of them is either designed or defaulted. And the difference between those two states is worth more than most organizations have ever calculated.

That calculation is where we begin.

CHAPTER ONE

My Car Talked to My House

And My Office Was Jealous

The Future of Connected Customer Experience — Which Is Already Here

"The future is already here. It's just not evenly distributed."

— William Gibson

Gibson wrote those words as a novelist. They have since become the operating thesis of competitive strategy. The future of customer experience is not arriving uniformly — it is landing in concentrated bursts, in specific industries, for specific customers, in isolated moments of breathtaking seamlessness surrounded by decades-old frustration.

Which means the most important question for any executive, manager, designer, or student reading this book is not whether the connected customer future will arrive. It already has. The question is whether your organization will be among those delivering it — or among those left explaining to customers why you still are not.

> ***"The future of customer experience is not a destination. It***

> ***is a competitive position — occupied now by some, and urgently available to others."***

To make this concrete, let's follow a day in the life of Neil — an ordinary customer living an increasingly extraordinary connected life. Neil's story is composite, drawn from technologies and experiences that exist today across automotive, energy, retail, healthcare, and financial services. Every interaction he has is real, or within twelve months of being real.

Pay attention not just to what delights him — but to what goes wrong. Because both are instructive. And in the gap between the two lies the entire business case for this book.

A Day in Neil's Connected Life

7:10 AM The Ecosystem Wakes Before He Does

Neil's alarm hasn't gone off yet when the coordination has already begun.

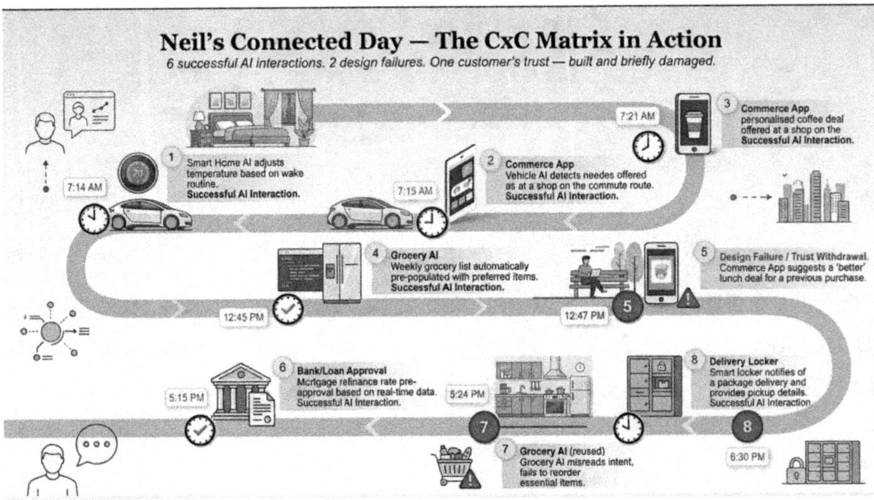

His electric vehicle, parked in the garage, finished charging overnight — not at 11 PM when he plugged it in, but at 2 AM, when the grid hit off-peak pricing. His utility company designed this benefit specifically to reward customers who allow intelligent scheduling. Neil didn't configure it. He simply said yes to the feature once, eighteen months ago, and has saved an estimated $340 since.

His thermostat, connected to the same home intelligence hub, registered his sleep pattern shift at 6:55 AM and began warming the house accordingly. The heating system didn't blast on when he finally got up — it was already there, invisible, effortless.

His smartwatch surfaces a single notification: "Your 9 AM client call is confirmed. Current route shows 23 minutes. Traffic is building — you should leave by 8:28. Want me to send a heads-up to the client?"

He blinks, mumbles "yes," and his office AI assistant — receiving the instruction through a single authenticated integration — fires off a polite, professional message to the client: a brief note that Neil may be two minutes late, no explanation required.

> **CXC MATRIX OBSERVATION**
>
> Before Neil has eaten breakfast, no fewer than seven distinct customer interactions have occurred: a utility rate optimization, a charging confirmation, a thermostat adjustment, a calendar-traffic cross-reference, a commute time calculation, a proactive notification, and an outbound client message. Six of the seven were machine-to-machine. Neil consciously participated in one. Each one was a contact. Each one either built or risked eroding his trust in the companies behind it.

This is not science fiction. It is the baseline expectation being established right now, in this decade, for customers who have experienced it once. Once Neil has lived this morning, he will never willingly return to a world where he has to call the utility company, manually check traffic, and draft his own "running late" emails. The companies that give him this experience have not merely satisfied him. They have structurally altered what he considers acceptable.

12:45 PM The Value Exchange That Feels Like a Gift

On his lunch break, Neil's car voice system surfaces an offer: "Hi Neil — your vehicle is approaching its 6-month service interval. Your preferred dealership has availability next Tuesday at 10 AM, which your calendar shows is open. Confirm?"

He confirms. The appointment is made, added to his calendar, and a confirmation lands in his inbox — all before he has finished his sandwich.

Fifteen seconds later: "There's a coffee shop 0.4 miles from your office offering 20% off to our vehicle owners through the end of the month. Interested?"

Neil says yes. The GPS routes him there. His digital wallet loads the discount code. He walks in, orders his usual, pays with his phone, saves $2.40, and leaves in under four minutes.

Trivial? Consider what just happened. The car company created a monetizable partnership with a local business. The coffee shop acquired a high-income customer it might never have reached otherwise. Neil received a frictionless perk that reinforced his positive feeling about his vehicle manufacturer — a feeling that, at renewal time, will be worth far more than $2.40. Every party won. No party was manipulated. The exchange worked because it was contextually relevant, transparently offered, and genuinely useful.

> ***"The best customer interactions feel less like commerce and more like someone who knows you doing you a favor. The companies that engineer this at scale will own the next decade."***

5:15 PM **When Automation Crosses the Line**

Not everything in Neil's day is seamless. And the failures are as instructive as the successes.

Driving home, a notification flashes across his dashboard console: "Annual solar panel permit renewal — $625 due. Approve?"

Neil, distracted, glances down and says "Approve." The system processes the payment from his saved card. It is done before he has processed what he agreed to.

Five minutes later, his spouse calls to ask him to stop for groceries. The car's AI — interpreting the word "groceries" as an actionable signal — begins reading off a suggested order from his household's most recent shopping list.

Neil shouts "Stop."

The system pauses. Recalibrates. Apologizes in a measured, friendly tone.

He appreciates the apology but is annoyed by the assumption. He was talking to his wife. He was not issuing a procurement instruction to an AI agent. The system could not tell the difference, and that gap — between a customer's intent and a system's interpretation — is where trust goes to die.

> **DESIGN PRINCIPLE: THE IRREVERSIBILITY PROBLEM**
> Automation that executes irreversible actions — payments, commitments, deletions — must operate at a higher consent threshold than automation that merely suggests. The $625 permit approval deserved a friction-positive confirmation, not a frictionless one. The engineering challenge for companies building AI-powered customer interactions is not just how to say yes on a customer's behalf. It is knowing precisely when to pause and ask. Every misread intent is a trust withdrawal. Overdraft enough of them and the account closes.

6:30 PM **The Quiet Satisfaction of Things That Simply Work**

The rest of Neil's evening requires nothing of him.

The package he ordered that morning is in his smart locker. The delivery app sends a confirmation and a single five-star rating prompt. He taps it without thinking — not because he was asked to, but because it genuinely reflected his experience. His utility app updates his dashboard: today's charging cost, projected monthly savings, current solar generation. His home, car, and energy systems present a unified picture of his household in a single interface.

He feels — without being able to articulate exactly why — that the companies serving him today earned their place in his life. Not because they asked him how he felt. Because they made it effortless to feel good.

That is the goal. That is the standard. That is what Customer Worthy means, operationalized.

What Neil's Story Teaches Us

Neil's day is not a fantasy. It is a composite of technologies and business models that are live, scaled, and already setting expectations across industries. The lessons embedded in it are not abstract — they are operational mandates.

Every Micro-Contact Compounds

Most companies manage a handful of interactions they consciously control: the outbound call, the renewal notice, the service response script. Meanwhile, dozens of micro-contacts — the charging confirmation, the route reroute, the permit payment, the delivery notification — accumulate invisibly into the customer's total experience of the brand.

Those micro-contacts are not noise. They are signal. Each one either reinforces or erodes the customer relationship. Companies that treat them as infrastructure — rather than experience — are managing only part of the system. And in a connected ecosystem, a partial system is a liability.

Ecosystems Outcompete Products

The car company that serves Neil well doesn't just sell him a vehicle — it becomes the hub through which he manages energy, scheduling, service, and commerce. The utility company that intelligently schedules his charging is not just an electricity provider — it is a financial advisor with a grid. Once a customer's life is woven into your ecosystem, you are no longer competing on features or price. You are competing on switching cost, and switching cost built on genuine utility is the most durable moat in business.

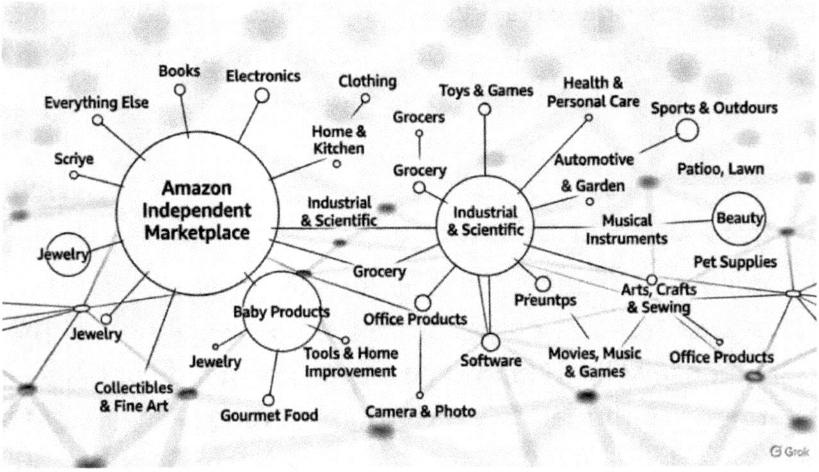

The data is instructive: 62% of Amazon's sales now come from independent marketplace sellers. Amazon's core competitive advantage is not its own inventory — it is its position as the customer's preferred starting point for commerce. Any company in any industry can pursue an analogous strategy by asking: how do we become the hub through which our customers experience not just our category, but adjacent ones?

Automation Must Serve, Not Assume

The grocery list incident and the $625 approval are not minor UX issues. They are early symptoms of a design philosophy that optimizes for automation without calibrating for consent. The most dangerous version of this is not a frustrated customer shouting at a car. It is a customer who quietly stops trusting the system, disables the features, and tells three people why.

> ***"Customers will forgive a company that makes a mistake. They will not forgive a company that makes it clear their preferences are an afterthought."***

Technology Is the Vessel. Humanity Is the Substance.

Neil's satisfaction at the end of his day did not come from the sophistication of the technology. It came from feeling understood. The car's AI apologizing gracefully. The coffee offer arriving at exactly the right moment. The delivery app asking for his feedback rather than assuming it. These are not technical achievements — they are design choices. Human-centered design choices, embedded in technical systems.

Every company building AI-powered customer interactions must hold both truths simultaneously: the technology must work flawlessly, and the human must feel seen. One without the other is either a broken product or a cold one.

The Challenge Ahead: Complexity at Scale

Neil's story illustrates the possibilities. It also reveals the operating complexity that organizations must be prepared to navigate. This is not a technology problem alone. It is a coordination, trust, data, and organizational design problem at simultaneous scale.

Data Coordination Across Competing Interests

For Neil's morning to work — for the car, the grid, the thermostat, the calendar, and the office AI to coordinate seamlessly — significant data sharing must occur across systems owned by different companies, operating under different privacy frameworks, with different security architectures. This is technically achievable today. It is legally and commercially complex, and getting more so as regulation matures.

The practical implication: your legal, IT, and partnership teams are now customer experience assets. Data-sharing agreements are customer experience decisions. API architecture is customer experience strategy. These conversations can no longer happen in silos — they must happen in the same room where customer journey design happens.

Trust as Infrastructure

Every automation is a trust wager. Most of the time, you win and the customer barely notices. When you lose — when the $625 clears before the customer has finished the word "approve" — the trust account takes a hit that advertising cannot repair.

Research consistently shows that more than three-quarters of consumers will abandon a company they no longer trust with their data. Security and transparency are not compliance functions. They are customer experience commitments. Customers need to understand, in plain language, what data flows through their connected life, who touches it, and what happens when something goes wrong. Companies that explain this clearly gain trust. Companies that bury it in terms-of-service documents lose customers the first time anything goes wrong.

Cross-Organizational Orchestration

Neil's seamless day required genuine coordination between his car manufacturer, his utility company, his employer's IT systems, a local coffee shop, a delivery service, and a permit authority. None of these organizations share an org chart. All of them contributed to his experience of the day.

The companies leading in connected customer experience are not merely building better internal systems. They are building the partnership architectures, shared data standards, and API ecosystems that allow multiple organizations to coordinate on a single customer's behalf. That is a different organizational muscle than most companies have yet developed — and building it is an urgent priority.

The Technology Making This Possible

Understanding Neil's world requires a working vocabulary of the technologies creating it. This is not a technology book — but executives and managers who cannot speak fluently about these tools are increasingly unable to lead the organizations building with them.

IoT and Ambient Intelligence: The Product Becomes the Channel

The Internet of Things has matured well beyond smart thermostats and connected refrigerators. Today's sensor ecosystems operate as ambient intelligence networks — continuously reading customer context without requiring explicit instruction. Today, the installed base of IoT devices has surpassed 18 billion globally, with projections exceeding 30 billion by 2030.

The practical implication for customer experience is architectural. Every physical product with a sensor becomes a live node in your customer relationship — capable of initiating contacts, responding to context, and updating data across multiple systems simultaneously. A connected medical device doesn't just measure — it alerts, schedules, and coordinates care. A connected vehicle doesn't just transport — it monitors, recommends, books, and pays. The product is no longer just the thing you sell. It is the ongoing service delivery mechanism through which the relationship lives.

AI Agents: From Assistants to Autonomous Actors

The era of voice assistants answering simple queries has given way to something far more consequential: autonomous AI agents that plan, decide, and act across multi-step tasks on a customer's behalf. Platforms emerging from OpenAI, Anthropic, Google, and Microsoft now enable agents that don't just retrieve information — they book travel, compare insurance, process returns, and negotiate contracts without human intervention on either side of the transaction.

For businesses, this creates both an obligation and a competitive threat. Your product listings, pricing logic, return policies, and support knowledge bases must now be legible to machines, not just humans. If an AI agent is shopping on a customer's behalf and your systems are not designed for machine readability, you will not be considered. You will simply be bypassed. Forward-thinking companies are already publishing AI-optimized catalogs, structured data schemas, and API-accessible knowledge bases designed specifically for agent-to-agent interaction.

> **STRATEGIC IMPLICATION: THE INVISIBLE COMPETITOR**
>
> When AI agents transact on behalf of customers, the traditional contact points you have engineered — the email campaign, the sales call, the in-store interaction — may be mediated or bypassed entirely. Companies that structure their customer-facing systems for machine readability today will be discoverable by AI agents tomorrow. Companies that do not will be invisible. This is not a five-year problem. It is a now problem.

Model Context Protocol: The Connective Tissue

One of the most significant under-reported developments reshaping enterprise AI is the emergence of Model Context Protocol — MCP. Introduced by Anthropic and rapidly adopted across the industry, MCP is an open standard that allows AI models to connect directly and securely to external tools, databases, APIs, and live data sources. Think of it as a universal language that lets an AI agent communicate simultaneously with your CRM, your inventory system, your customer service platform, and your fulfillment engine — in real time, across organizational boundaries.

For customer experience professionals, MCP is the connective tissue that finally makes the AI-powered CxC Matrix operational at scale. Instead of fragile point-to-point integrations that break when one system updates, companies can expose their core systems through MCP-compatible servers and allow AI agents to pull context, execute transactions, and update records fluidly across the entire customer lifecycle. Salesforce, Microsoft, Google, HubSpot, and dozens of enterprise software vendors have already launched or announced MCP-compatible integrations.

This is not a future capability. It is being deployed now. Organizations that lag in MCP readiness risk losing the ability to participate in agentic customer interactions entirely — not because competitors out-marketed them, but because their systems simply could not be found.

Platform Ecosystems and the Matter Standard

Apple HomeKit, Google Home, Amazon Alexa, and Samsung SmartThings are no longer consumer novelties — they are established distribution channels for customer experience. The more significant development is the Matter standard: a cross-industry protocol backed by Apple, Google, Amazon, and Samsung that allows devices from different manufacturers to interoperate natively. For companies selling physical products,

Matter compatibility has moved from competitive differentiator to baseline expectation.

The same ecosystem dynamics are consolidating in B2B settings through platforms like Snowflake's data marketplace and Databricks' lakehouse architecture. Companies that expose well-documented APIs and participate in relevant platform ecosystems dramatically expand the reach of their customer interaction channels without proportional increases in overhead. Those that remain closed face progressive marginalization as customers migrate toward integrated, AI-mediated experience environments.

Case Study: Tesla and the Art of Ecosystem Loyalty

Tesla is the most instructive example in the customer experience canon — not because of its vehicles, but because of what its vehicles are attached to.

Tesla sells electric cars, home battery storage (Powerwall), and solar panels. These products don't merely coexist — they think together. When your home battery runs low and your Tesla is plugged in overnight, the system automatically negotiates energy priority: the car yields charging to keep the house running. You didn't configure this. You didn't ask for it. It simply happened, correctly, because the system understood your actual priorities better than any manual setting could.

One app ties the entire ecosystem together — vehicle status, home energy usage, solar generation, climate control — a single window into a connected household. The more Tesla products a customer owns, the more indispensable the system becomes. This is not lock-in through contract — it is lock-in through genuine, compounding utility. The switching cost is not financial. It is functional. Leave the ecosystem and you lose the intelligence.

Amazon has built the same dynamic in the home. John Deere has built it in agriculture, where tractors, soil sensors, and irrigation systems coordinate to help farmers make better decisions faster than any combination of competing tools allows. The product has become the platform — and the platform has become the relationship.

> ***"When your products connect into a unified customer experience, you stop competing on features and start competing on ecosystems. That is a fundamentally harder race to run against you."***

The lesson is not specific to consumer electronics or automotive. It applies to any company in any industry willing to ask: how do we design our products and services to compound in value the more deeply a customer uses them together? The answer to that question is worth more than any single product improvement.

Early Indicators of Competitive Advantage

You do not have to wait for a quarterly results presentation to know whether your customer experience architecture is working. The signals are visible earlier — if you know what to look for.

Integration Depth

The clearest leading indicator is usage. How many of your customers have activated your connected features? How frequently are they using your app, your API integrations, your partner-linked services? Customers who have embedded your product into their daily connected life don't just have higher satisfaction scores — they have structurally elevated switching costs. Once Neil's car manages his energy, his calendar, his service appointments, and his coffee discount, the question is no longer "is he satisfied?" It is "what would it cost him to leave?"

Partner Ecosystem Momentum

When other companies begin approaching you to build integrations with your platform, you have crossed a critical threshold. You are no longer a vendor — you are infrastructure. Amazon's early lead in third-party voice integrations was not just a technical achievement; it was a market signal that Alexa was becoming the default starting point for connected commerce. Track the number and quality of external developers and partners building on your APIs. Growth in that number consistently precedes growth in customer adoption by twelve to eighteen months. It is one of the most reliable leading indicators in the ecosystem economy.

Retention in Connected Segments

Watch for measurable differences in retention between customer segments using your connected features and those who are not. Across multiple industries — automotive, healthcare, financial services, retail — early deployments of proactive, AI-coordinated service have produced measurable drops in customer attrition when compared with reactive, customer-initiated contact. This is not coincidence. It is the financial payoff of building an experience architecture that eliminates friction before the customer feels it.

Internal Conversations Crossing Old Boundaries

Here is an indicator that most leadership teams overlook: the conversations happening in your own hallways. When your hardware engineers talk regularly with your data scientists. When your marketing team brainstorms with product development about embedding AI into onboarding. When someone in finance asks whether your CRM could trigger proactive outreach based on a customer's IoT usage pattern.

That is a culture signal worth more than a strategy deck. The connected customer experiences that define markets rarely emerge from a single planned initiative. They emerge from organizations where curiosity and cross-functional collaboration have become daily operating habits — where someone, somewhere, is always asking: how does this decision affect our customers?

> **THE ORGANIZING QUESTION**
> These four signals — integration depth, partner momentum, connected-segment retention, and internal cross-functional energy — are your early warning system for whether you are building a customer experience architecture that compounds over time. The companies that will dominate the next decade are not necessarily the ones with the largest marketing budgets or the most advanced individual features. They are the ones engineering customer experiences so seamlessly useful, so genuinely woven into daily life, that leaving simply is not worth it.

What Comes Next

Neil's day introduced us to the operating terrain. The chapters ahead will give you the frameworks, the metrics, and the organizational design tools to build it.

In Chapter 2, we will introduce the CxC Matrix — the 15-stage, 6-channel, 90-cell framework that turns Neil's morning into a map of measurable decisions. You will see how each of his contacts plots to a specific cell in the matrix, and how that mapping transforms an intuitive story into an auditable economic model. In Chapter 3, we will extend that framework into the CxC Matrix 2.0 — the evolution from a static strategic grid to a dynamic, sensor-fed system that learns and optimizes in real time.

But before we go there, hold this: the connected customer future is not waiting for permission. It is being built right now, by companies in your industry and adjacent ones, by customers whose expectations are being reset with every seamless interaction they have. The question is not whether to engage with this transformation. The question is what role you will play in it.

Think Like a Customer.

Let's begin.

return form yourself. The company remained passive — processing you.

A customer today is, for the first time in commercial history, being actively choreographed. AI is beginning to orchestrate customer experience — at every lifecycle stage, across every channel, in every interaction — in ways that are simultaneously invisible and extraordinary. The right product reaches you before you go looking. The service call resolves before you make it. The renewal offer reflects what you actually value, not what the company wishes you valued. The delivery arrives when you are actually home.

> *"We are entering an era where customer experience is no longer left to chance, to whoever picks up the phone, or to whether the right employee is in a good mood. It is being engineered — deliberately, measurably, at a scale no human team could manage alone."*

That is an extraordinary statement. It is also entirely accurate. And here is the catch that makes this book necessary.

AI does not choreograph great customer experiences from thin air. It needs a framework — a coordinate system, a structure that tells it where the customer is in their relationship with you, what they have already experienced, what they are likely to need next, and what the optimal response looks like right now. Without that framework, AI does not solve your customer experience problem. It accelerates your existing one, at industrial scale.

That framework is the CxC Matrix.

What the CxC Matrix Actually Is

The Customer by Contact Matrix — the CxC Matrix — is a structured map of every meaningful interaction a customer can have with your organization, built on two dimensions that, when plotted against each other, reveal the complete architecture of your customer relationship.

CxC Matrix — Customer Life Stage by Contact

	1. Awareness	2. Information	3. Identification	4. Selection	5. Negotiation	6. Contract	7. Logistics	8. Delivery	9. Renewal	10. $ Collection	11. Use	12. Care/Support	13. Repair	14. Disposal	15. Community
Geography															
Digital															
Location															
Third Party															
One-on-One															
Community															

CxC Matrix by Customer Worthy, a ClientxClient Company 908.542.1134

The horizontal axis is the 15-stage customer lifecycle — from Stage 1: Awareness, the moment a need sparks into consciousness, through Stage 15: Community, where loyal customers become active advocates and your brand reputation compounds through peer-to-peer influence without additional marketing spend.

The vertical axis is your channel architecture — the six contact channels through which your company and your customer actually meet. Plot these two dimensions against each other and you get a grid — a matrix — with 90 distinct cells, each representing a specific type of interaction at a specific stage of the customer relationship.

Every Cell Is Three Things Simultaneously

Every cell in the CxC Matrix is a moment of truth — where the customer updates their impression of your brand. Every cell is an economic event — generating or destroying quantifiable value. And every cell is a competitive decision point — where the customer either advances toward deeper loyalty with you, or begins the quiet drift toward your competitor.

Most companies consciously manage perhaps 20 of their 90 cells. The other 70 are happening anyway — without design, without consistency, without measurement, and without accountability. The CxC Matrix makes all 90 visible. And once they are visible, they can be managed — and monetized.

There is a reassuring truth and a challenging one that belong together here. The reassuring truth: the fundamentals of what makes a great customer experience have not changed and will not change. Customers want to feel known. They want their needs met efficiently and with some degree of warmth. They want certainty — confidence they made the right choice. None of that is altered by AI. If anything, AI raises the stakes, because it raises the baseline expectation for how well a company should be able to know and serve each individual customer.

The challenging truth: the operational requirements for delivering great customer experience have changed dramatically, and they are going to keep changing faster than most organizations are currently prepared to manage. Channels multiply. Data volume explodes. The customer's synthetic representation starts making decisions before the human customer is even involved. The competitive bar lifts continuously. The CxC Matrix was built for exactly this environment — complex, multi-channel, data-rich, AI-enhanced, and relentlessly customer-centric.

The Competitor in the Room

Here is the conversation most customer experience frameworks never have — and the reason traditional journey mapping consistently underdelivers on its promise.

Your customer is not just moving through a relationship with you. They are simultaneously being pursued by every competitor you have. At every stage of the lifecycle, in every channel, your competitors are studying your customers, modeling your gaps, and crafting interventions designed to pull them sideways before they reach the next stage with you.

This is not a peripheral concern. It is the central drama of the customer lifecycle — and it is most acute in Stages 3, 4, and 5, before the relationship has deepened enough to create genuine loyalty. The CxC Matrix is designed to address both defection causes simultaneously: the reactive recovery of customers who have experienced problems, and the proactive reinforcement of customers who are perfectly happy — but not yet deeply committed enough to resist a well-timed competitive approach.

> *"Dissatisfied customers are not your only defection problem. Satisfied customers defect too — because a competitor made a better offer at exactly the right moment, in exactly the right channel, with exactly the right framing. You didn't lose because you failed. You lost because you weren't present."*

The Competitive Interception Window

A customer in Stage 3 (Identification) has not yet committed. They are, by definition, actively evaluating. Every day they spend identifying options without a clear, compelling reason to choose you is a day a competitor can insert a better narrative.

A customer in Stage 5 (Negotiation) is signals-rich: they have told you what they care about, what trade-offs they are willing to make, and where their threshold of acceptable value lies. Your competitors, if they are watching, can read those same signals. AI negotiation agents on the customer's behalf are arriving at Stage 5 with full information parity — real-time market pricing, historical discount patterns, knowledge of which terms are fixed versus negotiating positions. The CxC Matrix treats these high-defection windows not as sales problems to be solved by the commercial team — but as customer experience design problems the entire organization must address.

The 15-Stage Customer Lifecycle — The Architecture of Every Commercial Relationship

The 15 lifecycle stages of the CxC Matrix are not a theory derived from focus groups. They are the map of the commercial experience every customer has, in every category, in every industry — from the moment a need enters their awareness to the moment they become part of the community of advocates who extend your brand without additional cost to you.

What makes the framework operationally powerful is the direct correspondence between each lifecycle stage and the business functions and departments inside your organization that produce that stage's experience. The company that maps its customer stages to its organizational functions does not merely understand the customer journey better. It gains the ability to ask at each stage: Who owns this? Who is accountable for this customer's experience right here? And what does the performance of this cell cost us — or earn us — at full Customer Value Index?

Neil's Morning, Mapped

The story in Chapter 1 was intentional. Neil's morning is not a marketing scenario. It is a CxC Matrix audit. Every interaction he experienced maps to a specific cell — a coordinate defined by one lifecycle stage and one contact channel. Those coordinates are the unit of competitive analysis in everything that follows.

At **7:10 AM**, Neil's Tesla sent a notification that overnight charging was complete and pre-conditioning had begun. That is **Stage 11 (Use) × Digital channel**. The company designed this cell: an automated, proactive touchpoint during the use stage delivered through the digital channel. No human intervention. Zero marginal cost per interaction. Maximum relevance — exactly when Neil needed it, exactly because the system knew he would.

His **coffee shop mobile order** is **Stage 10 (Transaction) × Digital channel**. The transaction itself is a designed cell — an exchange with zero wait time, personalized order memory, and a loyalty mechanism built into the completion event. Compare that to the coffee shop that takes his order at the counter, hands him a receipt, and considers the transaction closed. Same Stage 10. Different cell design. Measurably different economic outcome.

The **insurance app's safe-driving acknowledgment** is **Stage 11 (Use) × One-to-One channel**. This cell is designed to interrupt the silence between renewal cycles — the long, unmanaged stretch of Stage 11 where most insurers are entirely absent. The company chose to be present. The design decision was deliberate. The financial implication — reduced churn at renewal, increased upsell probability, reduced claims cost from reinforced safe behavior — is calculable.

The **package delivery notification** that reached him before he noticed the box on his porch is **Stage 12 (Service) × Digital channel**. Proactive service contact, digital channel, at the exact moment the service event occurs. The alternative — the cell that is not designed — is silence followed by a customer wondering where their package is, then a support call, then an agent interaction that costs twelve dollars to handle what the automated notification prevented for twelve cents.

Four interactions. Four cells. Four design decisions — each one either made deliberately or left to default. Each one with a different economic consequence depending on whether the organization chose to be present, intentional, and intelligent at that coordinate. This is the unit of analysis the CxC Matrix was built to make visible. From here, we map all ninety.

Stage	Lifecycle Stage	Business Function	Primary Channels	Defection Risk	CxC Win-Rate Lever
S1	**Awareness**	Marketing / Brand / AI Signals	*Digital · Community*	**MODERATE**	Ambient need-detection; be present before the search begins
S2	**Information**	Content / Digital / AI Search	*Digital · Third Party*	**HIGH**	Machine-readable content; AI-retrievable authority
S3	**Identification**	Sales Engineering / AI Curation	*Digital · One-to-One*	**CRITICAL**	Intelligent shortlisting; stated + inferred preference matching
S4	**Selection**	Sales / Pre-Sales / AI Configuration	*Digital · Location · 1:1*	**CRITICAL**	Situational fit; prescriptive bundle; environmental configuration
S5	**Negotiation**	Sales · Legal · AI Agents	*One-to-One · Digital*	**CRITICAL**	Information parity; full-scope terms transparency; agent-ready pricing
S6	**Contract**	Legal / Finance / Operations	*Digital · One-to-One*	**HIGH**	Friction removal; one-click; every payment method; zero hesitation
S7	**Logistics**	Supply Chain / Fulfillment / 3PL	*Digital · Location*	**MODERATE**	Benefit-start timing; real-time visibility; buyer-type segmentation

Stage	Lifecycle Stage	Business Function	Primary Channels	Defection Risk	CxC Win-Rate Lever
S8	**Delivery**	Operations / Field Service	*Location · One-to-One*	**MODERATE**	Right-level delivery (bare-bones to white-glove); AI-configured
S9	**Acceptance**	Implementation / Onboarding / CX	*Location · Digital · 1:1*	HIGH	Shareability design; 9 Objectives; proper onboarding → +55% retention
S10	**Payment**	Finance / AR / Billing Platforms	*Digital · One-to-One*	**MODERATE**	Every currency; BNPL; loyalty points; community-contribution credit
S11	**Use**	Product / Customer Success / IoT	*Digital · All Domains*	**MODERATE**	Four domains: analog, digital, hybrid, synthetic; autonomous value
S12	**Care & Support**	Customer Service / AI / Self-Heal	*Digital · One-to-One*	HIGH	Self-healing products; 24/7 AI + expert escalation; proactive resolution
S13	**Repair**	Field Service / Tech Ops / Partners	*Location · Community*	**MODERATE**	Preventive IoT repair; hero-level recovery; intimacy in crisis

Stage	Lifecycle Stage	Business Function	Primary Channels	Defection Risk	CxC Win-Rate Lever
S14	**Disposal**	Reverse Logistics / ESG / Sustain.	*Third Party · Digital*	LOW	End-of-life = re-entry to S1; ESG transparency; refurbish/recycle
S15	**Community**	Marketing / Comm. Management / AI	*Community · All*	LOW	Social + digital + tech + empathetic layers; compounding flywheel

What the table above reveals — and what most org charts deliberately obscure — is that the customer lifecycle does not care how your company is structured internally. The customer moves through all 15 stages. The experience they receive at each stage is the product of your organizational choices, your technology investments, your partner relationships, and your culture. It is also the product of whether your competitors have shown up in that stage before you did.

Stage 1: Awareness — The Moment the Clock Starts, and It May Start Without You

Every customer relationship begins with a spark. But here is what has changed: that spark is increasingly lit not by your marketing department, but by the world around your customer — and increasingly, by AI systems operating quietly in the background of their lives.

A finance manager reads about a competitor's data breach and suddenly prioritizes the cybersecurity solution their IT team has been requesting for two years. A student stumbles across a 47-second TikTok of someone making perfectly crispy Brussels sprouts in an air fryer and a product category they'd never considered becomes an immediate want. These are the awareness stories we recognize. But here is the awareness story we are entering now, and it changes everything about how you think about Stage 1.

A customer's refrigerator camera captures a bottle of orange juice running low and cross-references it against health monitoring data suggesting increased Vitamin C consumption this week. Awareness of a need: created. A smart power meter registers that a twelve-year-old washing machine is drawing 40% more electricity than its rated consumption — a signature pattern that predicts imminent motor failure. Awareness of an impending problem: created, before the problem occurs. A safety notification published quietly by a product manufacturer is surfaced by an AI system scanning product registrations against published safety databases in the background. Awareness: created by machine, on behalf of human, before the human knew to look.

This is not science fiction. The component technologies — computer vision, IoT monitoring, AI-powered database scanning, purchase history integration — are operational today in various combinations across various industries. Their convergence into a seamless, ambient awareness layer is not a question of whether but when. What this means for your CxC Matrix at Stage 1: Awareness is no longer exclusively a marketing function. It is increasingly a data, AI, and product intelligence function. The question is not just 'where are we advertising?' but 'what signals in our customers' environments indicate an emerging need, and how quickly can we surface relevant awareness in a way that feels helpful rather than intrusive?'

> *The companies that answer that question well will be present at the moment of need creation. Everyone else will arrive three weeks later, after the customer has already formed a shortlist.*

Stage 2: Information — The Research Gauntlet, Now With an AI Co-Pilot

The need has been identified. Now the customer goes looking for answers. But 'looking' today looks nothing like it did five years ago. The Information stage is where a customer tries to understand how best to meet their need — and 'context' is the operative word. Not just 'what solves this problem' but 'what solves this problem for me, in my situation, with my constraints, at this moment.'

That context is rich and multi-dimensional: urgency, affordability, environmental fit, user aptitude, family or team dynamics, sustainability preferences, social context. In the previous era, assembling that picture required a skilled salesperson who had known a customer for years. In the AI era, behavioral data, situation analysis, device ecosystem data, purchase history, search patterns, and inferred preferences can assemble a remarkably accurate picture of this context automatically — and use it to surface information genuinely fitted to this specific person rather than a generic response to a generic query.

More than 80% of consumers research online before making a significant purchase, often consulting sources your company doesn't control. They're asking AI assistants that synthesize multiple sources into a single conversational answer. They're reading Reddit threads and industry forums where your brand's reputation is being shaped by people you've never spoken to. They're watching YouTube comparisons produced by creators whose editorial independence they trust more than your marketing copy.

The operational implication is twofold. First, your content must be machine-readable — structured for AI retrieval, accurate in third-party databases, present in the formats and platforms where AI assistants source their answers. If a customer asks an AI assistant to help them research options in your category and your product isn't accurately represented, you don't lose a consideration — you never enter one. Second, your AI-enhanced Information stage tools should be doing the context assembly work that previously required expert salespeople: understanding not just what the customer is asking, but why — and what information will genuinely help them make the best decision, even if that decision isn't your product. That last clause is the one most companies can't bring themselves to operationalize. The companies that can build trust no competitor's budget can easily undo.

Stage 3: Identification — The Cut List, Curated by Intelligence

The research phase generates options. The Identification stage narrows them. But the criteria driving that narrowing are more complex, more personal, and more AI-legible than most companies design for.

Identification includes both the preferences the customer can articulate and the ones they can't. The customer knows they want something under $400. They may not consciously know that they consistently choose products with minimal visual complexity — but their purchase history shows it. They know they want something that works with their existing smart home setup. They may not have explicitly stated a preference for sustainable materials — but their browsing and social engagement patterns suggest it strongly.

Expert AI identification works by integrating all of these signals — stated preferences, inferred preferences, behavioral signals, environmental constraints, and contextual requirements — to filter the universe of options down to a genuinely fitted shortlist rather than a keyword-matched list. A spatial AI cross-references product dimensions against the customer's known counter space or available installation area — eliminating options that physically don't fit before the customer wastes time considering them. A compatibility AI checks the product against every other device in the customer's ecosystem. A sustainability AI scores options against the customer's inferred environmental preferences. A social proof AI weights options based on the specific peer groups this customer actually trusts

— not aggregate star ratings, but the ratings of people whose taste and situation most closely matches theirs.

> *The Identification stage in its AI-enhanced form is not a filter. It is a curation — an intelligent narrowing that respects the full complexity of what 'right for this customer' actually means.*

Stage 4: Selection — The Arena, Equipped With Every Advantage

The customer has a shortlist. Now they are comparing finalists. And AI is transforming Selection from a passive evaluation into an active, dynamic, personalized experience that meets the customer exactly where they are — situationally, financially, temporally, and environmentally.

An AI-powered Selection experience knows this customer is currently standing near a retail location that has three of their shortlisted products in stock, available for immediate physical inspection. It knows the customer has an urgent timeline — the old appliance failed three days ago — which changes the weighting dramatically: in-stock availability and same-day pickup move up; features that require a two-week delivery wait move down. It knows a competing product is on sale this week at a nearby retailer. It surfaces all of this context automatically, without the customer having to research each variable separately.

Selection in the AI era also means prescriptive pricing and bundle configuration — not just 'here's what it costs' but 'here's the optimal configuration for your situation.' The customer who needs installation services, has two other devices that benefit from an extended warranty bundle, and whose usage patterns suggest they'll want the premium accessories within 90 days of purchase receives a configured offer that packages all of this with transparent pricing — ideally before they've asked for it. Upcoming release dates for next-generation models are flagged transparently, because a customer who buys the current model three weeks before a significant upgrade announcement becomes a dissatisfied customer, and an AI that surfaces that information proactively becomes a trusted advisor.

The Selection stage in its AI-enhanced form presents not just a product but the totality of a solution — product, configuration, services, financing, support resources, environmental fit, and timing — assembled specifically for this customer's complete situation. That is a categorically different experience than a product page with a star rating and an 'add to cart' button.

Stage 5: Negotiation — Expert Advocacy, Now on the Customer's Side

The customer has mentally selected. Now comes the negotiation — and in the AI era, the customer is no longer negotiating alone or underprepared.

For most of commercial history, negotiation was asymmetric. The seller knew their margin, their inventory position, their competitive situation, their authority to discount, and the full range of what was on the table. The buyer knew their budget and their desire. The seller almost always had the information advantage. That asymmetry is being dismantled — not gradually but rapidly.

AI negotiation agents operating on behalf of buyers now arrive at Stage 5 with information parity that no individual buyer could previously achieve: real-time market pricing across competitors, historical price trend data, knowledge of the seller's typical discount patterns, understanding of which terms are genuinely fixed versus negotiating positions, and the patience and consistency that no human buyer can fully maintain in a live negotiation. And the scope of negotiation has expanded: price, yes, but also warranty terms and what specifically they cover, service level agreements and their performance conditions, delivery timing and installation scheduling, add-on inclusions, trade-in credit, training access, data privacy terms, return and cancellation conditions, and performance guarantees with remedies attached.

> *The companies that win in AI-mediated negotiation aren't the ones that try to out-maneuver the customer's agent. They're the ones that make their genuine value so clear, their terms so transparent, and their configured solutions so well-fitted to the customer's situation that the agent concludes — accurately — that this is the best available deal.*

The Full Economic Cost of a Stage-5 Loss

A customer lost at Stage 5 costs far more than the immediate contract. Calculate the full CxC value: immediate contract revenue lost, plus the entire projected Customer Value Index (LTV + referral revenue + social advocacy + brand equity contribution). In most industries, losing a customer at Stage 5 to a direct competitor is a six-figure event when calculated at full CVI — even if the individual contract was modest.

For our mid-market B2B example: a $45,000 annual contract represents $857,000 in full CVI. A Stage-5 experience investment of $20,000–$50,000 is not a cost against a $45,000 sale. It is a return on an $857,000 relationship. The CxC Matrix makes this math visible — permanently changing every Stage-5 resource allocation conversation.

Stage 6: Contract — The Moment of Commitment

The deal is made. The customer clicks buy, signs the agreement, submits the purchase order. This should be the easiest stage in the entire journey — pure friction removal — and yet nearly 70% of online shopping carts are abandoned because something in the Contract stage created doubt or difficulty.

An unexpected shipping cost. A mandatory account creation. A payment form that didn't accept the customer's preferred method. A terms scroll that implied something the customer hadn't bargained for. These are not conversion optimization problems. They are Contract stage design failures with measurable revenue costs — losses from customers who had already decided to buy.

Leading companies treat Contract as sacred: one-click purchase, every payment method the customer might prefer, e-signature for anything requiring a signature, auto-fill everything possible, trust signals placed precisely where doubt tends to emerge. The economic calculation is simple: every friction point you remove at Stage 6 converts directly to revenue from customers who had already decided. The ROI on Stage-6 friction elimination is among the highest in the entire matrix.

Stage 7: Logistics — Time, Proximity, and the Experience of Waiting

Logistics has been revolutionized by Amazon and now needs to be rethought again — because what's being delivered, when the benefit starts, and how the customer measures 'arrival' are all more complex than a tracking number suggests.

Consider the temporal dimension: for a physical product, delivery means the product reaches the customer's door. But when does the benefit start? For software, benefit starts at download — potentially seconds after purchase. For a service subscription, benefit starts at account activation. For a product requiring professional installation, benefit doesn't start until a certified installer has completed their work — which might be two weeks after the box arrives on the porch. The CxC Matrix should map the logistics stage against benefit-start timing, not just delivery-completion timing, because the customer's experience of waiting is measured against when they expected to begin receiving value.

Proximity is increasingly a logistics variable — not just 'when will it arrive' but 'where is it right now and how does that affect my options?' A customer who discovers that three units are in a store 2.3 miles away and available for immediate pickup may choose a different logistics path than the one they initially selected — if your system offers that visibility and flexibility in real time. First-time versus repeat buyer logistics design is another dimension most companies flatten inappropriately. A first-time buyer needs guided options, clear explanations, and reassurance. A repeat buyer who has purchased the same product category twelve times wants previous preferences auto-applied and the minimum possible friction between decision and confirmation.

Stage 8: Delivery — From Bare Bones to White Glove, and Everything Between

The product arrives. The service begins. This is the first moment the customer encounters your company through something other than a screen, and the quality of that moment is your first opportunity to confirm that their decision was right.

The delivery experience exists on a spectrum, and AI can now configure that spectrum dynamically based on what each customer's situation and preferences actually call for. At the bare-bones end: fast, reliable, frictionless. The product arrives when promised, in good condition, with clear next steps. For repeat buyers of familiar products, elegance is speed and accuracy, not ceremony. At the white-glove end: the delivery team calls 48 hours ahead to confirm timing, arrives within a two-hour window, removes and disposes of the old product responsibly, installs the new one, tests it to full operation, walks the customer through key features in person, and doesn't leave until the customer confirms they're comfortable.

Between these poles lies a spectrum of configured options: curbside drop-off, in-home placement without installation, delivery-plus-unbox-assist, delivery with same-day installation scheduling, delivery with tutorial QR code and a follow-up call the next day. AI-configured delivery means the right option is offered to the right customer based on what the system knows about their situation, their previous delivery preferences, the complexity of the product, and the resources available in their geography. Nine in ten customers believe companies should 'know their needs' and deliver immediate value from the first moment of contact. The delivery stage, designed with this standard in mind, is not logistics — it is the opening act of the customer's experience with your product.

Stage 9: Acceptance — The Verdict, and the Broadcast

The customer has the thing. Now they are deciding whether it lives up to the promise. This is the Acceptance stage — the unboxing, the setup, the first use, the moment of truth that determines whether the gap between expectation and reality closes or widens.

The physical ritual of acceptance has been transformed by social media into a performance. Unboxing videos on YouTube collectively generate billions of views annually. The moment of opening a package is now frequently a broadcast — shared with followers, friends, and communities who are simultaneously experiencing the product vicariously and forming opinions about it. Your packaging, your presentation, your first-impression contents are not just functional — they are potentially broadcast content, and they should be designed with that reality in mind.

This connects directly to the 9 Objectives of Every Interaction framework that runs throughout the CxC Matrix — specifically the objective of creating a shareable experience. The Acceptance stage is one of the highest-shareability moments in the entire customer lifecycle. Companies that design acceptance experiences with shareability as an explicit objective — packaging that photographs beautifully, first-use moments that generate genuine delight, personal touches that feel worth commenting on — are creating marketing content at the customer's hands, at the customer's initiative, with a credibility no paid placement can match. And the data is unequivocal: proper onboarding at Stage 9 improves long-term product usage by 55% and dramatically increases retention. This may be the single highest-leverage intervention in the entire post-purchase experience.

Stage 10: Payment — Every Currency, Every Configuration

Money changes hands. And today, 'money' is a more creative concept than it has ever been.

Nearly one in five Americans used buy-now-pay-later services recently, reflecting a fundamental shift in how customers prefer to align payment timing with value realization. Subscription models have multiplied to the point where the average consumer has more recurring charges than they can name from memory. Cryptocurrency transactions are operational in enough retail and B2B contexts to require a policy position. Loyalty points as full or partial currency — Starbucks made this mainstream, but airlines, hotel chains, credit card programs, and an expanding range of retailers have followed.

But the truly creative payment frontier involves configurations most companies haven't considered. Bartering and in-kind exchange: a customer who generates significant referral traffic or content value might negotiate a partial exchange of that value for product or service credit — a configuration economically rational for both parties but requiring deliberate system design to execute. Community contribution credit: platforms that reward meaningful community participation — thoughtful reviews, tutorial content, peer support — with purchasing credit are turning Stage 15 Community behavior into Stage 10 payment currency, creating a virtuous cycle that compounds over time. The CxC Matrix imperative at Stage 10 is direct: do your payment options match your customers' actual preferences, or your company's operational convenience? The gap between those two things is a measurable source of friction, abandoned purchases, and churn.

Stage 11: Use — The Longest Stage, Across Four Domains

Here is the paradox at the heart of most customer experience programs: the stage that spans the longest period of the customer relationship receives the least deliberate design attention. Marketing obsesses over Awareness. Sales owns Contract. Operations owns Delivery. And then the customer starts actually using the product for months or years, and the company's attention largely moves on to the next new customer. This is backwards. And in the era of AI and connected products, it is also a significant missed revenue opportunity.

The Use stage must now be understood across all four customer domains. In the analog domain, use is the customer's physical interaction with the product — irreducibly human and the ultimate measure of whether the product delivers on its promise. In the digital domain, use generates a continuous stream of behavioral data — how often, how long, which features, in what sequence, with what outcomes — that the company can monitor to understand real usage patterns versus assumed ones. IoT telemetry and software usage analytics have given companies something unprecedented: visibility into actual use, not self-reported use. Companies using predictive analytics on usage data have documented up to 25% revenue growth from pre-empting churn and identifying expansion opportunities.

In the hybrid domain, use extends into AI-enhanced and device-connected experiences that go beyond the product itself. Tesla's over-the-air software updates that improve vehicle performance while the car sits in the garage are the canonical example — but the model applies broadly: embedded dynamic enhancements, downloadable feature expansions, AI-driven personalization that improves with time, and device ecosystem integrations that create value the customer didn't anticipate at purchase. In the synthetic domain, use enters genuinely new territory. The customer's synthetic representation may be using the product or service on their behalf — an AI agent managing a subscription, optimizing a smart home system, coordinating a service schedule — autonomously and continuously, with the human customer reviewing outcomes rather than directing individual actions. Autonomous use and autonomous benefit represent the frontier of Stage 11.

Stage 12: Care & Support — Self-Healing, Self-Enhancing, Always On

The customer needs help. How your company responds in this moment will determine more about long-term loyalty than almost anything else in the journey.

Ninety percent of customers say immediate response is important. 'Immediate' now means now — and AI-powered support available 24 hours a day across every channel is rapidly making instant response the standard expectation rather than a premium differentiator. By 2025, AI handles the first layer of customer interaction for the majority of support contacts across many industries — routing, triaging, resolving standard issues, providing contextually relevant guidance — with seamless escalation to human agents for complex, emotional, or novel situations.

But the Care stage is evolving beyond reactive AI support into something more profound: self-healing and self-enhancing products and services that identify, diagnose, and resolve issues before the customer experiences them as problems. A software platform that detects an impending database performance issue and automatically scales resources before the user experiences slowdown. A connected medical device that identifies a calibration drift and self-corrects while notifying the patient's care team. A home HVAC system that diagnoses a developing refrigerant issue, schedules a service appointment, and orders the required parts — all before the homeowner's home gets warm on a July afternoon. These are not incremental improvements to customer support. They are a redefinition of what support means — from a reactive function that responds to problems the customer reports, to a proactive function that prevents problems the customer would otherwise experience.

> *A support chat interaction at Stage 12 in the digital channel might cost $4 to deliver through an AI-assisted system. That same interaction, if it resolves the customer's issue completely and predicts continued subscription, protects $840 in annual recurring revenue. That is not a cost problem. It is a calculated return — and the CxC Matrix makes it visible.*

Stage 13: Repair — Preventive, Heroic, and Intimate

Something went wrong. Or — in the AI-enhanced world — something was about to go wrong, and your system caught it first.

Repair is the most intimate stage in the entire customer journey. It is the moment of maximum vulnerability — the customer is disappointed, possibly frustrated, possibly out of pocket, possibly facing consequences of the failure in their own life or business. How your company shows up in that moment is the purest expression of what your brand actually values, stripped of all marketing language.

The best Repair experiences are preventive — the failure is detected before it occurs, the maintenance scheduled before it becomes urgent, the part replaced before it breaks, and the customer's experience is that the product took care of itself with minimal disruption. When prevention fails and a genuine repair situation occurs, the standard should be nothing less than hero-level support — regardless of the cause. Zappos became a customer experience legend not through flawless products but through extraordinary recovery. Ritz-Carlton employees are authorized to spend up to $2,000 per guest to resolve any problem without manager approval — because the brand understands that the repair moment is where loyalty is either permanently earned or permanently surrendered.

Repair is rich with customer engagement potential. Advice, resources, and support channels should span every channel — in-app diagnostics, video tutorials, community forums with experienced users, manufacturer-authorized service networks, live chat with technical specialists, in-home service coordination, and for complex products, remote diagnostic sessions where a technician can see exactly what the customer sees. Used well, Stage 13 is one of the most powerful loyalty-building interactions in the entire matrix.

Stage 14: Disposal — End of Life, Beginning of Responsibility

Every product eventually reaches the end of its useful life. Every service contract eventually comes up for renewal or termination. Every relationship reaches a pivot point: deepen, transition, or end. The Disposal stage is where most companies fail their customers — and increasingly, fail the broader world — most visibly.

The creative and responsible treatment of product end-of-life spans a remarkable range: refurbishment programs that accept trade-ins, restore products to certified working condition, and resell them at accessible price points extend product life, reduce raw material demand, and create a new customer segment simultaneously. Take-back and recycling programs that make responsible disposal effortless — scheduled pickup, prepaid shipping labels, in-store drop-off — remove the guilt and inconvenience that cause customers to defer disposal. Self-dissolving packaging that biodegrades completely on contact with moisture. Printer ink cartridge programs with prepaid return envelopes in every box. Automotive parts programs where end-of-life components are returned for materials recovery.

ESG — Environmental, Social, and Governance — considerations are no longer optional appendages to disposal strategy. Environmental impact means accounting for carbon footprint and material recyclability. Social impact means considering how disposal programs can benefit disadvantaged communities — refurbished products donated to schools, repair training programs that create employment. The Disposal stage, managed well, is not the end of the customer story. It is an expression of the company's values at the moment when the commercial incentive to impress has passed. And critically: a customer who is actively managing the end of a product's life is simultaneously in the earliest stages of their next purchase decision. Stage 14 managed well is Stage 1 managed early.

Stage 15: Community — The Social, Digital, Empathetic Platform

And now the stage that feeds everything else. The stage most companies underinvest in most dramatically. The stage that is simultaneously a marketing channel, a product development resource, a trust infrastructure, a social platform, and an expression of the company's relationship with the world beyond its direct customers.

Community is where the customer's experience becomes public, permanent, and influential. Eighty-four percent of people trust online reviews as much as personal recommendations from friends. More than 75% of consumers read reviews before making almost any significant purchase. Referrals from community advocates convert at 30% higher rates and carry 16% higher lifetime value than customers acquired through other channels. These numbers are not marginal advantages. They describe a community-driven flywheel that, once turning, is one of the most powerful forces in customer acquisition and retention.

But community today is more than reviews and referrals. The most sophisticated community platforms are social, technological, digital, and empathetic platforms simultaneously. The social layer connects customers with shared interests and identities — creating genuine peer relationships that are emotionally attached to the brand ecosystem without being controlled by it. Sephora's Beauty Insider community, Salesforce's Trailblazer community, Harley-Davidson's owner networks — these are not company-managed broadcast channels. They are genuine communities where the company's role is host, resource, and occasionally participant, not broadcaster.

The technological layer integrates community with product — AI-curated community content surfaced at relevant moments in the customer journey, community-sourced expertise integrated into the support function. When a customer's support query is resolved not by a company agent but by a community expert whose answer the AI has surfaced from the community knowledge base, the community is functioning as a support channel, a recognition platform, and a trust signal simultaneously. The empathetic layer is the one most companies miss entirely: community is a place where customers face the same challenges, celebrate the same wins, and support each other through the same frustrations — with a shared experience of your product as the connecting tissue. Companies that understand and invest in this layer are not just building customer loyalty. They are building something customers genuinely value in their own right.

> *A single enthusiastic community post might require zero direct company investment to generate. It influences twelve prospective customers during their Stage 2 Information research, converts three of them to Stage 3 Identification, and contributes to one final purchase with a projected lifetime value of $2,400. The return on that single community interaction, traced back through the matrix, is extraordinary — and almost no company is currently calculating it.*

The Economic Engine — Value Per Customer, LTV, and Full CVI

The CxC Matrix is, at its foundation, an economic model. Every cell represents a financial event. Every interaction either creates or destroys value. And the decisions your organization makes about where to invest, what to improve, and what to measure should flow from a clear, honest accounting of what customers are actually worth — fully, honestly, completely.

Every cell in the matrix has a financial profile on both sides of the relationship. From the customer's side, every interaction has a cost: time spent researching, traveling, waiting, or navigating; money spent on the purchase itself and on the friction of a poor experience; cognitive effort spent understanding or troubleshooting; emotional energy spent on frustration or uncertainty. Customers are continuously, usually unconsciously, calculating whether the value they're receiving justifies what they're spending to get it. When that calculation tips — when the cost exceeds the perceived benefit — the customer leaves, often without explanation.

From the company's side, every interaction carries both cost and potential revenue: direct purchase revenue, subscription revenue, referral-generated revenue, upsell and cross-sell revenue, and the compounding lifetime value of a retained and deepening customer relationship. The CxC Matrix makes both visible simultaneously — and when you can see both, you can calculate something that most customer experience frame-works never reach: the actual return on investment of each individual interaction, in each channel, at each lifecycle stage. That is not theoretical. With AI-powered analytics and the 9 Objectives of Every Interaction, each interaction becomes measurable.

Mid-Market B2B Customer — Full CxC Value Calculation	Value
Annual Contract Value	$45,000
Average Relationship Duration	6.5 years
Baseline Lifetime Value (LTV)	$292,500
Referral Revenue — avg. 1.8 referrals	$526,500 additional LTV
Community & Social Advocacy Value	$38,000
Full Customer Value Index (CVI)	**$857,000+**
Cost of a Stage-5 Loss (CVI + transfer)	**$857,000 + full CVI transferred to rival**
Justified Stage-5 Experience Investment	**$20,000–$50,000 per high-value prospect**

The math changes everything. A Stage-5 negotiation process that costs an additional twenty thousand dollars to execute with exceptional quality — personalized proof architecture, dedicated competitive response, frictionless contract execution — looks expensive evaluated against a forty-five-thousand-dollar contract. It looks like a trivial investment evaluated against an eight-hundred-fifty-seven-thousand-dollar customer relationship.

> *"The support call that costs $40 to resolve but retains a customer worth $857,000 is not a cost problem. It is a return of over 21,000 to one. The CxC Matrix makes this math visible — so that every experience investment is evaluated at its actual economic return, not its line-item cost."*

This is how the CxC Matrix transforms 'customer experience' from a soft concept that sounds important but loses every budget fight, into a capital allocation framework that changes the economics of every decision — from hiring to technology to partner investment. When the economics of each cell are visible, the conversation shifts from 'can we afford to invest in customer experience?' to 'can we afford not to, given what we now know it returns?'

Two Levels, One Framework — Micro and Macro

The CxC Matrix operates simultaneously at two levels — micro and macro — and understanding both is the difference between incrementally better customer experience and genuinely transformative customer experience.

The Micro Level — One Customer. One Moment. One Decision.

The micro level is a single interaction. One customer. One contact. One precise moment in which your organization either creates value for this person — or fails to. At the micro level, the CxC Matrix asks: What exactly is this customer experiencing right now, and is that experience moving them forward in their relationship with us — or pushing them toward the exit?

Consider Stage 9 (Acceptance): a physical box arrives at the customer's door. Most organizations treat this as a logistics event. But consider what is actually happening. The customer picks up the box before they have touched the product. They are forming an immediate impression from the weight, the condition of packaging, the presence or absence of a personalized message, the quality of first-impression contents. They are experiencing either the confirmation they made a good decision — or the first whisper of buyer's remorse that a well-timed competitor follow-up will find and amplify. Apple understood this two decades ago. The original iPhone box was engineered to open slowly, with deliberate resistance, building physical anticipation. That was micro-level CxC Matrix thinking applied to cardboard. And it was a designed experience for a stage most companies treat as pure logistics.

Micro-level thinking today is informed by AI in ways that were previously impossible: the packaging insert dynamically generated to reflect purchase history, loyalty status, and the logical next product in the customer's journey. The follow-up — email, app notification, prompt to share — timed to when this specific customer historically engages after receiving an order. One box. Dozens of micro-level decisions. All engineerable. All measurable. All economically consequential.

The Macro Level — The Symphony, Not the Note

If the micro level is a single note played with precision, the macro level is the symphony — and a symphony's power comes not from any individual moment but from the coherence of the whole arc. At the macro level, the CxC Matrix is the complete, orchestrated customer journey — every interaction across all 15 stages, every channel, designed and sequenced as a coherent progression toward a specific destination: a customer who values the relationship, deepens their commitment over time, is actively resistant to competitive approaches, and becomes a genuine advocate who expands your market without additional acquisition cost.

At the macro level in an AI-enabled organization, your systems incorporate contextual depth that was previously impossible. Not just purchase history, but the behavioral trajectory of the past 90 days — content engaged, timing patterns, competitor signals in the digital domain, lifecycle position. The macro-level

CxC Matrix is not a static map reviewed quarterly. It is a dynamic, continuously updated model of each customer's position, momentum, competitive exposure, and next-best experience — operating across your entire customer base, in real time.

Above the Line and Below the Curtain

Here is a visualization that will permanently change how you think about the CxC Matrix in operation.

Imagine a line across the middle of the page. Everything above the line is what the customer sees, feels, experiences, and remembers. The unboxing. The invitation to an exclusive event. The complimentary trade show pass that arrives at precisely the right calendar moment. The support call. The renewal offer. The hand-written note from the account manager after a difficult situation was resolved. These moments are simply the customer's experience of your company — seamless or clunky, personally relevant or tone-deaf, memorable or instantly forgettable.

Everything below the line is everything the customer never sees — but that determines the quality of everything they do. The CRM architecture that carries their history accurately across channels. The AI model that predicted what they would need before they asked. The logistics API that routed their shipment. The competitive intelligence system that flagged they had been visiting your competitor's pricing page. The orchestration engine that triggered the event invitation at precisely the right moment because the system knew the customer was in an active consideration window and a competitor was exhibiting at the same show.

The Systemic Failure Most Organizations Are Making Right Now

Most organizations invest heavily in above-the-line execution and underinvest dramatically in below-the-line infrastructure. They hire exceptional customer service people and deploy them into broken systems. They design powerful marketing campaigns and send them to poorly segmented lists. They build loyalty programs with insufficient behavioral data to make them feel personal.

The result is customer experience that is inconsistent, expensive, and impossible to scale — not because the people are wrong but because the architecture is absent. The CxC Matrix forces accountability for both layers. Every above-the-line experience maps to a set of below-the-line requirements. Trace every customer-facing interaction to its infrastructure dependencies and you find your gaps. Those gaps are where experience breaks down — and they are almost always invisible until you map them this way.

The Six CxC Contact Channels — Where the Customer Already Is

Before we define the six channels, here is the most important thing to understand about them — and the reframe that changes everything about how the CxC Matrix's channel dimension should be read.

> *"Your customer exists in all six channels. You don't get to decide that. You do get to decide which channels you invest in, which you manage deliberately, which you monitor, and which you choose to leave unattended. Those are real strategic choices with real financial consequences. But the customer's existence in those channels — their life in a geography, their access to digital platforms, their relationships with third parties, their participation in communities — none of that waits for your organizational decision to engage."*

The six channels are not a menu of distribution options your company selects from. They are the landscape of human life in which your customer is already living — and within which they will seek to fulfill every one of the 15 lifecycle stages, with or without your participation, using whatever resources they can find, in whatever channel is most convenient, available, and suited to their situation at that moment.

A customer at Stage 2 (Information) will gather information somewhere. If you haven't invested in your digital channel presence at Stage 2, they'll find information from your competitors, from third-party review sites, from community forums, from AI assistants synthesizing sources you don't monitor. Your absence from the channel doesn't eliminate the customer's need. It just means someone else fills it. The six channels are not yours to create. They are yours to manage — or to abandon.

And abandonment has a cost that is just as real as the cost of investment, even if it's harder to see on a balance sheet.

Channel	What the Customer Experiences	What the Company Chooses	The Economic Reality
Geography	Their physical world — location, access, culture, regulation, competitive options. The invisible envelope that shapes every other channel.	*Coverage, localization, geo-targeted pricing, regional service configuration*	Determines cost-to-serve baseline. Geography-adjusted lifetime value is the only honest calculation.
Digital	The always-on environment where most research, consideration, and increasingly autonomous purchasing occurs — never closed, always generating data.	*Presence, content quality, AI readiness, machine-readable data architecture, agent accessibility*	Highest scale, lowest marginal cost, highest measurability. The primary arena for AI-mediated interaction.

Channel	What the Customer Experiences	What the Company Chooses	The Economic Reality
Location	Physical spaces where they touch, evaluate, and experience with full senses — and their own environment as a channel through connected products.	*Real estate investment, staff quality, in-store experience design, hybrid digital-physical integration*	Highest fixed cost, highest conversion for complex or high-consideration purchases. Justified only when physical adds what digital cannot.
Third Party	Brokers, marketplaces, influencers, comparison tools, and AI agents that shape discovery, evaluation, and purchase through entities that aren't you.	*Partner selection and standards, brand representation monitoring, AI channel readiness*	Lower direct acquisition cost, higher long-term relationship risk. Third-party customers need a pathway to direct relationship to maximize lifetime value.

Channel	What the Customer Experiences	What the Company Chooses	The Economic Reality
One-to-One	Being recognized as an individual — history known, preferences reflected, situation understood — in every interaction, regardless of channel or medium.	*Which customers receive individualized service, at what level of human vs. AI delivery, at which lifecycle stages*	Highest per-interaction cost, highest lifetime value return. The channel that turns transactions into relationships.
Community	Peer conversations, shared expertise, collective reviews, and mutual advocacy — the most trusted source of information and deepest sense of brand belonging.	*Community platform investment, moderation standards, recognition programs, authentic vs. artificial engagement*	Highest ROI per dollar invested, lowest direct cost, most credible content. Runs continuously whether you're present or not.

The Channel Decision — Invest, Monitor, or Cede

Every company, for every lifecycle stage, in every channel, is making a choice — explicitly or by default. That choice has three states: Invest and manage — actively designing, funding, and optimizing your presence at this stage in this channel. Monitor without fully engaging — maintaining awareness without the investment required for full management. Cede the channel — explicitly deciding not to invest, accepting that the customer's experience will be shaped by whatever they find from other sources.

Ceding can be a rational economic decision when the stage-channel combination doesn't justify investment given your customer profile and business model. It is only a problem when it's not a decision but a default — when the channel is unmanaged not because you chose to cede it but because you never thought to look. The CxC Matrix makes all three states visible, across all 90 cells, simultaneously. It reveals the pattern of your investment, the gaps in your coverage, and the cells where the customer's experience is being shaped by the absence of your presence rather than the quality of it.

Person to Person. Person to Machine. Machine to Machine to Person.

We are entering a new era of customer interaction that no previous framework was designed to handle. Understanding the full arc of this evolution — where we came from, where we are, and where we are unmistakably going — is essential to building a CxC Matrix that will be competitive not just today but across the next decade.

Era One — Person to Person

For most of business history, customer experience was person to person. Quality depended on people — their training, judgment, emotional intelligence, authority, and mood. Consistency was a management challenge. Scale was a staffing challenge. Excellence was personal and therefore fragile. The extraordinary account manager who remembered every client's preferences, the service representative who could de-escalate any situation, the advisor who had seen every scenario — these people existed, and they created extraordinary customer experiences. But they didn't scale, they didn't replicate, and when they left the company, their knowledge walked out with them.

Era Two — Person to Machine

The first digital wave introduced person-to-machine interaction at scale. Quality shifted from depending on people to depending on design and technology. Consistency became more achievable through engineering. Scale became a technical architecture problem rather than a headcount problem. Excellence became a product discipline. The CxC Matrix emerged from this era as the framework that made the machine layer manageable — mapping every stage and channel so that the technology serving each one could be designed, measured, and optimized rather than improvised.

Era Three — Machine to Machine to Person

We are now entering the era in which AI agents operating on behalf of customers communicate directly with AI systems operating on behalf of companies — researching, comparing, negotiating, and transacting, with human involvement reserved for decisions that genuinely require it and eliminated from routine transactions that do not. A shopping agent acting on behalf of your customer will engage with a sales system acting on behalf of your company. Those agents evaluate options, negotiate terms, execute transactions. The human customer reviews a summary — or pre-authorized the parameters and simply receives a confirmation. The interaction will have happened, the relationship will have moved forward or backward, the economic event will have occurred, and there may not have been a single human conversation.

This is early-stage operational reality in financial services, B2B procurement, travel, and e-commerce today. By the end of this decade it will be standard across most industries. And it requires every cell in the CxC Matrix that previously assumed a human interaction to have a machine-readable version — one in which your value proposition, pricing logic, and service recovery process are legible to an AI agent evaluating them on a customer's behalf.

What Machine-to-Machine Interaction Means for Your Competitive Position

In the machine-to-machine era, companies that structure their customer-facing systems for agent readability will be discoverable, evaluable, and selectable by AI shopping agents. Companies that do not will be systematically bypassed — not because their product is inferior but because their information architecture is invisible to the agents making the selection.

> The CxC Matrix survives this transition because it was always about the interaction and the outcome, not the specific humans or systems delivering it. The fundamental question does not change: Is this interaction, however it is occurring, creating certainty and winning the next stage of the relationship?

The VMAO Engine — How the Matrix Comes to Life

The CxC Matrix is the map. VMAO is how you navigate it — and how you continuously improve the territory while you travel. Four disciplines, applied continuously and in sequence, transform a static framework into a dynamic management system that learns, adapts, and compounds in competitive effectiveness over time.

V	**Visualize**	See the customer experience as the customer actually lives it — not as your org chart imagines it is delivered, and not as your last survey described it. Map every cell: stage by stage, channel by channel. Critically, visualize with competitive awareness — which cells is the customer navigating while simultaneously evaluating a rival? Where are the blank spots your competitors have made their home? Visualization requires empathy, honest data, and the organizational courage to look clearly at the gap between the experience you intend and the one you are delivering.

M	**Monetize**	Attach economic value to every interaction. Quantify the cost of poor execution and the return on excellent execution — including the full Customer Value Index implications of each cell. This is the discipline that transforms customer experience from a soft aspiration into a capital allocation argument. When you monetize the matrix, resources follow the highest-return cells rather than the loudest internal advocate. The executive who previously deflected CX investment with 'we can't measure that' is now presented with a contact-level profit-and-loss statement for every customer relationship.
A	**Analyze**	Use behavioral, transactional, contextual, competitive, and AI-generated data to understand what is actually happening in each cell, why it is happening, what patterns reveal about customer needs and defection risk, and where the highest-leverage improvement opportunities exist. In an AI-enabled matrix, analysis extends beyond what happened to what is about to happen: which customers are approaching competitive vulnerability windows, which lifecycle stages are showing declining win rates, which channel interactions are consistently preceding defection three interactions before the customer consciously decided to leave.

O	**Optimize**	Act on what the analysis reveals — redesigning interactions, reallocating resources, updating AI models, refining competitive response playbooks, and continuously improving the quality and economic return of every cell. Optimization is not a project with an end date. It is a discipline with a cycle. The customer evolves. The technology evolves. Your competitors are optimizing simultaneously. The matrix is never optimized once — it is optimized continuously, at speed, or it falls behind the organizations that treat it as a perpetual discipline.

And Then — Materialize

Materialization is where thinking becomes reality — the execution of the designed experience, at scale, consistently, across all 90 cells, through all six channels, at all 15 lifecycle stages. It is the hardest part. Not because the concepts are unclear but because organizations are complex, resources are finite, and the gap between strategic clarity and operational reality is almost always larger than leadership expects.

Think of deep space missions. Years of observation, hypothesis formation, instrument calibration, trajectory modeling, simulation. All of that invisible, painstaking work happens before a single rocket leaves the ground. The launch — the materialization — is only possible, only safe, only likely to succeed, because of the rigorous preparation that preceded it. Organizations that attempt to skip to the launch without the framework discover the same thing that hastily designed rockets do.

> *"The matrix is not a destination. It is a discipline. The companies that will define the next era of customer experience make Visualize-Monetize-Analyze-Optimize a continuous operating rhythm — not a one-time strategic initiative."*

The Kernel of Every Customer Interaction

At the center of every cell in the CxC Matrix — micro or macro, analog or synthetic, a box arriving at a doorstep or a machine negotiating a renewal — is a single, irreducible dynamic:

The customer has a need. You have the opportunity to fulfill it. The question is whether you do so in a way that creates certainty, builds memory, and wins the next stage of the relationship — before a competitor does.

'Creating certainty' is the operative phrase. Beneath every specific request, what a customer is fundamentally seeking is confidence that they made the right choice. That they chose the right company. That their need will be met. That they will not regret this. Every exceptional customer experience delivers that certainty. Every poor one erodes it. And every competitive vulnerability is, at its root, a certainty gap — a moment where the customer's confidence in your organization is less than total, and a well-positioned competitor can insert a better story.

AI transforms this dynamic in a profound and specific way. For most of business history, creating certainty required extraordinary people — the brilliant salesperson who could read a room, the empathetic service representative who knew exactly when to escalate, the experienced advisor who had seen every situation. Those people still matter enormously. But they do not scale.

> *"AI can scale certainty in ways human teams cannot. It can make every customer, at every stage, in every channel feel genuinely known — in a way that was previously only possible for your most valuable customers, served by your most experienced people."*

But AI can only scale certainty if the framework is right. If the lifecycle model accurately reflects how your customers move. If the channel architecture maps where they actually are. If the data is integrated, current, and trustworthy. If the economic value of each interaction is understood. If the objectives of each stage are clearly defined and owned.

The CxC Matrix provides all of that. It is the score. AI is the ensemble that plays it at a scale and consistency no human team could match. Without the score, the ensemble produces noise — however sophisticated the individual instruments.

What This Chapter Has Built

You now have the full foundation of the CxC Matrix framework: the 15-stage lifecycle structure and the AI-era transformation of each stage from ambient awareness creation at Stage 1 to the compounding community flywheel at Stage 15. The six channel architecture and the fundamental truth that the customer already exists in all six, whether you are present or not. The competitive logic that makes every stage a defection window as much as a relationship opportunity. The economic model that turns customer experience from a soft aspiration into a capital allocation discipline. The VMAO operating cycle that keeps the matrix alive. And the understanding of how AI transforms each layer — from reactive response to proactive orchestration to machine-to-machine transaction.

More importantly, you have a new lens for every business decision you will make after closing this chapter. When a competitor launches a new campaign, you will ask: which lifecycle stages and channels are they targeting, and what is our designed response? When someone proposes cutting the customer success budget, you will ask: what is the Customer Value Index of the relationships that investment protects? When a technology team proposes a new digital capability, you will ask: which cells in the matrix does this improve, and what is the measurable return? When your Stage 12 AI support system gets proposed as a cost-cutting measure, you will ask: what is the retention value of the interactions it handles, and what does a 5% improvement in resolution quality translate to in lifetime value across the customer base?

The CxC Matrix is not a customer satisfaction tool. Not a journey mapping exercise. Not a technology implementation plan. It is a complete operating system for the customer relationship — designed to make every interaction, at every stage, in every channel, an intentional, measurable, economically justified act of genuine service. One that builds value for the customer, competitive advantage for the organization, and resistance to the constant competitive pressure that is the permanent condition of modern markets.

That is what it means to be Customer Worthy.

Contact by contact. Stage by stage. Channel by channel. Domain by domain.

Think Like a Customer.

> *"If a car shopper has read dozens of owner reviews documenting that the back seat is cramped and a salesperson denies it, the salesperson does not lose a debate. They lose a sale — and a customer who goes home and writes their own review about the experience."*

The implications for customer experience design are significant. Customers value honesty and demonstrated expertise over enthusiasm and optimism. They arrive pre-skeptical, pre-informed, and pre-comparing. The interaction that wins them is not the one with the best pitch — it is the one that acknowledges what they already know, respects the quality of their research, and adds something genuine to it. Something they couldn't get from the thirteen content pieces they already read.

And the empowered customer increasingly brings tools to the encounter. AI shopping agents that research options overnight and present synthesized recommendations by morning. Price comparison algorithms that run continuously in the background. Peer networks that can be polled in minutes. Procurement bots — already deployed by organizations like Walmart and Maersk — that negotiate supplier contracts without a human buyer directly involved. Gartner projects a significant rise in 'machine customers' — algorithms that act on behalf of human customers — and that organizations will need deliberate strategies to serve them.

Thinking like a customer today, increasingly means thinking like the customer's AI assistant. What does your product information look like to an algorithm evaluating it? Is your pricing architecture coherent to a negotiation system? Is your value proposition legible to a machine, or only to a human who has been briefed by your sales team? These are not theoretical questions. They are the new front line of competitive differentiation.

The New Dimension of Customer-Centricity

Companies spent two decades adapting their content and operations for search engine optimization — structuring information so algorithms could find and surface it accurately. The next adaptation is AI optimization: ensuring that your product information, pricing logic, terms, and value proposition are structured and accurate in the databases that AI assistants and shopping agents draw from.

If a customer asks an AI assistant what the best option is in your category and your product is inaccurately represented — or simply absent — you do not lose a consideration. You never enter one. This is not a future problem. It is a present competitive vulnerability, operating right now in every category where AI-assisted purchasing has taken hold.

From Contacts to Continuous Sensors — The CxC Matrix in Practice

Understanding how the customer thinks and feels is the foundation. But to apply that understanding at scale — across thousands or millions of customers, through dozens of interaction types, over a relationship that may span years — you need more than empathy. You need a system.

That system is the CxC Matrix — and in this chapter, we are going to make it operational. Not as a theoretical framework. As a working tool you can build, populate, and use to find the opportunities and failures hidden in your customer relationships right now.

Recall the structure from Chapter 2: the horizontal axis maps 15 lifecycle stages, the vertical axis maps 6 contact channels, and each of the resulting 90 cells represents a specific interaction at a specific stage. Each cell is an opportunity. Some are generating extraordinary value. Some are costing more than they are worth. And some are completely blank — moments in the customer's journey where your organization is not present and the customer is navigating alone, or worse, with a competitor's help.

The goal of mapping your CxC Matrix is to make all of that visible simultaneously. Because what you cannot see, you cannot improve. And what you cannot measure, you cannot justify investing in. The matrix does not ask you to guess where the value is. It shows you.

The Matrix in Motion — A Complete SaaS Example

Here is the CxC Matrix mapped for a subscription software company — fifteen contacts across the full lifecycle, every one with a cost, an outcome, and an economic signal. Read this table sequentially and notice what becomes visible that would remain completely invisible inside separate departmental reports.

#	Stage	Channel	Cost	Outcome / Revenue Signal
C1	Awareness	Social Ad — LinkedIn	$2.00	Click-through to website. First impression of brand credibility, ad copy, and targeting precision.
C2	Information	Website	Negligible	Customer self-qualifies. Enters email, requests pricing. The decisive moment — do they believe what they see?
C3	Information	Email — Welcome Sequence	$0.02	Customer clicks through to pricing page. Tone and content set the relationship expectation from this first exchange.
C4	Identification	Website — Pricing Page	Infrastructure	Customer determines tier of interest and compares competitors. Often the last moment before a decision — or a defection.
C5	Negotiation	Sales Call	~$10.00	Potential $10K deal negotiated to $8K annual. Information parity test: is the rep more knowledgeable than the customer?
C6	Contract	E-Signature / CRM	Overhead	$8,000 annual contract value — REVENUE EVENT. Every second of friction here has a calculable dollar cost.

#	Stage	Channel	Cost	Outcome / Revenue Signal
C7	Logistics	Email — Onboarding Confirmation	$0.05	Customer confirms ready to start. The gap between C6 and C7 is where buyer's remorse either forms or evaporates.
C8	Delivery	Platform Access	Server infra	Customer gains access; first login. The product meets the promise — or the first disappointment occurs, here.
C9	Acceptance	In-App Tutorial / Onboarding	Platform cost	Customer completes guided setup. Proper onboarding here improves long-term usage by 55% and dramatically reduces churn.
C10	Use	Daily Product Engagement	Server + support	Ongoing value extraction captured in usage data. Behavioral signals here predict churn weeks before the customer decides.
C11	Care & Support	Live Chat	~$3.00	Issue resolved — or the first churn signal is created. A $3 interaction protecting an $8K relationship: 2,667:1 ROI.
C12	Care — Proactive	Email Check-In	$0.05	Expansion opportunity identified — or missed. This contact costs a nickel. Silence here costs a renewal.

Fifteen contacts. A complete business relationship in a single view. Now let us look at what the mapping reveals — because the power of the CxC Matrix is not in the listing. It is in what becomes visible once everything is visible at once.

Five Things the CxC Matrix Makes Visible That Nothing Else Does

1. Where Value Is Actually Created

Contact C14 — the Annual Business Review where you demonstrate ROI and discuss expansion — is obviously high-value. Contact C11 — the support interaction that prevents churn — is equally high-value, even though it costs only three dollars. Both of these contacts are protecting or generating revenue that can be calculated precisely. Contact C1 — the LinkedIn ad — is necessary, but only valuable if it leads to Contact C2. Without tracking conversion rates between contacts, you have no way to know whether your awareness spend is generating returns or simply generating traffic that disappears into the information stage and never comes back.

Most organizations have no single view of these relationships because each contact lives in a different system owned by a different team. The matrix creates that single view — not by replacing those systems, but by layering the customer's experience across all of them simultaneously.

2. Where the Pain Points Are

If a significant percentage of prospects drop off between Contact C4 (pricing page) and Contact C5 (sales call), you have a funnel leak. Maybe the pricing isn't transparent enough to justify the commitment of a sales conversation. Maybe the wait for a demo is a week, and the customer found an alternative in those seven days. Maybe the pricing page itself triggers comparison shopping at the exact moment the customer was closest to committing.

The matrix makes these gaps visible as specific, addressable failures rather than aggregate statistics that obscure the cause. 'Our conversion rate dropped 8% this quarter' is a report. 'We are losing 40% of prospects between Contact C4 and Contact C5, and the average gap between those contacts is eleven days' is a diagnosis — and a roadmap.

3. Where Costs Accumulate Unnoticed

Contact C11 costs three dollars per support interaction. If you are handling 100 support requests per month from a 500-customer base, that is $300 per month in visible support costs. The important question the matrix forces is: what is causing those requests? Can you trace them back to Contact C8 — the delivery and platform access experience — and find that 40% of support tickets originate from onboarding confusion that a better guided setup would have prevented?

A $10,000 investment in Contact C8 that eliminates $3,600 in annual support costs is not a customer experience upgrade. It is a financial decision with a calculable 2.8-year payback period —

independent of the retention value of the customers whose frustration you've prevented. The matrix makes both calculations visible and connects them. Most organizations only see the first.

4. Where Messages Compete or Contradict

Are you sending a customer an email and a direct outreach from a different department in the same week, with different tones, different offers, and different assumptions about where the customer is in their journey? This happens constantly in organizations where the CxC Matrix has never been built, because no single person can see the full sequence of contacts the customer is experiencing.

The matrix makes these redundancies and contradictions visible. And in large organizations, eliminating them often produces immediate improvements in customer satisfaction that have nothing to do with adding new capabilities, new technology, or new headcount. The improvement comes entirely from removing the noise that your own organization is generating in your own customer relationships.

5. Where Silence Occurs — The Most Dangerous Finding of All

This is the insight that most organizations find most uncomfortable — and most valuable — in equal measure.

Look at the gap in the SaaS example between Contact C10 (daily use) and Contact C11 (support). There is no company-initiated contact in that period unless the customer reaches out with a problem. For customers who are using the product without issues, the company is simply absent — until the annual renewal conversation in Contact C14 arrives. By then, if a competitor has been more present, more proactive, and more demonstrably interested in this customer's success during that silence, the renewal conversation is far harder than it needed to be.

> *"Most companies focus on the customers who make noise. They escalate complaints, reward high-NPS respondents, and celebrate new logos. The silent customer — the one who is using the product without complaint, without enthusiasm, without strong connection — represents the largest single pool of defection risk in most organizations. They leave quietly, and often surprisingly."*

The matrix shines light on the silence. Every blank space between company-initiated contacts is a period when the customer is forming opinions, being approached by competitors, and experiencing whatever their usage reality actually is — without any input from you. Some of those silences are appropriate. Many are not. And the ones that are not appropriate have a calculable cost — which brings us to the most important economic exercise this framework enables.

From Matrix to Monetization — The Language of Business

Here is where the CxC Matrix transforms from a customer experience tool into a capital allocation framework. Once you have mapped your contacts and assigned costs and revenue impact to each one, you can calculate something that most customer experience programs never reach: the actual return on investment of each individual interaction.

Metric	Definition	From the SaaS Matrix
Cost Per Contact (CPC)	The fully loaded cost to deliver this interaction — labor, technology, overhead.	Sales contact: $10. Support chat: $3. Proactive email: $0.05. Platform delivery: server infrastructure + fractional overhead.
Revenue Per Contact (RPC)	The direct or protected revenue attributable to this interaction.	A support contact that prevents an $8K/year customer from churning: RPC = $8,000 in protected revenue. The contact costs $3. The math is not subtle.
Net Value Per Contact	Revenue or protected revenue minus the cost to deliver the contact.	Support contact: $8,000 – $3 = $7,997 net value. The $3 support interaction is not a cost. It is a $7,997 return. This is the calculation that changes every budget conversation.

Metric	Definition	From the SaaS Matrix
Contact Efficiency Ratio (CER)	The expected value generated per dollar invested in this contact.	Sales contact at 20% conversion on a $10K deal: $2,000 expected value ÷ $10 cost = 200:1 ROI. Proactive email at 2% repeat purchase rate on $200 order: $4.00 ÷ $0.05 = 80:1 ROI.

This is not theoretical economics. This is the language of every budget conversation, every investment committee presentation, every argument for why customer experience deserves a larger allocation. When you can demonstrate that a $3 support interaction generates $7,997 in protected revenue, the conversation about whether to invest in better support tools becomes very different from the conversation about 'improving customer satisfaction.'

'Improving customer satisfaction' is a soft goal that competes with every other priority in the room. 'This $3 contact generates a 2,665:1 return and we currently handle 100 of them per month, meaning the $300 in monthly support costs is protecting $799,700 in annual recurring revenue — and we need a $50,000 technology investment to ensure we handle them consistently at scale' is a capital allocation argument. The matrix gives you the second conversation. Most organizations are still having the first.

> *The matrix doesn't make customer experience more important. It makes customer experience impossible to dismiss. Those are different things — and only one of them survives a budget negotiation.*

Case Study — How a Regional Insurer Found $11 Million in the Silence

Here is a real example that illustrates every principle in this chapter — the empathy gap, the economics of mapping, the cost of silence, and the extraordinary return on showing up.

A regional insurance company mapped the customer journey for a standard auto insurance policy across a base of 500,000 active customers. The matrix revealed 18 contacts across the entire lifecycle, from initial quote request to annual renewal. Their analytics team then analyzed a full year of customer data, assigning costs and revenue impact to each contact.

What the Matrix Revealed — The Known Costs

Contact 5 (Payment Processing): $2 per transaction × 500,000 customers = $1,000,000 annual cost.

Contact 11 (Claims Support): $50 per claim × average 0.3 claims per customer per year = $7,500,000 annual cost.

Contact 15 (Renewal Negotiation): $20 per contact × 400,000 renewing customers = $8,000,000 annual cost.

Total: known, manageable, expected. The real discovery came from what was between the contacts — and what was not there at all.

Between Contact 8 (Policy Issued) and Contact 11 (First Claim), there was a gap that looked like this for 70% of the customer base: twelve months of complete silence. No company-initiated contact. No proactive value demonstration. No check-in. No recognition that the relationship existed. The company had issued the policy, collected the premium, and essentially disappeared — until the renewal conversation, at which point customers who had been approached by competitors during that silent twelve months were significantly more likely to leave.

The solution was elegantly simple: introduce a Contact 10.5 — a Proactive Value Check-In at the six-month mark. An automated touchpoint with a conditional follow-up call for at-risk segments, reminding customers of their coverage, sharing a relevant safety insight, and demonstrating that the company was present in the relationship — not just present at billing time.

The Economics of Filling the Silence — Contact 10.5	Calculation
Cost of Contact 10.5	$2 per customer × 500,000 customers = $1,000,000 total annual investment
Expected renewal rate improvement	3% — based on benchmark data from comparable proactive contact programs
Additional renewals generated	500,000 customers × 3% = 15,000 customers retained who would otherwise have left
Value per retained renewal	$800 average annual premium per retained customer
Revenue from additional retentions	15,000 × $800 = $12,000,000
Net gain after investment	**$12,000,000 − $1,000,000 = $11,000,000**
Time to identify this opportunity	**Less than one day of matrix analysis**
Tool required	**A contact map. A gap. And the decision to show up.**

> *"$11 million in additional net revenue. Found by looking at a twelve-month gap in a customer journey map. Not by launching a new product, not by hiring a new executive, not by spending more on marketing. By identifying where the customer was alone — and deciding to show up."*

The insurance case study is not unique in its structure. It is representative of what the matrix reveals in every industry where it is applied rigorously: the highest-return opportunities are almost never in acquiring new capabilities. They are in filling the silences in existing relationships that have already been paid for — customers who chose you, stayed with you, and are being left alone in the gaps between the contacts your organization thought were sufficient.

Containers and Slots — Every Interaction Is a Message

Here is a concept that will permanently change how you look at every customer touchpoint — from the most sophisticated AI-driven personalization campaign to the most mundane operational artifact your organization produces.

Every customer interaction has two structural components: the container and the slots.

A container is the structure through which the customer receives and interprets the interaction. An email. A receipt. A support call. An onboarding sequence. A product box. A store environment. An invoice. Containers are the channels and formats through which value — or its absence — is delivered.

Slots are the specific elements within that container where value can be created, deepened, or destroyed. Every container has multiple slots. Some slots are filled with purpose and precision. Many are filled with default content — functional, accurate, completely devoid of any sense that a human being is on the other side. And some slots are simply empty — left blank in a container that reaches every customer who completes a transaction.

> *"Every container is a conversation. Most organizations design their containers as if they are legal documents — accurate, functional, and completely impersonal. The Customer Worthy organization designs them as if they matter — because to the customer, every single one does."*

The critical insight is this: the customer does not experience your internal categories. They experience the container as a unified message from your organization. The receipt is not a financial record to them. It is the last thing your company said to them before they left. The onboarding email sequence is not a logistics communication. It is the first extended conversation your company has with them after they committed. The invoice is not an accounting artifact. It is a monthly reminder of whether the relationship is worth the cost.

When you see containers and slots, you begin to see something most organizations have never systematically looked at: the aggregate message your company is sending through the artifacts that leave the building every day — invoices, confirmations, receipts, shipping notifications, renewal reminders — artifacts that receive no strategic attention and reach every single customer you have.

** Store Phone Number (908) 231-8100
THANK YOU FOR VOTING US BEST
SUPERMARKET 27 YEARS IN A ROW!
NOW HIRING!!
APPLY ONLINE: SHOPRITE.COM

ShopRite
we are here.

Welcome to ShopRite
of SOMERVILLE

11/10/25 07:12am S468 R78 T6 C78

Regular Items

A 1 SAUCE 5.79 F
REALEMON LEMON JUI 2.79 F
Valued Customer 48101070784
TAX 0.00
**** BALANCE 8.58

ShopRite Credit Receipt
Store # 468 of SOMERVILLE , NJ
Terminal: 78 Operator: 78 Trans: 6
Date: 11/10/25 Time: 07:13am

Purchase: $ 8.58
Acct#: ************9803 CONTACTLESS

Response : APPROVED
Approval : 010468
Prepaid Card Balance: 0.00

VISA CARD 8.58
CHANGE 0.00
TOTAL NUMBER OF ITEMS SOLD = 2
11/10/25 07:13am 468 78 6 78

Present your card with every order
and save with Price Plus discounts!

Questions or comments?
Contact us at 1-800-SHOPRITE or
on the web at www.shoprite.com

HOLIDAY PROMOTION
YOUR HOLIDAY POINTS:$ 24.35 of $400
QUALIFY & REDEEM 10/26 - 11/27

HOW WAS YOUR VISIT TODAY?

Please take our survey within
7 days for a chance to win
$100 in ShopRite Gift Cards.
Scan the QR Code or visit
MyShopRiteExperience.com
Use This Code: 468 S 78 R 6 T
Thank you for your feedback!

A Receipt as a Case Study — $8.58 and a Masterclass in Missed Opportunity

Let us make the containers-and-slots concept concrete with the most humble customer container in commercial life: a grocery store receipt.

November 10, 2025. 7:13 AM. ShopRite of Somerville, New Jersey. Two items: A1 Sauce, $5.79. ReaLemon Lemon Juice, $2.79. Subtotal: $8.58. Tax: $0.00. Payment by Visa, contactless. Cashier: Scot Lane.

surface, entirely. But look at what is actually t strip of thermal paper. The organization has omplete attention for the thirty seconds they spend reading it. They know exactly what was purchased. They have a loyalty program relationship. They have the cashier's name. They have a survey mechanism already printed on the paper. They have a holiday promotion running. And they have done almost nothing with any of it.

Container Slot	What It Represents	Customer Worthy Evaluation
Header: 'Welcome to ShopRite of Somerville'	*Store identity; first impression slot*	Generic. Costs nothing to personalize. 'Good morning, Michael — your Somerville ShopRite team thanks you for starting your day with us.' The slot is wasted on a greeting that could have been printed in 1987.
Item List: A1 Sauce, ReaLemon Juice	*Proof of purchase — functional accuracy*	Accurate. Entirely transactional. A1 Sauce is going on something at dinner. That story is completely ignored. The bridge from what was purchased to why it matters: missing.
Loyalty Mention: 'Present your Price Plus card'	*Customer relationship signal*	Acknowledges the program. Offers nothing personal. How much has this customer saved this year? How close to their next reward? All known. None shared. Instruction replaces recognition.
Survey Invitation	*Post-purchase engagement slot*	'Tell us how we did.' Framed as a favor to the store. Customer Worthy framing: 'Help us make your next visit better — your opinion shapes your store.' One sentence, written from the customer's perspective.
Holiday Promotion: '$24.35 of $400 in Holiday Points'	*Progress and reward slot*	'You have $24.35 of $400 in Holiday Points' is a data point. 'You've earned $24.35 toward your holiday goal — only $375.65 to go by November 27' is a story. A timeline and destination change everything.

Container Slot	What It Represents	Customer Worthy Evaluation
Cashier Name: Scot Lane	*Human connection and accountability slot*	Currently: a transaction identifier. Potential: 'Scot thanks you for starting your morning with us — he hopes the A1 Sauce makes dinner great.' Scot becomes a character in the customer's story. Costs nothing.

None of those changes require a technology investment. They require a decision — a deliberate choice to treat the receipt as a customer container with valuable slots, rather than as a financial document that happens to leave the building with the customer. The container is already reaching the customer. The question is what it says when it gets there.

Default Slot — What It Says Now	Customer Worthy Upgrade — What It Could Say
'How was your visit today?'	**'Your opinion shapes your store — help us make your next visit better.'**
'Holiday Points: $24.35 of $400'	**'You've earned $24.35 toward your holiday goal — $375.65 to go by Nov. 27!'**
'Cashier: Scot Lane'	**'Scot thanks you — he hopes the A1 Sauce makes dinner perfect tonight.'**
'Visit ShopRite.com'	**'Need a recipe? Scan here — we've matched a few to what you just bought.'**

The Hidden Marketplace for Micro-Container Data

Here is something most organizations have not fully considered: the receipt data they treat as wastepaper is actively purchased by retail data aggregators, consumer analytics firms, and behavioral modeling platforms. Anonymized receipt data is worth fractions of a cent per transaction — but aggregated at scale across millions of transactions, the same data sells for tens of millions of dollars annually.

Retail media networks, loyalty-card platforms, and AI consumer-insight engines all pay for it. They are not buying the paper. They are buying the behavioral pattern embedded in every transaction. The Customer Worthy organization asks a different question: not 'who wants to buy this data?' but 'how can we use this signal to create worth for the customer who generated it?' The data belongs to the relationship. The question is whether the organization treats it that way.

The CxC Matrix 2.0 — From Static Document to Continuous Operating System

The traditional CxC Matrix — even when fully populated and economically calibrated — has one limitation: it is a photograph of a moving situation. Customer behavior changes. Products evolve. Competitive dynamics shift. A matrix reviewed quarterly is already partially obsolete by the time the review happens.

The CxC Matrix 2.0 is dynamic. It is fed continuously by four categories of data that, combined, give your organization something it has never had before: real-time visibility into the health of every customer relationship, at every stage, in every channel, simultaneously.

Event Data — When Action Happens, and When It Stops

Every login, every purchase, every support ticket, every opened email, every unanswered outreach is a timestamped signal about where the customer is in their relationship with you. The gaps between events are often the most revealing data of all. A customer who logged in daily for ninety days and then went silent for two weeks is not a steady-state customer. They are a customer in transition — and the matrix, fed with event data in real time, surfaces that signal before the transition completes.

Behavioral Data — What Customers Do vs. What They Say

Feature adoption rates, time-on-task, the sequence in which they navigate, the workarounds they create when something doesn't work intuitively. This is use-stage intelligence that reveals whether the product is delivering its promise — long before the customer articulates any dissatisfaction. A customer using three of twelve available features for six consecutive months is not a satisfied customer. They are an underserved customer whose unmet potential is also unmet revenue.

Sentiment Data — What Customers Feel at the Interaction Level

Extracted from support transcripts, email language, chat interactions, and review text through AI-powered sentiment analysis. Not just positive or negative — but the specific emotional registers: frustrated about billing, confused about a feature, delighted by a response time, anxious about an upcoming renewal. Sentiment data mapped to specific contacts in the matrix tells you not just where experience is failing, but how it is failing — and which failures carry the highest emotional cost.

Financial Data — The Economic Pulse of Every Contact

Revenue, cost, margin, and lifetime value calculations updated with each interaction. When AI algorithms analyze this data continuously, the matrix stops being a report and becomes an alert system — flagging the contacts that are underperforming, the customers who are showing early churn signals, and the cells where a modest investment would generate a disproportionate return. The financial data layer is what turns customer experience management from a reporting function into a capital allocation discipline.

When these four data streams feed a live matrix, AI can generate the alerts that no human team could monitor at scale. 'Customers in Stage 7 are taking three days longer than average to confirm implementation. Recommend follow-up.' 'Support contact resolution time is increasing. Root cause: new feature complexity introduced six weeks ago. Recommend additional tutorial at Stage 9.' '30% of customers go silent after their first support interaction. These are elevated churn risks. Trigger proactive retention contact at the 72-hour mark.'

That is not a customer experience program. That is an operating system for the customer relationship — one that learns, adapts, and improves continuously, without requiring a quarterly review cycle to update. The matrix built once and reviewed periodically is a tool. The matrix fed continuously with four categories of live data is a competitive infrastructure.

Building the Culture That Makes All of This Possible

The CxC Matrix is a framework. The contact economics model is a language. The container-and-slot analysis is a discipline. None of them work without a culture that consistently asks one question — and has the organizational courage to act on the answer.

If I were the customer in this situation, what would I want? And are we delivering it?

Amazon famously leaves an empty chair in meetings to represent the customer — a physical reminder to ask how every decision impacts the person who will ultimately experience its results.

These are not customer empathy programs. They are cultural commitments — organizational decisions that the customer's perspective is not an input to the decision process but the starting point of it. The difference between those two positions determines whether the CxC Matrix becomes a living operating system or a document that was built once, presented once, and filed.

Early Indicators That the Culture Is Working

Watch for these signals: Employees use customer-centric language unprompted — 'How will this affect our customers?' becomes a standard meeting question rather than an exceptional one. Customer stories appear in internal communications alongside metrics. Support teams share real customer interactions with product teams, and product teams actually change priorities as a result.

Customer satisfaction improvements are tied to executive compensation — not as a peripheral metric but as a primary one. And most tellingly: when a proposed internal policy or process change is questioned on the grounds of customer impact rather than departmental convenience, someone in the room has started thinking like a customer — and is making it safe for others to do the same. That moment is the one that compounds.

Customer-obsessed organizations grow faster. The data on this is consistent and significant: companies that systematically prioritize the customer perspective see 49% faster revenue growth and 51% better retention than peers who treat customer experience as a downstream function of operational efficiency. Those are not soft metrics. Those are compounding competitive advantages — the kind that accrue over years and eventually become structural moats that new entrants cannot easily bridge.

The Matrix Is Industry-Agnostic — Four Sectors, One Framework

The CxC Matrix applies to any organization with customers — which means every organization. The stages adjust in name and sequence. The channels vary in relative importance. The economic values per contact differ dramatically. But the fundamental structure — lifecycle stages plotted against contact channels, every cell an economic event — applies universally.

Financial Services — **The 100-Contact Mortgage Journey** — Where Systems Failed Before the Customer Said a Word

A major bank used the CxC Matrix to map a customer's journey through a standard mortgage application. They found more than 100 contacts — from initial website research through branch visits, phone consultations, document uploads, underwriting status updates, closing meetings, and welcome calls after funding. The mapping revealed two critical findings.

First: customers were being asked to submit the same documentation twice at different stages due to a system handoff failure — a friction point invisible inside any single department but immediately obvious when the customer's full contact sequence was mapped as a unified experience. Second: after loan servicing started — Stage 11, Use — there was essentially zero company-initiated contact. Customers were left entirely alone to manage their mortgage relationship until something went wrong.

The fix — a personalized new-borrower onboarding program with a proactive check-in after the first payment — produced measurable improvements in satisfaction and a significant reduction in support calls, both traceable to revenue through higher cross-sell rates on ancillary products. The mortgage was the same. The containers around it were redesigned to fill the silences the matrix revealed.

Healthcare — When Clinical Excellence Is Not Enough — The Experience Surrounding the Care

A hospital network plotted the patient journey for a surgical procedure across 100 patients using empathy mapping alongside the CxC Matrix. The clinical care — Stage 11, in this case the procedure and recovery — was rated excellent across the board. The surrounding experience was not.

Pre-admission paperwork was confusing and redundant, triggering significant patient anxiety that clinical staff were absorbing in pre-op conversations that were not designed for it. Post-discharge, patients felt completely abandoned — discharged with a folder of instructions and no proactive follow-up from the institution that had just performed surgery on them. The container around the care was failing the patient experience in exactly the stages that clinical excellence couldn't compensate for.

The solution: a digital pre-admission portal that streamlined paperwork and a post-discharge mobile app that checked on recovery and answered FAQs in the patient's own timeline.

Patient satisfaction scores improved 23 points on NPS. Hospital readmission rates — a key quality and cost metric — decreased by 40%. The clinical work was always excellent. The matrix revealed where the experience surrounding it was not.

Retail — When Community Becomes Your Best Sales Channel — The Stage 15 → Stage 1 Discovery

A direct-to-consumer fitness equipment company mapped their customer journey and discovered something their marketing team had suspected but never quantified: their Stage 15 (Community) was their most powerful Stage 1 (Awareness) driver. Existing customers in their branded community were actively selling to prospects by sharing transformation results, posting comparison content, and answering product questions with more credibility than any marketing campaign could match.

The company responded by investing deliberately in community management — seeding topics, offering referral incentives for community members, and creating structured programs that made advocacy easy and rewarding. The result: referral-driven sales grew to represent a significantly larger share of new customer acquisition, and referred customers demonstrated 25% higher lifetime value than customers acquired through paid channels.

The matrix made the connection between Stage 15 investment and Stage 1 outcomes visible — a connection that no departmental P&L would have revealed, because marketing owned Stage 1 and customer success owned Stage 15, and the two departments had never been asked to look at the full arc simultaneously. The matrix forced that conversation. The investment followed. The revenue followed the investment.

B2B SaaS — **Engineering the Handoff, Eliminating the Cliff** — The Failure Point Every Software Company Recognizes

A B2B SaaS provider used the CxC Matrix to coordinate across marketing, sales, customer success, and product teams for the first time in a systematic way. The mapping revealed a critical failure point that every sales-driven software organization recognizes: the handoff from Sales to Customer Success at the Contract stage was a cliff.

Customers signed a contract with one team's promises and then met a completely different team at implementation, often without any context transfer. The customer's experience was not of a single organization honoring a commitment — it was of two separate organizations, the second of which had never been introduced and had no visible connection to the first. Buyer's remorse, seeded at contract and nourished at handoff, is one of the primary drivers of early churn in SaaS — and the matrix made it visible as a structural design failure, not a performance problem.

The fix was structural: Customer Success Managers were introduced before contract signature, creating relationship continuity across the commercial and implementation phases. The matrix also revealed that mid-contract customers received no proactive value demonstration until renewal conversations began — by which time they had already formed their opinions about whether renewal was worth it. Adding a formal Value Review at the six-month mark, using predictive analytics to demonstrate usage outcomes and ROI, improved renewal rates significantly. Companies applying this level of systematic CX to B2B relationships have documented up to 25% revenue growth and 50% lower churn — not from better products, but from better presence across the full lifecycle.

> *The matrix does not reveal what is wrong with your products. It reveals what is wrong with your presence — the stages where you are absent, the silences where competitors fill the space you left, and the containers that reach every customer you have while saying nothing worth remembering.*

Building Your Own CxC Matrix — Seven Steps, Starting Monday

The principles in this chapter are compelling. The case studies are instructive. Neither is worth anything if you close this book without building the map. Here is a practical sequence for getting started — not as a multi-quarter initiative, but as a working draft you can produce in a focused workshop. The first version doesn't need to be perfect. It needs to exist.

#	Step	How to Execute It
1	**Identify Your Stages**	Map the 15 lifecycle stages to your specific business context. The names may differ — 'Awareness' might be 'Referral Introduction' in a professional services firm; 'Logistics' might be 'Provisioning' in a software company. The principle is identical: name every distinct phase from first awareness to deepest advocacy, and name who inside your organization owns each one.
2	**List All Current Contacts**	For each stage, list every way your organization currently initiates or responds to contact with the customer. Email, phone, in-product notification, sales outreach, support interaction, invoice, third-party channel, community. Do not filter for quality. List what actually happens — not what the process document says should happen.
3	**Assign Costs**	Using your actual or estimated cost per contact — labor, technology, marketing spend, overhead — assign a fully loaded cost to each contact. Be honest. A sales call that takes 45 minutes of a $150,000-per-year representative's time costs more than $10. Calculate it at the actual cost. The honesty is what makes the economics useful.
4	**Assign Revenue or Protected Revenue**	If the contact directly generates revenue, use that figure. If it prevents churn, estimate the annual revenue of the customer relationship at risk. If it is brand-building or relationship-deepening, estimate the downstream impact on lifetime value. Be conservative. Even conservative estimates will reveal return ratios that change how resources are allocated.

#	Step	How to Execute It
5	**Identify the Silences**	Where are customers alone? Where are the gaps between company-initiated contacts that last more than 30, 60, or 90 days? In the silence, competitors are present, opinions are forming, and commitment is quietly eroding. Every silence longer than 30 days in a high-value customer relationship is a potential Contact X.5 waiting to be designed.
6	**Prioritize Improvements**	Use the Contact Efficiency Ratios to rank improvement opportunities. The highest-return improvements are almost always the same three: eliminating a friction point at a high-defection stage, adding a proactive contact in a high-silence period, and ensuring at least one human-initiated contact exists at each stage for your highest-value customers.
7	**Measure and Iterate**	Update the matrix quarterly with new data. Track conversion rates between contacts, changes in cost, and revenue impacts. The matrix is not a strategic artifact filed after a workshop. It is an operational tool. The organizations that generate the most value from it treat it as a living document — updated with every meaningful shift in customer behavior, competitive dynamics, or channel economics.

A working matrix — even an imperfect first draft — changes the conversation in organizations that have never had one. It surfaces silences that were invisible inside departmental reports. It creates a shared language between teams that previously managed separate slices of the same customer relationship. It generates investment arguments that no single department could make alone. And it forces the question that the entire CxC Matrix framework is built to answer: what is the customer actually experiencing — and is it worth what they are paying for it?

What This Chapter Has Built

You now have three things that most organizations lack.

First: a framework for seeing your customer's experience as they actually experience it — not as five departments describe it from the inside, but as a continuous story with emotions, assumptions, and competitive pressures built into every stage. The empowered customer is not waiting for your sales process to begin. They are already several contacts into their own research, already comparing you to alternatives, already forming the opinions that your contacts will either confirm or contradict. The matrix makes that reality visible — and designable.

Second: an operational model for mapping that experience with economic precision — contacts plotted against stages, costs and revenues assigned to each cell, silences identified and priced, and improvement priorities ranked by return rather than executive intuition. The insurance company found $11 million by mapping a gap and filling it. The SaaS provider found revenue growth by eliminating a handoff cliff and filling a silence at month six. The fitness retailer found its most cost-efficient acquisition channel by quantifying what Stage 15 customers were already doing at Stage 1. None of these discoveries required new technology. They required the map.

Third: a way of looking at every customer touchpoint — from the most sophisticated AI-driven interaction to the most mundane operational artifact — as a container with slots, each slot representing a choice between building a relationship and processing a transaction. The receipt at ShopRite. The welcome email after contract. The invoice at month three. The renewal reminder at month eleven. Every one of these containers already reaches every customer you have. Every one of them has slots that are currently empty or filled with defaults that say nothing worth remembering. That is an inventory of opportunity waiting to be claimed.

The next chapter moves from understanding and mapping to measuring — real-time, behavioral, financial metrics that tell you exactly how well you are serving customers at every stage and in every channel, without relying on surveys that are backward-looking, incomplete, and often systematically misleading.

Because thinking like a customer is where this work begins. Measuring like an economist is where it pays.

Think Like a Customer.

Chapter Four

Choreographing the Customer

Containers, Slots, and the Architecture of Every Win

Every interaction is binary. Every slot is a choice. Every container is a stage — and the performance is always for an audience of one.

Every Interaction Is a Performance. Most Organizations Improvise.

Think about the last truly exceptional customer experience you had. Not just a good one — an exceptional one. The kind that made you stop and think: how did they know to do that? How did every element arrive in exactly the right sequence, at exactly the right moment, calibrated precisely for you?

That experience was not an accident. It was not luck. It was not even a single talented person performing well under pressure. It was choreography — a deliberate sequence of designed interactions, each one engineered to build on the last, each element chosen for its specific effect on a specific audience, all of it moving together toward a single intended outcome: your next step deeper into the relationship.

the CxC Matrix. The language is containers and slots. The mathematics is precise. But the principle is ancient: know your audience, design your stage, deliver every beat with intention, and never leave a moment to chance when you can engineer it to win.

The Meeting Place — What Actually Happens Inside Every Cell

Each cell in the CxC Matrix is not a task, a campaign, or a channel. It is a meeting place — a specific location in time and space where a human being at a specific stage of their journey encounters your company's best attempt to move them forward.

That human being has a status. They are somewhere on the arc from complete stranger to passionate advocate — a suspect, a prospect, a new customer in the fragile early weeks, a long-term customer whose relationship is quietly deepening or quietly eroding, a community advocate actively selling your product to their network with more credibility than any marketing campaign can match. In each of those cells, in each of those moments, the interaction is binary.

Not binary in the sense that a digital transaction either completes or errors. Binary in the deeper sense that matters: the customer's next step is either toward deeper commitment or toward the exit. There is no standing still. There is no neutral. The customer is always forming an impression, always updating their internal calculus of whether this relationship is worth continuing.

↑ The Interaction Advances	↓ The Interaction Stalls or Ends
The customer feels understood, valued, and confident. The message arrives at the right moment, in the right channel, with the right framing for where they are in their journey. The experience confirms their best intuition about your organization. Consciously or not, they take another step toward deeper commitment, higher value, and longer tenure. **The story is coherent. The promise is being kept. The next container is already being earned.**	The customer encounters friction, irrelevance, or the quiet indifference of an organization that doesn't know who they are or where they've been. A competitor's message — better timed, better designed, or simply more present — occupies the space your organization left empty. The journey stalls, reverses, or ends. **The cost is not the lost sale. It is the entire Customer Value Index of the relationship that no longer exists.**

There is no neutral. Every slot in every container in every cell either contributes to a story that advances commitment — or subtracts from one. And the customer experiences all of it as a single, continuous narrative — not as your sales deck, your email program, and your support queue. As one story, either coherent or fragmented, about whether your organization deserves their trust, their loyalty, and their money.

The Six Channels — Six Venues Where Your Brand Meets the Customer's Life

The six channels of the CxC Matrix are not distribution options. They are the six arenas where your company's messages, brand signals, offers, and human presence meet the customer's world — across all 15 lifecycle stages, in all 90 cells. Your choreography must work in all six simultaneously. Most organizations have designed for one or two and improvised the rest.

Geography	The invisible envelope of location, culture, access, and regulation that shapes every other channel. The rules of engagement are set here — before a single word is spoken, before a single slot is filled.
Digital	The ambient, always-available environment where most modern decision-making begins — and increasingly ends. Never closed. Always generating data. The primary arena for AI-mediated interaction in every industry.
Location	The physical spaces where the customer has chosen to invest their body, time, and presence. The highest conversion ceiling in the matrix — and the highest cost of mediocrity.
Third Party	The brokers, platforms, marketplaces, and AI agents through which your customer navigates discovery and evaluation — with or without your participation. Full of containers you didn't design and slots you may be leaving empty.
One-to-One	The channel where the individual is fully recognized and served as a specific person with a specific history. The only channel where every slot can be personalized to one. The highest per-interaction cost. The highest lifetime value return.
Community	The channel that runs whether you manage it or not — generating peer testimony that carries more weight than anything your marketing team produces. Your most credible voice. Your least controlled asset. Your highest-leverage underinvestment.

Across all six venues, across all fifteen lifecycle stages, 90 cells await design — or await default. What separates the organizations that lead their categories from those that wonder why they keep losing is, at its root, a single decision: the decision to treat the choreography of customer interactions as the core competitive discipline it is.

Containers — The Architecture of the Moment

A container is the specific structure through which a customer interaction is delivered. It is the form that carries the content — the vessel that shapes not only what is communicated but how it is received, in what context, with what emotional register, and with what implicit signal about how much care your organization invested in the moment.

A web page is a container. An email is a container. A phone script is a container. A product package is a container. An invoice is a container. A hotel check-in greeting is a container. A factory floor walkthrough with an account engineer is a container. A support chat window is a container. A community forum post is a container. A push notification arriving on a phone at 7:14 in the morning is a container. A receipt — two items, $8.58, handed across a counter — is a container.

What makes a container more than a format is that it arrives in context. The customer brings to every container the history of every interaction that preceded it — the emotional residue of previous experiences with your brand, the specific stage they occupy in their lifecycle journey, and the competitive environment they are simultaneously navigating. The container either acknowledges that context or ignores it. And that choice — acknowledge or ignore — is one of the most powerful determinants of whether the interaction advances the relationship or diminishes it.

Before a Word Is Read	The Signal Your Container Is Already Sending
Production quality	signals your regard for this customer's attention — and your regard for your own brand.
Timing	signals whether you understand where they are in their journey — or whether you are broadcasting on a schedule designed for your convenience.
Medium	signals whether you know how this customer prefers to be reached — or whether you chose the channel that costs you least.
Personalization	signals whether you know this individual at all — or whether they are a record in a database receiving the same message as 200,000 others.
Consistency	signals whether anyone in your organization is coordinating — or whether the left hand cannot see the right, and the customer pays the price.
Relevance	signals whether this was designed for this customer — or broadcast to everyone because designing for one felt too expensive to justify.

Every container is a composite of elements — visual, textual, structural, sensory, temporal. A great email is not great because it has good copy. It is great because the subject line earns the open, the layout earns the read, the first sentence earns the second, the offer arrives at the moment the reader is most receptive, and the call to action requires minimum effort to complete. Each of those elements is a separate engineering challenge. Each occupies a slot.

Slots — The Atomic Unit of Experience Design

A slot is the specific element within a container where a message, offer, image, sound, or signal is delivered. Slots are the atomic unit of customer experience design — the smallest meaningful component that can be individually engineered, tested, personalized, and optimized.

An email has eight or more slots: sender name, subject line, preview text, header image, headline, body copy, call-to-action button, footer. Each slot carries a different message. Each can be personalized independently. Each can be tested against a variant. And the failure of any single slot — a subject line that fails to generate an open, a CTA that fails to generate a click — cascades through the container's entire ability to advance the customer's journey.

A retail web page has 50 to 100 or more monetizable slots. An Amazon product page has exceeded 263 individually engineered slots — each one positioned, sequenced, and dynamically populated based on real-time intelligence about the specific visitor: their session behavior, purchase history, behavioral profile, and hundreds of contextual signals that combine to determine which message in which slot has the highest probability of advancing this specific customer's journey at this specific moment.

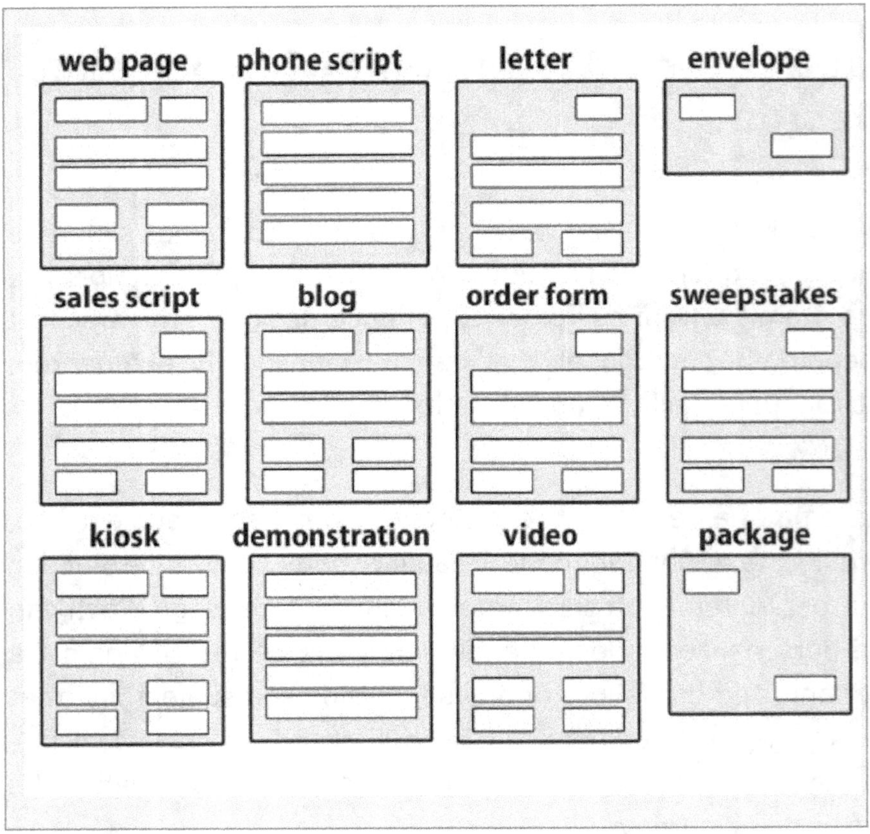

Figure 4.1 — Customer Contacts as Containers *Each contact type is a container with distinct slot architecture. Web page, phone script, letter, email, sales script, blog, order form, kiosk, demonstration, video, package — every one is a stage with designed positions waiting to be filled or defaulted.*

Notice that each contact type above is divided into sections — those sections are slots: message blocks that can be customized, personalized, and optimized using modern technology, digitized content, and AI-driven analytics. The right content for each slot can be determined by the customer, the time and location of the contact, competitive signals, inventory levels, or the strategic goals of your organization. Every slot in every container is a decision waiting to be made — either by design or by default.

Container Type	Slots	What Those Slots Include
Email	**8+ slots**	Sender name · Subject line · Preview text · Header image · Headline · Body copy · CTA button · Footer
Web Page	**24–100+**	Hero · Navigation · Search · Social proof · Product grid · Offers · Recommendations · Checkout path · Trust signals · ...
Mobile App	**12+ slots**	Splash · Onboarding · Navigation · Push notifications · In-app offers · Support access · Profile · Review prompt · Referral

IoT / Physical	**3–20+**	Packaging · Unboxing experience · Setup guide · First-use prompt · Error state · Warranty registration
Amazon Product Page	**263+**	**Every module independently engineered. Dynamically populated. Continuously A/B tested for the specific visitor at the specific moment.**

> *"The monetization of customer contacts is implemented through the monetization of slots. A slot is not a design element — it is an asset. Every unfilled, default-filled, or poorly-designed slot is a missed revenue opportunity your organization is already paying for at exactly the same cost as a slot engineered to win."*

Your organization pays for every container whether you design it intentionally or not. The invoice goes out whether it is engineered to deepen the relationship or simply to request payment. The confirmation email arrives whether it is designed to reduce buyer's remorse or simply to confirm the transaction. The phone script is delivered whether it is crafted to advance the lifecycle stage or simply to route the call. The cost is identical either way. The return is not.

Amazon — 263 Decisions on One Page

Amazon is the canonical example of single-channel slot mastery. No other organization has more visibly demonstrated what it looks like to treat every pixel of a customer interaction as an engineered economic decision. Look at Amazon's homepage not as a shopper but as an experience architect, and what you see is not a web page — it is a decision matrix. A choreographed sequence of 263 or more individually optimized messages, each one dynamically populated based on real-time intelligence about the specific visitor, their session history, their purchase history, and hundreds of contextual signals the algorithm weighs simultaneously.

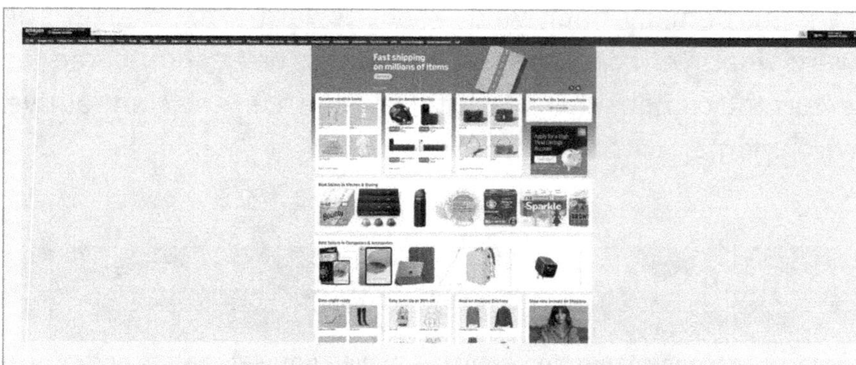

Figure 4.2 — Amazon Homepage as a Container *Every visible section is a designed slot, dynamically populated per visitor in real time. Best Sellers modules, hero banners, sign-in prompts, and category recommendations are individually engineered and continuously A/B tested. No two visitors see the same page.*

The Amazon homepage is not shown to any two visitors the same way. The 'Best Sellers in Kitchen & Dining' section appears because the system has determined this category is relevant to this specific visitor at this moment. The Prime banner is positioned where research indicates hesitant non-members are most likely to convert. The 'Sign in for the best experience' module appears at the exact viewport location where behavioral data shows undecided visitors are most likely to be sitting when they decide whether to proceed.

Every slot is the product of continuous experimentation. Amazon runs hundreds of simultaneous A/B and multivariate tests at any moment — testing headline copy, button color, module position, personalization algorithm versions. The winning configuration deploys incrementally, the losing version retires, and a new test begins immediately. The result is a page that is perpetually improving — not toward a fixed ideal but toward whatever configuration generates the best outcome for the current composition of visitors in the current competitive environment.

The Compounding Return of Slot Optimization

Amazon's recommendation engine — which populates slots across product pages with personalized suggestions — has been estimated to generate 35% of Amazon's total revenue. The mechanism that generates that return is not the algorithm itself. It is the slot the algorithm fills.

Every product page contains a 'Customers who bought this also bought' module, a 'Frequently bought together' module, and a 'Customers also viewed' module — each occupying a distinct slot with distinct copy, distinct positioning, and a distinct algorithmic logic. Remove any one of those slots and you remove a measurable fraction of total revenue. A single 0.3% improvement in the primary CTA slot across a 2-million-email program, at $8 average click value, generates $576,000 in annual incremental value. That is what a slot is worth when it is engineered properly and tested continuously.

What Amazon Cannot Do — and Why That Matters for Your Strategy

Amazon's mastery of the digital channel is real and worth studying. But Amazon's strategy also reveals the hard limit of single-channel optimization. There is no phone number on Amazon's website — deliberately. No chat for general shopping assistance. No human expert available for a $10,000 television purchase. Amazon has calculated that the cost of a human interaction in its digital channel exceeds the revenue benefit for its customer base and its business model. That is the right answer for Amazon.

It is the wrong answer for most businesses. The customer considering a luxury purchase, a complex B2B software contract, a healthcare decision, or any high-consideration product needs more than 263 slots on a web page. They need a conversation — a container that operates in real time, adapts to their specific situation, and delivers the one thing no algorithm has yet fully replicated: the felt experience of being heard by a person who genuinely understands their situation.

> *Amazon's lesson is not 'maximize your slots.' It is: engineer every slot in every channel you operate in with the same rigor Amazon applies to its single channel — and be clear-eyed about which channels your customers actually need that Amazon has deliberately decided not to serve.*

The Ritz-Carlton — When Every Sense Is a Slot

Amazon's 263 slots are visual and behavioral. The Ritz-Carlton's slots include everything you can see, hear, smell, feel, and remember. Understanding how a luxury hotel engineers the complete sensory, interpersonal, and operational experience is essential to understanding the full spectrum of what container-and-slot design means — and why the concept applies with equal power in every industry, from hospitality to healthcare to heavy manufacturing.

Figure 4.3 — The Ritz-Carlton Website as Container *The digital container signals the brand's design philosophy before a single page loads: every visible element communicates aspiration, warmth, and the promise that attention to detail extends from the website to every property worldwide. The website is not marketing. It is the first slot in the guest journey.*

The Container Is the Property — and Everything Within It

Walk into a Ritz-Carlton and the container activates immediately. The lighting is a slot — calibrated to create warmth without dimness, luxury without ostentation. The lobby scent is a slot — a proprietary fragrance developed specifically for the brand, present in every property worldwide, creating a sensory anchor that triggers brand association the moment a returning guest enters. The music is a slot — a curated playlist updated by season and time of day, designed to match the energy of the moment without demanding attention. The furniture arrangement is a slot — intimate conversational groupings that signal this is a place to be at ease, not merely a place to pass through.

Then the greeting begins. A staff member makes eye contact from twelve feet away — deliberate, warm, intentional. At nine feet, they acknowledge with a smile. At conversational distance, they engage with a greeting that reflects what the system has already prepared them to know. Returning guest? Preference history has been surfaced: room type, pillow firmness, dietary restrictions, previous special occasions, complaints resolved, compliments given. The greeting is not scripted in the sense of being read from a card. It is scripted in the sense of being prepared — every slot populated with the best available intelligence about this specific person before they arrived.

> *"The Ritz-Carlton does not have a customer service program. It has a customer choreography system — designed containers, deliberately filled slots, a story of recognition, care, and luxury that compounds with every interaction. Employees are not just empowered to deliver great service. They are trained to understand and execute a choreography."*

The $2,000 Slot — Empowered Recovery

Every Ritz-Carlton employee is authorized to spend up to $2,000 per guest per incident to resolve a problem — without management approval. This is not a generous expense policy. It is a slot design decision. The recovery interaction is a container. The slot that determines the container's outcome is the employee's ability to act decisively, generously, and immediately. The $2,000 authority fills that slot. Without it, the slot is occupied by hesitation, escalation, and the customer's growing certainty that the organization's policies care more about cost control than about them.

Service recovery research consistently shows that customers who experience a failure followed by extraordinary recovery often exhibit stronger loyalty than customers who never experienced a failure at all. The Ritz-Carlton knows this calculation. The cost of losing a luxury hotel customer in lifetime value terms dwarfs the recovery investment by orders of magnitude. The slot is engineered accordingly — not as a customer service gesture but as a precise financial decision that generates a measurable return.

Ritz-Carlton Slot	What It Is Engineered to Deliver
Lobby Scent	Proprietary fragrance, consistent across every global property. A sensory anchor that triggers brand association before the first word is spoken.

Greeting Distance Protocol	Three engineered stages: eye contact at 12 feet. Acknowledgment at 9. Personal engagement at conversation distance. Not scripted from a card — prepared from a system.
Guest Recognition	Preference history surfaced before arrival: room type, pillow firmness, dietary restrictions, previous occasions, complaints resolved, compliments given.
Room Preparation	Personal preferences applied before the guest enters. The room knows who is arriving. The guest has not had to ask for anything.
Turndown Service	Personalized by guest profile, not executed by rote. The same slot. A different performance for every occupant.
Recovery Authority	$2,000 per incident. No approval required. No justification demanded. The slot filled — decisively, generously, immediately.
Departure Anticipation	Proactive, personalized farewell that references specific interactions from the stay. Not 'thank you for staying.' A real goodbye.
Post-Stay Contact	Personal, not templated. References the specific experience. Signals the relationship continues beyond the physical stay.
Story Documentation	Notable interactions captured and accessible at every property worldwide. The next staff member inherits the story. The guest never has to reintroduce themselves.

The Ritz-Carlton's choreography is warm, human, and deeply personal precisely because it is engineered. The engineering does not make it feel mechanical. It makes it feel inevitable — as if every element of the experience was designed for you specifically, because it was. That is the difference between a great service culture and a choreographed customer experience system. Both value the customer. Only one can scale.

Facebook Marketplace — Engineering Slots in the Channel You Don't Own

Not every container is one your organization designed. Not every slot is one you fill. The third-party channel — the marketplaces, platforms, comparison tools, AI shopping assistants, and social networks through which customers encounter your brand and category — is full of containers your competitors are using and slots you may be leaving empty.

Figure 4.4 — Facebook Marketplace as a Third-Party Container *Each listing is a sub-container with engineered and default slots: primary photo, price display, title, description, seller reputation badge, location signal, response time indicator. The difference between a designed primary photo slot and a default upload is 30–50% in conversion rate. The product is identical. The slot is not.*

Facebook Marketplace is a container. Every listing is a sub-container with specific slots: the primary product photo, the secondary photos, the price display, the title, the description, the seller reputation badge, the location signal, the response time indicator. Each slot is a decision point for the prospective buyer — and each one is either engineered with intention or defaulted to whatever the seller happened to upload at 11:00 on a Sunday night.

The slot that generates the most dramatic conversion differential on Facebook Marketplace is the primary product photo. Not the description. Not the price. Not even the seller's review score, though that matters significantly. The single most powerful slot in the listing container is a high-quality, well-composed photograph that communicates the product's condition, scale, and desirability in a scrolling environment where the viewer forms an impression in approximately 0.3 seconds.

This principle scales throughout the third-party channel universe. Amazon sellers who invest in professional product photography — engineering that one most visible slot — routinely see conversion improvements of 30 to 50% over sellers using manufacturer images. The product is identical. The slot is different. The revenue is not.

The Third-Party Channel Slot Imperative

In every third-party channel where your product or brand appears — marketplace listings, review aggregators, comparison platforms, reseller sites, partner portals, AI shopping assistant databases — there are slots. Some you control directly: your product images, pricing, description copy, structured data feeds. Some you influence: your customer review velocity and quality, your response rates, your fulfillment performance that feeds star ratings. Some you monitor but cannot control: competitor comparisons, editorial content, algorithmic placement.

Your third-party channel strategy is not a partnership strategy. It is a slot strategy — an explicit, deliberate decision about which slots in which containers you are going to engineer, which you are going to influence, and which you have made a conscious choice to cede. Unmanaged third-party slots are not neutral. They are occupied by default content, competitor positioning, or the absence that a competitor will eventually fill.

The Story Arc — How Containers Build on Each Other

The transformative insight that separates organizations that improve incrementally from those that build compounding competitive advantage is this: containers do not exist in isolation. They exist in streams. The customer experiences them as a continuous narrative. And the organizations that engineer that narrative — not just individual containers, but the connections between them — are the ones that build the kind of customer relationships that resist competitive pressure and generate disproportionate lifetime value.

Great customer experience choreography works like great storytelling — or like a great symphony. Each movement picks up where the last one ended. The earlier movements create the emotional expectation that the later movements either fulfill or betray. Remove one and the whole loses its shape. Improvise one and the audience hears the seam. The best organizations design not just individual containers but the transitions between them: what the customer is expected to remember, what question they are likely to have, what competitor they are likely to be hearing from, and exactly what the next container needs to say to advance the story.

The Customer Journey as Symphony *Like instruments in an orchestra, each container plays its part at precisely the right moment — not in isolation, but as one movement in a continuous composition.*	
Awareness	Sets the opening theme — the first impression that tells the customer what kind of story this will be.
Information	Develops the melody — evidence and detail that confirms and deepens the expectation the awareness contact created.
Selection	Builds harmonic context — the comparative framing that lets the customer place your offering above the alternatives.
Contract	Resolves the tension — the moment friction gives way to commitment and the relationship officially begins.
Delivery/ Use	Sustains the primary theme — either delivering on the story told before the sale or revealing it as a promise not kept.
Community	Becomes the encore — what satisfied customers play back to the world, recruiting the next audience for the first movement.

A great symphony is not the sum of its instruments. It is the story they tell together. A great customer experience is not the sum of its contacts. It is the narrative they build.

When these containers are engineered as a sequence — when each one picks up the thread of the last and advances it — the customer experiences something that feels like being understood. Because they are being understood. Their journey is being tracked, their stage is known, their context is informing the design of every slot in every container they encounter. The experience feels personal because it is personal.

When these containers are improvised independently — when the awareness campaign is owned by the brand team, the welcome email by operations, and the renewal communication by finance, each built in isolation without reference to the others — the customer experiences the seams. They feel the organization's internal structure as their problem. They feel each handoff as a small abandonment. They feel the inconsistency across channels as a signal that the organization they chose is more interested in its own processes than in them.

The Competitive Dimension — What Happens Between Your Containers

Your customer is not sitting still between your contacts. Between your awareness message and your information container, they are seeing your competitor's information. Between your contract and your first post-sale contact, they are reading community forum posts where your brand's post-sale performance is being evaluated by people who paid what they paid and felt what they felt.

Between your use-stage communications and your renewal conversation, they are being approached by competitive sales teams who are acutely aware that renewal windows are when relationships are most vulnerable. Your choreography does not only need to be compelling in itself. It needs to be present — occupying the customer's attention, building the story, filling the slots — during the windows when the alternative is that your competitor occupies them first.

The Technical Architecture — How Enterprise Systems Engineer Slots at Scale

Understanding containers and slots conceptually is one thing. Building the technical infrastructure to engineer, personalize, test, and optimize thousands of slots across hundreds of containers, for millions of customers, in real time — that is the competitive frontier where the gap between leading and lagging organizations is widening fastest.

Adobe Commerce — the platform powering a significant share of the world's enterprise retail — publishes technical documentation that gives a precise view of how enterprise-grade slot architecture is implemented in production. Examined through the CxC Matrix lens, it reveals both how far advanced slot engineering has come and what it makes possible for organizations willing to build the infrastructure.

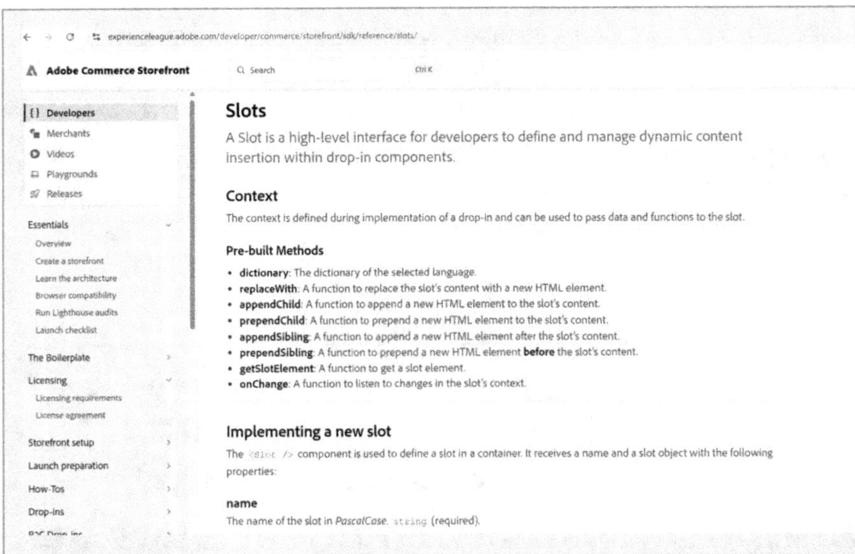

Figure 4.5 — Adobe Commerce Storefront SDK: Slots as Programmable Interfaces *The official Adobe documentation defines a Slot as 'a high-level interface for developers to define and manage dynamic content insertion within drop-in components.' Pre-built methods — replaceWith, appendChild, prependChild, appendSibling, onChange — are each a distinct type of choreographic move: a different way of responding to the customer's real-time behavior.*

Adobe defines a slot as 'a high-level interface for developers to define and manage dynamic content insertion within drop-in components.' This is the technical translation of the CxC Matrix's slot concept — a named location within a container where content can be inserted, replaced, or modified dynamically based on any combination of contextual signals. Read the API methods not as developer documentation but as a choreographic vocabulary — five different ways of adapting the stage to the audience in real time:

Method	Choreographic Function	What It Does	AI Application — The Choreographer in Action
replaceWith	**Complete Slot Replacement**	Replaces a slot's entire content, enabling full customization for a specific customer context or test variant.	*Which of 47 tested versions of this slot generates the highest conversion for this customer profile at this exact moment?*

appendChild	**Progressive Slot Enrichment**	Appends additional content to an existing slot as behavioral signals accumulate during the session.	*As the session deepens, AI appends increasingly targeted offers to the recommendation slot without disrupting what is already visible.*
prependChild	**Priority Injection**	Prepends content before existing slot content so urgent, high-relevance messages appear above standard content automatically.	*Customer abandoned cart in previous session. Recovery offer prepends before standard hero content the moment they return.*

appendSibling	**Slot Extension**	Appends content adjacent to an existing slot without disrupting the existing architecture, creating new real estate from detected opportunity.	*High cross-sell probability detected. appendSibling creates a complementary offer module instantly, without touching the existing page design.*
onChange	**Reactive Slot Updating**	Listens for changes in slot context and enables real-time reconfiguration as customer behavior shifts within the session.	*Customer adds item to cart. onChange triggers immediate recalculation of every recommendation slot on the page, optimized for the new basket.*

These five methods represent five different types of AI-driven choreographic response. Together, they constitute a performance infrastructure that enables the container to respond to the customer rather than simply broadcasting at them. This is a single component of a single platform in a technology ecosystem that includes hundreds of similar capabilities across analytics, personalization, testing, and experience orchestration tools.

> *Adobe's slot architecture is the technical implementation of a concept that predates it by decades: every customer interaction is a stage, every element of that stage is a design decision, and the best organizations never stop optimizing those decisions based on evidence from every performance.*

The Three Generations of Slot Design

The evolution of slot design follows a clear progression that maps directly onto an organization's customer experience maturity — and reveals the magnitude of the performance gap between organizations at different stages of this evolution.

Genera-tion 1	**Static**	Every customer receives identical slot content regardless of context, history, or stage. This is baseline — but it is broadcasting at a stadium without knowing who is in the seats.

Generation 2	**Personalized**	Slot content is determined by known customer attributes: segment, lifecycle stage, stated preferences, historical behavior. The right message for this type of customer in this context. Most organizations currently operate here.
Generation 3	**Predictive**	Slot content is determined by real-time AI integration of behavioral signals, contextual data, session intelligence, and competitive environment. The optimal message for this individual at this exact moment — before they even know they need it.

Most organizations are operating somewhere between Generation 1 and Generation 2. The organizations driving the competitive gaps that define category leadership are operating at Generation 3. The distance between where most organizations are and where the leaders are is not primarily a technology gap — it is a strategic commitment gap. The tools exist. The data exists. The mathematical frameworks exist. What is missing, in most organizations, is the decision to treat the choreography of customer interactions as the core competitive discipline it is.

The Mathematics — Yield, Testing, and the Optimization Engine

The organizations that lead their categories combine design excellence with a mathematics of continuous improvement that most organizations have not yet built — and that, once built, creates compounding advantages that become increasingly difficult for competitors to close.

Yield Per Customer — The North Star Metric

The foundational metric of slot optimization is yield per customer — the total economic value generated by the complete stream of interactions a specific customer experiences, divided by the total cost of delivering those interactions. Every slot-level design decision can be evaluated against its impact on this metric. A small improvement in a high-traffic, high-leverage slot can generate extraordinary returns at scale.

The Mathematics of a Single Slot Optimization	Value
Slot Optimized	Primary CTA button in flagship email program
Change Made	Subject line + CTA copy rewritten; button color tested in 3 variants
Click-Through Rate Improvement	0.3% — from 4.1% to 4.4%
Email Program Size	2,000,000 sends per month

Additional Clicks per Send	6,000
Average Click Value	$8.00
Incremental Monthly Value	$48,000
Incremental Annual Value	**$576,000**
Time to Design, Test, Deploy	**3 weeks**
Annual ROI on That One Slot	**Substantial. Permanent. Compounding.**

That slot improvement took perhaps three weeks to design, test, and deploy. The annual value on that investment — in a single slot — compounds with every send, every open, every customer relationship that advances one step further because the right message was in the right place at the right moment. This is not hypothetical. It is the economic case for continuous slot-level testing that Amazon, Netflix, Booking.com, and a widening circle of category leaders have been executing for a decade or more.

The CxC Matrix makes this calculation visible at every level: individual slot, individual container, individual lifecycle stage, individual channel. When you can see yield per customer at every level simultaneously, investment priority becomes a calculation rather than an opinion.

Multivariate Testing — The Science of Configuration

A/B testing evaluates one variable at a time. Multivariate testing evaluates multiple variables simultaneously, determining not just which version of each element performs best in isolation but which combination of elements performs best together. The subject line that converts best with one hero image may not be the same subject line that converts best with a different hero image. The offer that performs best in the left slot may not be the most effective offer in the right slot. Multivariate testing reveals these interaction effects and finds the optimal configuration across all variables simultaneously.

Booking.com runs over 1,000 simultaneous A/B tests at any given moment. Each test is a slot-level hypothesis: if we change this specific element of this specific container, does the customer's journey advance more effectively? Each result feeds a continuously improving optimization model that makes every subsequent container iteration more effective than the last. This operational posture — treating every slot as a testable hypothesis rather than a settled design decision — is not a startup behavior. It is the operational posture of an organization that has fully internalized the premise that every slot is an asset and every suboptimal slot is a permanent, compounding revenue leak.

AI Personalization — Individual-Level Choreography at Scale

The third-generation slot design model — predictive, individual-level personalization — is achievable at scale through AI systems that maintain comprehensive behavioral and contextual profiles for millions of customers and use those profiles to determine, in real time, the optimal slot configuration for each individual interaction.

This is beyond segmentation. Segmentation divides your customer base into groups and assigns the same slot configuration to everyone in a group. True individual-level personalization means point in time, point in lifestage contextualization, that the specific 47-year-old B2B procurement manager who has visited your product page three times in two weeks, requested a demo once and cancelled it, and whose search history signals they are also evaluating your primary competitor, encounters a slot configuration — across every container in every channel — that is designed specifically for their exact situation, their exact hesitations, their exact stage in the decision process, and the specific competitive vulnerability this moment represents.

Morgan Stanley deployed AI with a custom knowledge base to give financial advisors instant access to the firm's complete research library — surfacing the right information, in the right format, for the specific client conversation happening right now. The slot is the advisor's response. The AI is the system that fills it. The container is the client relationship. The choreography is the ongoing design of that relationship as a deliberate sequence of value-adding interactions that deepen trust, expand assets under management, and reduce attrition. This is the model: AI as choreographer's assistant — not replacing the human in the performance, but ensuring every slot is prepared before the curtain rises.

Designing for Memory — What the Customer Carries Away

The ultimate output of a choreographed customer experience is not a conversion metric, a satisfaction score, or an NPS number. It is memory — specifically, the emotional residue the customer carries from each interaction into the next one, and ultimately into every conversation they have about your brand with the people in their lives.

The science of customer memory has a precise finding that should guide every container design decision: customers do not remember the average of an experience. They remember the peak — the single most intense emotional moment, positive or negative — and the end. Nobel laureate Daniel Kahneman called this the Peak-End Rule, validated across hundreds of studies of experience evaluation. The implication for container and slot design is consequential and immediately actionable.

A single poorly designed slot at the end of an otherwise excellent container can define the customer's memory of the entire interaction. The checkout page that demands mandatory account creation after an excellent browsing experience becomes the defining memory of a shopping trip that was otherwise seamless. The support call that resolved the issue perfectly but ended with 'Is there anything else I can help you with today?' defines the call as transactional rather than caring — and that definition persists.

Conversely, a single extraordinary slot can elevate the memory of an entire interaction that was otherwise merely adequate. The handwritten note inside the package. The support agent who, after resolving the technical issue, noticed from the account history that it was the customer's company anniversary and acknowledged it. The follow-up email that arrived two weeks after a large purchase to ask not 'how are we doing?' but 'how is the product performing for you?' — a question that signals genuine investment in the customer's outcome rather than interest in a satisfaction score.

> *"Design the peak. Design the end. Everything in between serves to make both more powerful — because the customer's memory of the experience, not the experience itself, is what drives every subsequent decision they make about your brand."*

Fear, Uncertainty, and Doubt — The Choreography of Competitive Defense

Advanced choreography also operates in a dimension most organizations prefer not to discuss explicitly but that the most effective practitioners design for with precision: the deliberate, honest, evidence-based communication of genuine differentiation — delivered at the exact moments when the customer is most actively considering alternatives.

Every organization's product has genuine advantages over alternatives. The question is whether those advantages are communicated — deliberately, specifically, at the moments when the customer is most actively considering alternatives — or left unarticulated in the hope that loyalty persists without reinforcement. The best CxC Matrix practitioners map their competitor's interaction design alongside their own. They identify the moments in the customer lifecycle when competitive switching is most likely — around unresolved support issues, significant price events, and renewal conversations — and they design containers specifically for those moments.

Not defensive containers that communicate insecurity. Confident, evidence-rich containers that remind the customer what they would be giving up — and that make visible that the alternative they are considering has limitations that become apparent when examined with the same rigor applied to the incumbent. This is choreography as competitive strategy — and it is one of the most underutilized slots in most organizations' customer experience design.

The Choreography Audit — Seven Questions for Every Container

Building a choreographed customer experience begins with a clear-eyed assessment of every container your organization currently operates. These seven questions apply to any container — web page, email, phone script, physical environment, service interaction, packaging — and reveal immediately whether it is performing at its potential or running on default.

1	**Does this container know who it is talking to?**	Is the content adapted to the specific individual receiving it — their lifecycle stage, channel preference, history with your organization? A container that treats a new prospect and a ten-year customer identically has left the most powerful slot of all — the recognition slot — perpetually empty.
2	**Does this container know what happened before it?**	Is this container aware of the interactions that preceded it, and does it build on that history? A renewal communication that ignores 24 months of successful engagement misses the most powerful loyalty reinforcement available. A support email that ignores three previous unresolved contacts communicates organizational amnesia.
3	**Is every slot filled with intention?**	Go through the container element by element: why is this message in this slot? What outcome is it designed to advance? Every slot that cannot answer these questions is running on default — the minimum possible return from a contact your organization is already paying for.

4	**Has this container been tested?**	Is there empirical evidence that this configuration generates better outcomes than alternatives — or is the design based on whoever last edited it? Untested containers are hypotheses. Tested containers are assets. Every untested slot is a missed optimization compounding indefinitely, at zero additional cost to fix.
5	**Does this container advance a story or interrupt one?**	Does the message this container delivers connect coherently to preceding and subsequent containers? Or does each interaction feel like a first contact — as if the organization has no memory of having met this customer before?
6	**Does this container design for the memory it will create?**	Is there a deliberate peak — an element designed to create the most positive possible emotional moment? Is the end designed to leave the customer with a feeling that advances the relationship? Has anyone explicitly asked: what do we want the customer to remember from this interaction?
7	**Does this container create momentum toward what comes next?**	Does this container make the customer's next step obvious, easy, and compelling? Does it anticipate the objections that typically arise at this stage and address them before they cause hesitation? Does it open the next door — or simply close without pointing toward it?

Apply these seven questions to the ten containers your organization relies on most heavily, this is the Prioritize step. The results will be instructive — not because they reveal that your organization is doing everything wrong, but because they reveal exactly where the highest-return improvements are. The containers that fail these questions most dramatically are not necessarily the most complex or expensive to fix. They are often the most default-laden — containers that have never been intentionally designed, merely inherited.

From Improvisation to Orchestration

The organizations that win the customer experience competition in the AI era will not be the ones with the largest marketing budgets, the most sophisticated technology stacks, or the most customer service headcount. They will be the ones that have built the most intentional, most precisely engineered, most continuously improving choreography of customer interactions — contact by contact, container by container, slot by slot.

This is not a vision of a cold, algorithmic customer experience. The Ritz-Carlton's choreography is warm, human, and deeply personal precisely because it is engineered. Amazon's 263 slots feel useful and relevant rather than intrusive because the engineering serves the customer's actual interests rather than the organization's short-term conversion metrics. The organizations that get this right understand that the purpose of precision is not efficiency — it is intimacy at scale. The goal of engineering every slot is not to reduce the customer relationship to a transaction. It is to ensure that every moment of the relationship carries the weight and care of an organization that genuinely understands who its customers are, where they are in their journey, and what they need to take the next step forward.

The CxC Matrix is the architecture. Containers and slots are the vocabulary. The choreography is the practice — continuous, intentional, evidence-driven, and never finished. Because the customer's journey is never finished. And the opportunity to make the next interaction better than the last is always present — in every slot, in every container, in every cell of the matrix.

> *"Every contact your company has ever had with every customer was paid for. The only question is whether it was designed — or defaulted. The difference, compounded across every customer, every stage, every channel, every slot, is the entire gap between the organizations that lead their categories and the ones that wonder why they keep losing to them."*

Think Like a Customer. Design Like a Choreographer. Win Like a System.

CHAPTER FIVE

Think Like a Customer, Measure Like a CEO

Empathy, Behavioral Data, and the Financial Metrics That Actually Predict What Happens Next

The customer is always right — not because they're always rational, but because their experience is always real. The question is whether you understand it well enough to measure it, respond to it, and profit from it.

The Gap That Costs You Millions — Without Anyone Noticing

Here is a scenario that plays out thousands of times a day inside well-run companies with competent people who genuinely care about their customers.

A product manager sits down for the weekly team review. The dashboard looks fine. Net Promoter Score: 54. Customer Satisfaction: 78%. Support tickets closed on time: 91%. The team feels good. Maybe a little proud. Someone mentions they should keep up the good work.

Meanwhile, 340 customers quietly reduced their usage this month. Sixty-two of them have started researching alternatives — you can see this in their browsing patterns, if anyone is looking. Eleven have already made the decision to leave. They just haven't told you yet.

The NPS score didn't catch any of that. The satisfaction survey didn't catch it either. The support metrics certainly didn't — these customers stopped contacting support months ago, not because their problems were resolved, but because they stopped expecting anything to change. Their silence isn't satisfaction. It's departure in slow motion.

> ***"The customer who tells you they're unhappy is giving you a gift. The customer who goes silent is giving your competitor one."***

This is the challenge this chapter addresses. Not just how to understand what your customers are thinking and feeling — though that matters enormously. But how to translate that understanding into measurement systems that actually see what is happening, in real time, before the revenue impact is already done. How to move from the lagging indicators of traditional customer satisfaction measurement — backward-looking scores that tell you how last month went — to the leading indicators that tell you what next month is going to look like, with enough time to change it.

We will cover both sides of this equation: the empathy that reveals what customers actually experience, and the behavioral metrics that turn those experiences into numbers your finance team can act on. Because customer experience without measurement is guesswork. And measurement without empathy produces numbers that can't explain themselves.

PART ONE

Think Like a Customer

Why the Inside View Is Always Wrong — and How to Fix It

The Inside View vs. the Outside View

Every morning, millions of business professionals show up to work and make decisions about their customers — without actually thinking like their customers. Not because they don't care. Because it's genuinely difficult. Our brains default to the inside view: the organization's perspective, the internal process, the metric on the dashboard. We know what we built. We know what we intended. We know what it cost. And all of that knowledge, paradoxically, makes it harder to see what the customer actually experiences.

Your marketing team spent six weeks designing a customer onboarding sequence. Forty-seven touchpoints, three ad networks, eighteen emails, two webinars. They're proud of the architecture. The customer experienced none of that architecture. They experienced one thing: 'I needed something. I looked for it. I bought it. It worked, or it didn't.'

Your operations team optimized fulfillment to 1.8 days. Genuinely impressive. The customer experienced one thing: 'It arrived on Thursday. I expected it on Wednesday.' The objective improvement was real. The customer's experience of it was not what you expected.

This is not incompetence. It is the natural consequence of being inside the organization. The inside view sees the process. The outside view sees the experience. And these two perspectives are almost never the same thing — which is why companies that systematically cultivate the outside view consistently outperform those that don't. Customer-obsessed organizations grow 49% faster and retain customers 51% more effectively than their peers. Not because they work harder, but because they see clearly what their customers actually experience, rather than what they intend for them to experience.

THE EMPTY CHAIR

Amazon famously leaves an empty chair in senior leadership meetings. Not a metaphorical chair — a real, physical, empty chair at the table. It represents the customer. Before any major decision is finalized, someone is expected to speak for the person in that chair. What does this decision look like to them? How does it change their experience? What does it cost them in time, money, or frustration? The chair is a reminder that the most important stakeholder in the room is the one who isn't there — and that their perspective will not represent itself without someone deliberately choosing to hold it.

The Customer's Story — Five Chapters Your Organization Didn't Write

However many stages your CxC Matrix contains, however many channels you manage, however many contacts you have engineered — the customer experiences all of it as a story with five chapters. Understanding this simplified narrative is not about dismissing your operational complexity. It is about remembering what all that complexity is supposed to produce.

The Five-Chapter Customer Story		
Chapter 1	***"I had a problem"***	The customer doesn't experience your marketing campaigns. They experience a personal moment — something ran out, something broke, something got frustrating enough to address. Forty-seven touchpoints later, their story starts: 'I had a problem.'
Chapter 2	***"I looked around"***	The customer researches — but from their perspective, all sources are equal. Your website, a Reddit thread, a friend's recommendation, a competitor's content, a three-year-old review on a platform you don't monitor. They don't distinguish. It all blends into 'I looked around.'

Chapter 3	***"I made a choice"***	The 15-stage sales process your team orchestrated becomes one moment: 'I bought it, and it worked or it didn't.' Frictionless experiences don't get remembered — they feel natural. Friction gets remembered forever.
Chapter 4	***"I'm using it"***	This is the longest and most consequential chapter. Months or years of forming an opinion. If you're present during this period — proactive, relevant, helpful — you are part of their story. If you're absent, you leave a gap that erodes loyalty without any single dramatic event.
Chapter 5	***"I told people"***	This happens whether you're listening or not. A friend asks for a recommendation, a colleague complains about their current vendor, someone posts a question in a forum. The customer answers — based entirely on chapters 1 through 4. Your Community stage is not a program you launch. It's what happens when the first four chapters create a story worth telling.

The Empathy Map — Hearing What Customers Won't Say Out Loud

There is a fundamental problem with relying on what customers tell you: they often don't tell you the most important things. Not because they're being difficult. Because the most important things are often the hardest to articulate, the most emotionally sensitive, or simply the things they assume you already know.

Empathy mapping is a tool developed at Stanford's d.school that gives you a structured way to capture not just what customers say — the part you're probably already tracking — but the three dimensions underneath it that drive actual behavior. Done well, it transforms a feature comparison into an emotional portrait of the person you are trying to serve.

The Four Dimensions of the Empathy Map	
SAYS	The customer's explicit statements, the language they use, the feedback they give when asked. 'I'm not sure this will work for my team.' 'The implementation was painful last time.' 'Can you match this competitor's price?' This is the layer most organizations capture — and then stop.
THINKS	Their internal thoughts, worries, hopes, and assumptions — the things they are not saying out loud, often because they don't feel safe saying them or assume you already know. 'I've been burned before. I don't trust implementation promises.' 'I'm worried the CEO is going to kill this project.' 'I like this but my team will never adopt it.' This layer drives 70% of the decisions that the SAYS layer doesn't explain.
DOES	Their actual behaviors — what they click, search, compare, delay, and avoid. Reading competitors' case studies. Requesting three demos and showing up to one. Building a parallel Excel workaround because they don't trust the system. The gap between what customers say and what they do is where the most valuable intelligence lives.
FEELS	Their emotional state — the anxiety, the hope, the frustration, the quiet relief when something finally works the way they expected. Burdened by the evaluation process. Anxious about choosing wrong. Hopeful, but guarded. Emotion is not soft data. It is the engine that drives every decision in chapters 1 through 5 of the customer's story.

Here is a concrete example. A hospital system was genuinely puzzled. Their clinical outcomes were excellent. Patient satisfaction scores were mediocre. They ran an empathy mapping exercise across 100 patients who had undergone the same procedure, and what they found was not a clinical problem at all.

Hospital Case Study — The Empathy Gap That Was Killing Satisfaction Scores	
SAYS	'The surgery went well. The medical care was excellent.' Patients were not complaining about the clinical experience.
THINKS	'That was the most expensive thing that has ever happened to me. How am I going to pay for this? Will insurance cover it? What if there's a dispute?' The financial anxiety was enormous — and invisible to the clinical team.
DOES	Called billing three times. Visited the hospital website repeatedly looking for cost information. Requested payment plans. Avoided calling back because every call felt like the beginning of a financial negotiation.
FEELS	Grateful for the clinical care. Simultaneously frightened about the financial aftermath. Frustrated that no one had prepared them for the cost conversation. Abandoned by an institution that saved their life and then left them to navigate a billing labyrinth alone.

The fix was not clinical. It was structural: a price estimator on the website before procedures, billing staff trained to discuss payment plans proactively during pre-op visits, and a financial summary sent before the surgery rather than after. Patient satisfaction increased 23 points on NPS. Medical bill default rates decreased by 40%. The clinical work was always excellent. The container around it — the financial experience — was not designed at all.

> ***"The product works great, but the onboarding was confusing." Most organizations hear 'the product works great' and feel relieved. The customer's real message is in the second half of the sentence."***

The Empowered Customer — They've Already Done Their Homework

Here is something that should keep every sales and marketing leader slightly uncomfortable: by the time your customer engages with you directly, they have often already formed a strong opinion — based largely on sources you don't control.

The average B2B buyer consumes 13 pieces of content before making a purchasing decision, and most of it is vendor-agnostic: analyst reports, peer reviews, Reddit discussions, LinkedIn posts from people who actually use the product. In B2C, 93% of consumers read online reviews before purchasing. Not some consumers. Ninety-three percent. Your customer arrives pre-researched, pre-skeptical, and often pre-comparing you to your top two competitors.

This changes everything about how customer interactions need to work. The customer who has read 27 owner reviews noting your product's weak mobile app does not want a salesperson who denies the problem or pivots away from it. They want to be respected. They want acknowledgment: 'Yes, you're right about the mobile interface — here's exactly what we're doing about it and here's why the desktop experience still makes us the right choice for teams like yours.' That response doesn't just address the concern — it builds trust, because it proves you're honest.

TRADITIONAL SALES RESPONSE	CUSTOMER WORTHY RESPONSE
'Our mobile app is actually very well-designed for the use cases our customers care about most.' The customer, who has read 27 reviews contradicting this, files your company under 'organizations that aren't straight with me' and immediately moves you down their shortlist.	'You're right — our mobile experience has been a work in progress. Here's specifically what we've shipped in the last two quarters and what's coming next. And here's why seventeen of our customers in your exact situation chose to stay with us anyway.' Honesty isn't a concession. It's a competitive advantage.

The empowered customer also increasingly brings AI tools to the encounter. Shopping agents that research options overnight and synthesize recommendations by morning. Price comparison algorithms that run continuously in the background. Procurement bots — already deployed by Walmart and Maersk — that negotiate supplier contracts without a human buyer directly involved. Gartner predicts a significant rise in what they call 'machine customers': algorithms that act on behalf of human customers, making purchases and negotiating terms autonomously.

Thinking like a customer today, increasingly means thinking like the customer's AI assistant. What does your product information look like to an algorithm evaluating it? Is your pricing architecture legible to a negotiation system? Is your value proposition structured in a way that can be parsed by the databases that AI shopping agents draw from? This is not a future problem. It is a present competitive vulnerability for any organization whose product information is inconsistent, incomplete, or buried in PDFs that no algorithm can read.

> **THE NEW DIMENSION OF CUSTOMER-CENTRICITY: AI OPTIMIZATION**
>
> Companies spent two decades adapting their content for search engine optimization — structuring information so algorithms could find and surface it accurately. The next adaptation is AI readiness: ensuring that your product information, pricing logic, terms, and value proposition are machine-readable and accurate in the databases that AI assistants draw from. If a customer asks an AI assistant what the best option is in your category and your product is misrepresented or absent, you don't lose a consideration. You never enter one. Start by auditing how your brand, products, and reviews appear to AI-driven research tools — not just how they appear on your own website.

What It Looks Like in Practice —

Understanding the customer's perspective is easier to describe than to institutionalize. Here are three organizations that built systematic practices — not one-time initiatives, not customer satisfaction campaigns — for staying inside the customer's experience on an ongoing basis.

Starbucks — Feeling the Friction Before the Customers Do

Starbucks executives regularly spend time in their stores not as executives, but as customers. Ordering in line, using the app on a real phone, waiting for pickup in a real pickup area, noticing what a customer notices when they're balancing a bag and a phone and trying to find their name on a cup. This practice produced two major innovations that transformed the business: mobile ordering (born from executives personally experiencing the frustration of long wait times) and store layout redesigns (born from watching customers physically struggle with cramped pickup areas while holding laptops and umbrellas).

Neither of these improvements came from a customer survey. Surveys ask customers what they experienced. Standing in the line and feeling it yourself reveals what customers experience but often don't bother articulating — the micro-frictions that accumulate into the slow erosion of loyalty.

Building the Culture — Empathy as a Repeatable Organizational Practice

Individual empathy is a personality trait. Organizational empathy is a system. The difference between companies that occasionally produce great customer experiences and companies that consistently produce them is not talent or intention. It is whether thinking like a customer has been institutionalized — baked into how decisions get made, how performance gets measured, and how language works in internal meetings.

Five Practices That Work at Scale

Customer Council Meetings bring real customers into direct conversation with decision-makers — not to pitch to them, but to listen. The rule is simple: customers talk 70% of the time. Leaders listen. This sounds obvious but violates the instinct of almost every organization, which wants to use customer time to present plans and get approval rather than to genuinely interrogate assumptions.

Employee Shadowing expands beyond customer service. Every person in the organization — product managers, finance analysts, engineers — spends time with customers. Not on service calls (though those are valuable). In the customer's environment, watching them use the product, solve the problem, live with the consequences of every design decision made from the inside.

Making Customer Feedback Visible means NPS comments, support tickets, social media mentions, and app store reviews are not sequestered in a CX department report that gets circulated quarterly. They live on screens in common areas. They get shared at the beginning of team meetings. One retail chain starts every morning huddle by sharing a single customer anecdote from the previous day — not sales numbers, not operational metrics. What happened with one real person, and what did we learn?

Language Monitoring is unglamorous but powerful. Listen for how your team talks about customers internally. 'User error.' 'They just don't understand how to use it.' 'We need to educate customers.' Every one of those phrases is a diagnostic of an empathy gap. The customer is not wrong. The design is unintuitive. The process is confusing. The moment you catch an employee saying 'customers don't understand' and replace it with 'we haven't made this clear enough,' you have changed the organization's fundamental orientation toward customer experience.

Incentive Alignment is the capstone. Everything else in this list is soft until the organization puts money behind it. Companies that tie 20-30% of executive variable compensation to customer satisfaction improvements are not making a symbolic gesture. They are changing what executives pay attention to on a daily basis — and therefore what gets resourced, what gets escalated, and what gets deprioritized when tradeoffs must be made.

THE ONE QUESTION THAT CHANGES EVERYTHING

Steve Jobs famously articulated the principle that drives Apple's design obsession: you have to start with the customer experience and work backwards to the technology. Not the other way around. This sounds like a philosophical preference. It is actually a process instruction. Before any product decision, any policy change, any operational redesign, ask one question first: 'If I were the customer in this situation, what would I want?' Not what would be operationally efficient. Not what would reduce cost. Not what would be technically easiest. What would the customer want? Build that question into your team's decision-making vocabulary, and the rest of the cultural shift follows.

PART TWO

Measure Like a CEO

Beyond Surveys — The Behavioral Signals and Financial Metrics That Actually Predict Revenue

Why Your Survey Score Is Lying to You

There is a reason your customer satisfaction score looks fine while your retention numbers are quietly declining. NPS, CSAT, Customer Effort Score — these are all survey-based metrics, and surveys have a structural problem that no question design or sample size can fully fix: they measure what customers say about their experience, not what customers do as a result of it.

Consider what this actually means. A customer gives you an 8 out of 10 after a support interaction. You log a positive result. What you don't know is that this customer has quietly started evaluating your primary competitor, has reduced their usage by 40% over the past month, and has already recommended a colleague look elsewhere. Their 8 reflects a single interaction that was competently handled. It does not reflect the trajectory of their relationship with your organization.

FOUR STRUCTURAL PROBLEMS WITH SURVEY-BASED MEASUREMENT

Self-reported data is unreliable — people recall and rate experiences inaccurately, especially days after the fact

Surveys sample 2-3% of your customer contacts — 97% of interactions go unmeasured

Response bias skews results — extreme experiences (very positive, very negative) over-represent; the at-risk middle often doesn't respond

No tie to revenue — a satisfaction score doesn't tell you whether satisfaction drives repurchase, referral, or churn

The most damaging characteristic of survey-based measurement is that it is backward-looking. You measure satisfaction after the interaction. You can use that data to improve the next interaction. But you cannot change the one that already happened. And by the time the score gets reported, aggregated, and reviewed in a leadership meeting, you are three weeks removed from the events that produced it.

Leading companies have largely shifted from asking 'how did we do?' to watching what customers actually do — and using behavioral signals that update in real time to catch problems before they become exits.

Six Behavioral Signals That Tell You More Than Any Survey

Behavior doesn't lie the way self-report does. When a customer stops logging in, that signal is unambiguous. When they increase their order frequency, that signal is unambiguous. When they open seven support tickets in the first month, that signal is unambiguous — even if every one of those tickets gets resolved to their stated satisfaction. Here are the six behavioral dimensions that, together, give you a real-time portrait of customer health.

Signal	What to Measure	Real-World Example
Engage-ment	Login frequency, feature usage depth, session length, time in product. Are they using more of what you built, or less?	*A productivity platform tracked daily active users per account. When DAU dropped 50% in a month, 78% of those accounts churned within 90 days. The behavioral signal predicted churn three months before the renewal conversation.*
Conversion	Do customers complete the goals you designed for them? Free-to-paid, trial completion, onboarding milestones, stage-to-stage progression.	*An e-commerce platform moved shipping cost disclosure to the first screen of mobile checkout. Cart abandonment dropped 22%. Revenue impact: $15 million. No survey would have identified the cause.*

Return Behavior	Repeat purchase rate, frequency, interval between purchases, order value trajectory over time.	*A coffee subscription service found that customers who didn't place a second order within 45 days had a 60% churn rate. A proactive email at day 40 reduced churn by 19%. The behavioral window — 45 days — was only visible in the data.*
Help-Seeking	Support volume, escalation rate, self-service resolution rate, repeat contacts on same issue.	*A B2B software company found customers opening more than 3 support tickets in their first month had 80% annual churn. Assisted onboarding for high-risk accounts dropped that churn rate to 20%. The early warning existed in ticket data for months before anyone looked.*
Expansion	Tier upgrades, additional product adoption, seat additions, wallet share growth.	*A project management tool found that customers who adopted the advanced reporting feature within 30 days had 94% annual retention vs. 67% for non-adopters. They built automated prompts to drive feature discovery. Retention improved across all accounts.*

Advocacy	Referral link usage, public review submission, case study acceptance, event attendance, community participation.	*A financial platform found customers who referred even one other customer had 5x higher lifetime value and 85% higher retention. They built referral rewards and simplified the referral process. Referral rate doubled within a year.*

From Signals to Revenue — The Customer Lifetime Value Calculation

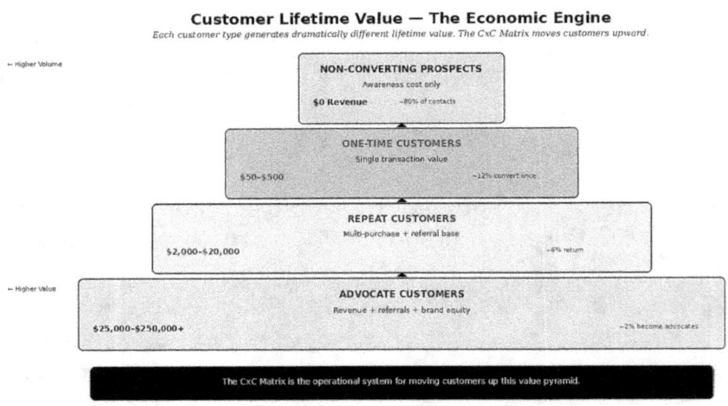

Figure: Customer Lifetime Value Layers — Customer Worthy: Future Edition

Behavioral signals are powerful diagnostics. But they become strategic when you translate them into the language your CFO uses. Customer Lifetime Value — CLV — is the bridge between customer experience and financial performance. It answers the question that ultimately matters: what is this customer relationship actually worth to the business?

The standard CLV formula is straightforward:

> **CLV = (AVERAGE ANNUAL REVENUE PER CUSTOMER) × (EXPECTED RETENTION YEARS) – (CUSTOMER ACQUISITION COST)**
>
> A customer paying $10,000 per year, retained for an expected 4 years, with a $5,000 acquisition cost has a CLV of $35,000. Straightforward — but static. The more powerful version updates dynamically based on behavioral signals.

Dynamic CLV incorporates behavioral intelligence to give you a real-time estimate rather than a historical average:

Dynamic CLV = (Current Annual Revenue) × (Probability of Retention, based on engagement score) × (Expansion Potential, based on usage patterns)

Example: A customer pays $10,000 this year. Their engagement score — based on login frequency and feature usage — indicates an 80% probability of one-year retention. Their usage of only 40% of available features suggests an expansion multiplier of 1.3x. Dynamic CLV for the next year: $10,000 × 80% × 1.3 = $10,400.

Compare that to a different customer also paying $10,000, whose engagement has dropped 40% in the past month and who has opened three support tickets with unresolved issues. Their behavioral signals suggest 35% retention probability and 0.9x expansion potential. Dynamic CLV: $10,000 × 35% × 0.9 = $3,150. Same revenue today. Dramatically different value tomorrow. Which customer gets the CSM's attention this week? The calculation is unambiguous.

> ***"CLV is not an accounting metric. It is a decision-making tool. When you calculate CLV dynamically — updated by behavioral signals rather than set by contract history — you turn your customer base into a portfolio, and every customer into an investment with a current valuation."***

The Silent Customer — Your Biggest Opportunity Is the One Who Isn't Complaining

Most organizations build their customer experience improvement systems around the customers who speak up. They track complaint resolution. They monitor negative reviews. They escalate high-NPS detractors. And all of that is necessary. But it focuses attention on the loudest signals while the most dangerous ones operate in silence.

The silent customer is not happy. They are done expecting things to change. They have stopped reaching out to support because the last time they did, it didn't help. They have stopped responding to surveys because they feel performative. They are quietly using your product less, quietly researching alternatives, and quietly preparing to leave — without ever triggering a single alert in your current monitoring system.

How do you find them? Four behavioral signatures: zero engagement (no logins, no activity, no contact initiated by them); declining frequency (they used to purchase monthly, now quarterly); no expansion (on the same plan or tier for three-plus years despite multiple price increases); and no advocacy (never referred anyone, never left a review, don't attend events or participate in community).

THE PROACTIVE INTERVENTION WINDOW

Every customer's behavioral arc has a window — a period during which a single, well-timed contact can re-engage them before the departure decision is made. That window varies by industry and product type: it might be 45 days for a subscription service, 90 days for a SaaS platform, 6 months for a B2B enterprise contract. Identifying your window — the period between behavioral disengagement and irreversible decision — is one of the highest-value analytical investments your customer experience team can make. Once you know the window, you can design a proactive contact specifically for customers who enter it, delivered at the exact moment when intervention is most likely to succeed.

Real-Time Measurement — Building a Dashboard That Sees Tomorrow

The shift from survey-based to behavioral measurement is also a shift from periodic to continuous. Traditional customer experience measurement happens in cycles: quarterly NPS surveys, annual account reviews, post-interaction CSAT requests. Behavioral measurement happens in real time — every login, every click, every support ticket, every purchase, every period of silence is a data point that updates the customer's health score the moment it occurs.

An insurance company built a real-time customer health dashboard with four live views: customers with high churn risk (based on engagement drop plus open issues); customers with unresolved problems (support tickets open more than three days without resolution); customers eligible for upgrade (based on usage patterns indicating need for higher tiers); and customers at risk of escalation (based on sentiment analysis of recent support communications). The dashboard didn't just report what had happened. It generated specific action triggers for the customer success team: call this account, escalate this ticket, notify sales of this opportunity, route this conversation to a senior representative.

The results were precise and measurable: churn decreased 8%, satisfaction increased 12%, and revenue grew 6% — without adding a single headcount. The improvement came entirely from acting on signals that were always present in the data but had never been organized into a system that made them actionable.

From Signals to Action — The Trigger Architecture

Behavioral signals are only as valuable as the actions they trigger. Here is the trigger architecture that connects measurement to outcome:

Behavioral Signal	Trigger	Expected Outcome
Engagement drops >30% in 30 days	**Re-engagement email + CSM flag for personal outreach**	*Proactive contact before the departure decision is made*
>5 support tickets in one week	**Escalate to product team (pattern signal) + senior support**	*Identifies systemic problem; prevents frustration from becoming exit*
Usage pattern indicates unmet need	**Targeted feature education + usage tutorial**	*Captures expansion opportunity before customer builds workaround or looks elsewhere*
Customer hits usage limit	**Proactive upgrade offer before they feel constrained**	*Converts a potential frustration event into a revenue and loyalty win*
45-day silence from previously active customer	**Personalized re-engagement: 'Here's what's new for you'**	*Recovers disengaged customers before departure window closes*
Advanced feature adoption in first 30 days	**Celebration + deeper feature pathway prompt**	*Accelerates the path to high-retention behavior*

The Contact-Level P&L — What Every Interaction Is Worth

The most sophisticated version of behavioral measurement connects individual contacts to their financial impact — not just in aggregate, but interaction by interaction. When you can quantify the revenue impact of a single support call, a single check-in email, a single feature tutorial, you transform customer experience from a cost center managed by intuition into an investment portfolio managed by ROI.

Here is how the math works for a single support interaction. An agent spends 15 minutes resolving a customer's issue. Fully loaded cost: $8. Now measure the downstream behavioral impact by comparing customers who received this contact to matched customers who didn't.

What Happened	Behavioral Impact	Financial Value
Issue resolved immediately, customer felt heard	15% less likely to churn — based on behavioral comparison with similar customers who received slow/poor resolution	**15% of $500 annual value = +$75 in protected revenue**
Agent acknowledged frustration, offered follow-up	10% more likely to expand wallet share within 12 months	**10% of $200 expansion potential = +$20 in incremental revenue**

Issue reached support but was not resolved	70% churn risk within 90 days	**70% of $500 annual value = -$350 in threatened revenue**

Net value of a successful support interaction: $75 + $20 - $8 cost = $87 net positive return. Net risk of a failed support interaction: -$350 in threatened revenue for an interaction that cost the same $8 to deliver. That gap — $437 in financial difference between a good and a bad support contact — is the business case for investing in support quality, training, staffing levels, and systems. Not as a customer satisfaction initiative. As a capital allocation decision with a calculable return.

> ***"The $8 support call is not a cost. It is an $87 investment — or a -$350 liability. Which one it becomes depends entirely on whether the contact was designed and executed with intention, or handled by whoever happened to pick up the phone."***

Building Your Measurement System — Six Steps, Starting This Quarter

The principles in this chapter are only as valuable as the systems you build to implement them. Here is a practical sequence for moving from survey-based, backward-looking measurement to behavioral, real-time measurement — not as a multi-year digital transformation, but as an incremental capability you can build in stages.

Step 1: Identify Your Predictive Behaviors

For your specific business, which behavioral patterns correlate most strongly with retention, expansion, and advocacy? Login frequency? Feature adoption? Purchase interval? Referral activity? This is not a universal list — it is specific to your product, your customer base, and your lifecycle. Start by analyzing your best customers and your churned customers. What behavioral differences existed six months before the churn event? That gap is your signal library.

Step 2: Build the Data Infrastructure

You cannot act on signals you cannot see. This step requires connecting your product usage data, your CRM, your support system, your billing data, and your marketing engagement data into a unified view of each customer. This does not require a massive platform replacement. It requires deciding that customer behavioral data is as strategically important as financial data — and therefore deserves the same integration discipline.

Step 3: Calculate CLV Dynamically

Build a model that estimates CLV for each customer based on current behavioral signals, not just historical averages. This model does not need to be perfect to be valuable. A rough CLV that updates weekly based on engagement signals is dramatically more useful than an exact CLV calculated at acquisition and never revised.

Step 4: Set Up Behavioral Triggers

Define the specific behavioral events that trigger a response. The drop in engagement that triggers a check-in. The feature adoption milestone that triggers a deeper education prompt. The silence window that triggers a re-engagement contact. Automate the ones that are scalable. Escalate to humans the ones that require judgment.

Step 5: Measure Contact-Level Impact

Begin tracking how individual interactions affect downstream behavioral signals. Does a proactive check-in at 45 days improve 90-day retention? Does advanced feature education in the first week improve 12-month retention? You cannot answer these questions from a survey. You can answer them from behavioral data — but only if you are tracking it at the contact level.

Step 6: Iterate Continuously

Customer behavior changes. Competitive environments shift. Product capabilities evolve. No measurement system built today will be optimal in two years. Build iteration into the process: quarterly reviews of which behavioral signals most predict retention and churn, semi-annual recalibration of CLV models, continuous A/B testing of trigger designs and response contacts.

The Awareness Forfeiture — The Billion-Dollar Stage Nobody Measures

There is a number that sits quietly inside almost every organization's marketing report, accepted as normal, rarely questioned, and almost never connected to the revenue it represents. It is the response rate on awareness-stage contacts. Email: 1.8% open-to-click. Direct mail: 0.5% response. Display advertising: 0.1% click-through. Social media reach: 2% engagement. Signage and location visits: conversion rates so low they are rarely tracked at all. Partner mentions, referral traffic, affiliate touches, trade show visits — measured in fractions of a percent.

These numbers are treated as the cost of doing business. Industry benchmarks. Acceptable performance. The marketing team compares their 1.9% click rate to the industry average of 1.7% and calls it a win. What almost nobody does is look at the 98.1% — the overwhelming majority of people who received the communication, registered some level of exposure to the brand, and then disappeared into a journey the organization never tracked, never followed, and never attempted to recapture. That 98.1% is not waste. It is unmonetized potential. And in aggregate, across the full volume of awareness-stage contacts a typical organization generates, it represents one of the largest concentrations of forfeited revenue in the modern business.

Consider what actually happens during the awareness stage. A prospect sees your social media post and pauses for 3 seconds before scrolling on. A potential customer clicks your display ad, spends 22 seconds on your landing page, and leaves without converting. A buyer receives your email, opens it on their phone at 6:47 AM, reads the subject line and the first sentence, and then their train stops and they close it and never return. A retailer's customer walks past an in-store display, picks up the product, reads the back panel, puts it down, and walks away. A conference attendee stops at your booth, takes a brochure, and says 'I'll look at this later.' Later never comes. Each of these micro-interactions is a real person who had a real moment of attention directed at your brand. Each represents a relationship that began and then was abandoned — not by the prospect, but by an organization that had no system for catching them.

Modern technology has closed the gap between awareness contact and recoverable intent in ways that most organizations have not yet fully operationalized. Retargeting pixels follow the display ad visitor across the web and surface a second, third, and fourth exposure calibrated to what they viewed. Email automation detects the open without click and sends a different message the next day with a different subject line. Location intelligence identifies the store visitor who lingered in a product category and sends them a mobile offer within the hour. Partner attribution tracks the referral visit that didn't convert and enrolls it in a nurture sequence. Social listening identifies the person who commented on a competitor's post and enters them into a targeted awareness program. The technology is not theoretical — it is available, affordable, and already deployed by the organizations that are capturing the revenue their competitors are forfeiting. The question is not whether you can recover value from awareness-stage contacts. It is whether you have built the system to do it, and whether you understand what that system is worth.

The math is revealing. If a company generates 500,000 awareness-stage contacts per month across all channels — email sends, social reach, ad impressions, location traffic, partner referrals — and converts 1.5% of them, that is 7,500 customers acquired. Increase the recovery rate by one percentage point, to 2.5%, and you produce 12,500 customers from the same marketing spend. The additional 5,000 customers cost nearly nothing to acquire because the awareness contact was already paid for. The entire 98.5% who didn't convert represent a pool of partially-warmed prospects that a structured recovery system — retargeting, lookalike modeling, behavioral re-engagement, AI-optimized follow-up sequencing — can work against continuously. Every one percentage point of improvement in awareness-stage recovery is worth, at scale, the equivalent of a significant increase in marketing budget. Except it comes from spending smarter on contacts you already own rather than buying new reach you haven't earned.

THE AWARENESS STAGE CONTACT INVENTORY — WHERE THE FORFEITURE LIVES

Most organizations cannot answer a simple question: of every awareness-stage contact we generated last month across all channels, how many eventually became customers, and which channel touched them first? Without that answer, you cannot calculate the forfeiture — and you cannot prioritize the recovery. Building a unified awareness-stage contact log is the first step. It requires connecting your ad platform impression data, email send records, website session analytics, social reach metrics, partner attribution data, and location traffic estimates into a single view. The result is not just a number. It is a map of the revenue sitting untouched in your awareness pipeline, and a starting point for the system that begins to recover it.

Case Study — The Hotel Chain That Recovered $6.2 Million From Guests Who Almost Visited

A mid-market hotel chain was running a standard awareness marketing program: display ads, social campaigns, email blasts to a rented list of travel-intent households, and partnerships with travel booking platforms. Monthly awareness reach: approximately 2.4 million contacts. Conversion to booking: 0.8%. By industry standards, acceptable. By the CxC Matrix framework, a map of forfeited revenue.

The chain's marketing team had never tracked what happened to the 99.2% of awareness contacts who didn't convert. So they built the system to find out. Using pixel retargeting on display visitors, behavioral email sequences triggered by opens-without-clicks, travel intent data purchased from a third-party provider to identify anonymous site visitors, and a partner attribution model that tracked booking platform visits linked to prior ad exposure, they built a picture of the full awareness pipeline.

What they discovered was a segment they hadn't known existed: 340,000 contacts per month who showed genuine purchase intent — they visited the website, viewed room pages, checked dates, or clicked to a booking platform — but did not complete a reservation. These were not cold prospects. They were warm prospects who had self-identified as interested and then been abandoned by an organization that had no recovery system in place. The conversion rate on this identified intent segment, with a structured three-touch retargeting sequence, was 11.4% — compared to 0.8% on the general awareness pool. The incremental bookings generated from this single recovery program, over twelve months, produced $6.2 million in additional revenue from contacts the organization was already generating and previously leaving entirely unrealized.

The insight is not just that recovery programs work. It is that the revenue was always there. Every month for the years before this program was built, $6.2 million in annual revenue was walking through the awareness stage and walking out the other side — not because the prospects weren't interested, but because no system existed to catch them. The awareness stage was treated as a broadcast mechanism whose job was to spray reach and hope some of it converted. The CxC Matrix view transforms it into something far more valuable: the first stage of a managed journey, where every contact — regardless of whether it converts immediately — is a relationship that has begun and can be continued.

The hotel chain's next step was to apply the same lens to their partner channel: travel agents, corporate booking platforms, affinity group referral partners. Every partner mention or partner-driven visit that didn't convert was logged, tagged, and entered into a partner-specific nurture sequence. Upgrade and affiliate revenue from this channel — offers for room upgrades, dining packages, and loyalty enrollment surfaced to partner-referred visitors who didn't initially book — added another $1.1 million. Revenue that had always been present in the pipeline. Revenue that had always been forfeited for lack of a system to capture it.

THE AWARENESS STAGE MULTIPLIER — WHAT EVERY 1% RECOVERY IS WORTH

Before moving on, do this calculation for your own organization. Estimate your total monthly awareness contacts across all channels: email sends, social reach, ad impressions, partner referrals, location traffic, website sessions. Multiply by your current conversion rate. That is your current baseline. Now multiply the total contacts by a conversion rate one percentage point higher. The difference in customers — and in CLV-weighted revenue — is the value of one percentage point of improved awareness stage recovery. For most mid-market organizations, this number is in the millions of dollars annually. For enterprise organizations, it is in the tens of millions. And the cost of the recovery system that captures it is typically a small fraction of that value — because the awareness contact was already paid for.

Bringing It Together — Empathy and Evidence

Empathy without measurement is a feeling. Measurement without empathy is a spreadsheet. Neither is sufficient on its own, and most organizations lean too hard toward one or the other.

Organizations that lead in customer experience combine both: the systematic cultivation of genuine understanding of what customers experience, think, feel, and fear — and the rigorous measurement of what customers actually do as a result, translated into financial terms that justify investment, prioritize action, and demonstrate return.

The customer who tells you they're unhappy is giving you an opportunity. The customer who goes silent is bleeding revenue through a wound you can't see. The NPS dashboard that says you're at 57 is reporting last quarter's story while this quarter's story is being written in behavioral data you may or may not be reading. The $8 support call that either generates $87 or threatens $350 is happening right now, dozens or hundreds of times today, with no one calculating which outcome it produced.

This chapter gives you the tools to change all of that. Think like your customer — systematically, structurally, continuously, with the humility to know that what you intend to deliver and what they actually experience are not the same thing until the evidence says they are. Measure like a CEO — in behavioral signals that predict the future, financial terms that justify investment, and real-time systems that let you intervene before the story ends badly.

The next chapter applies this dual discipline to the most critical phase of the customer lifecycle: the moments after the sale, when the customer's story about whether you delivered on your promise is being written, chapter by chapter, in the experience of actually using what they bought.

Think Like a Customer. Measure Like a CEO. Act Before the Story Is Over.

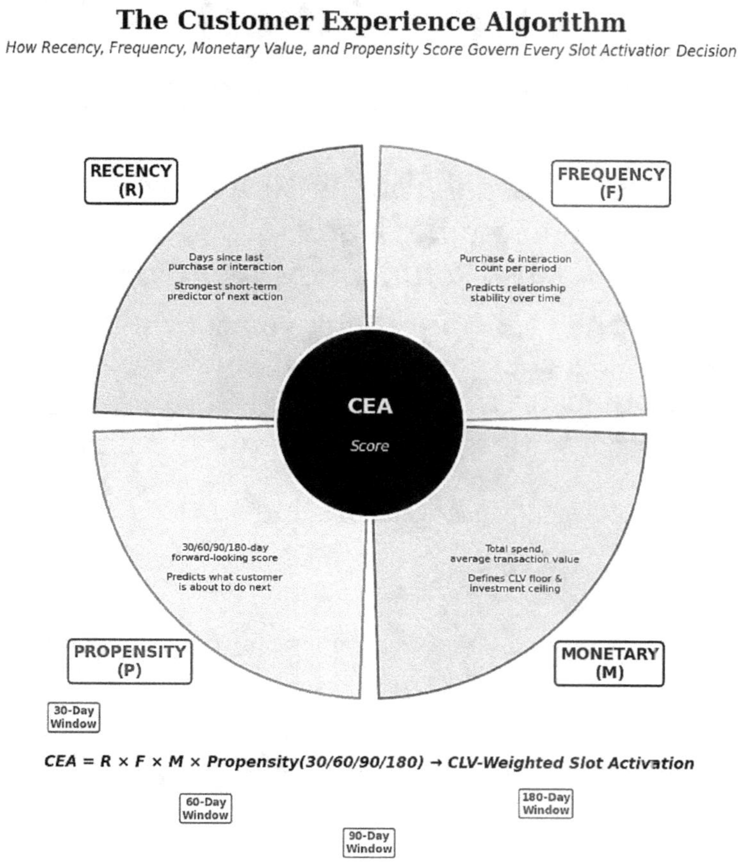

Figure: *The Customer Experience Algorithm — RFM × Propensity Score governs every slot activation decision in the CxC Matrix.*

CHAPTER SIX

The Physics of a Perfect Moment

How World-Class Organizations Turn Operational Complexity Into Customer Magic — and Why That Magic Is the Highest-Return Investment in Business

One swipe. One tap. One 'Thank you for calling.' Behind every effortless customer moment is an organization that chose to make it look easy.

> *"We don't rise to the level of our intentions. We fall to the level of our systems. A customer-centric culture isn't built on values alone — it's built on systems that make the right thing the easy thing, for every employee, in every interaction, every single day."*

One Swipe. One Miracle.

Watch a customer pay with their phone at a coffee counter. One tap. Done. Three seconds, start to finish. They pick up their drink and walk out the door, probably already thinking about something else.

What just happened in those three seconds is, without exaggeration, one of the most complex coordinated sequences of technology and human decision-making in the modern economy. A payment request left the customer's device, traveled through encrypted channels to a payment processor, was verified by a bank's fraud algorithm against hundreds of behavioral signals in real time, returned an authorization, triggered an inventory update, created an order record, notified the fulfillment system, and scheduled a digital receipt — all before the customer's hand dropped back to their side.

Multiple companies, dozens of systems, hundreds of decisions — all choreographed to produce a three-second experience that the customer registered as simply: it worked.

This chapter is about the extraordinary discipline behind extraordinary simplicity. It is about understanding what it actually takes to deliver those three seconds consistently, at scale, across every channel, for every customer. And it is about the transformative truth that sits underneath that understanding: the organizations that master this complexity don't experience it as burden. They experience it as competitive advantage — because they have learned something their competitors haven't yet grasped. When every system, every person, and every process is aligned to protect the customer's experience of effortlessness, three things happen simultaneously. The customer wins. The employee wins. The company wins. Not as a nice sentiment on a values poster. As a measurable, predictable, compounding economic outcome.

> ***"Effortlessness is not a feature. It is a culture — expressed in operations, technology, training, incentive design, and the ten thousand daily decisions made by people who understand exactly whose experience they are protecting."***

The Iceberg Beneath the Moment

To most customers, the experience is the iceberg's tip. Visible, clean, apparent. What they never see — what most employees never see, either — is the nine-tenths of the structure that makes the visible part possible.

Here is a rough accounting of what lives behind a single e-commerce purchase. A customer finds a product, spends three minutes reading reviews, clicks Buy, and enters their payment information. From their perspective: simple. From the organization's perspective: at least eight interconnected systems must succeed in precisely the right sequence, within tolerances measured in milliseconds, coordinated across at least three departments and potentially three external partners, simultaneously.

> **THE TRUE COST OF A SINGLE PURCHASE — WHAT THE CUSTOMER NEVER SEES**
>
> Marketing upstream: if this customer arrived through paid search at a 2% conversion rate, their acquisition cost is $50 ÷ 2% = $2,500 attributed to this transaction. If they came through organic referral, near zero. The cost of the awareness stage matters enormously to the economics of every transaction downstream. Website infrastructure: server costs, CDN delivery, session analytics, personalization rendering — approximately $0.10 per visit. Payment processing: the standard gateway fee of 2.9% plus $0.30 means a $100 purchase costs $3.20 in processing alone. Order management: $0.05 to create and route the record. Fulfillment: $3–5 to pick, pack, label, and hand off to a carrier. Shipping: $2–15+ depending on method, speed, and destination. Customer communications: three triggered messages — confirmation, shipped, delivered — together costing approximately $0.05. Customer service overhead: factoring in average support contacts per order, $0.50–2.00 depending on complexity and exception rate. Total organizational investment in a single seamless purchase: $8 to $20 before a dollar of revenue is recognized. That investment either generates a profitable, loyal customer — or it vanishes entirely the moment any single system in the chain fails.

Understanding this cost structure is not an exercise in anxiety. It is a design principle. When every person in the organization understands what a single successful customer interaction actually costs — and what a single failed one actually loses — the conversation about customer experience stops being about satisfaction scores and starts being about economics.

The support agent who knows that a failed delivery doesn't just create a frustrated customer, but triggers a return, a reshipping cost, a churn risk, and a potential negative review with a long-tail impact on future acquisition — that agent makes different decisions. The engineer who knows that a 200-millisecond increase in checkout load time correlates with a measurable drop in conversion rate — and can translate that conversion drop into lost revenue per day — prioritizes differently. The operations manager who sees that inventory inaccuracy generates an average of $15 in downstream costs for every $2 it saved in simplifying the count process — makes different tradeoffs.

> ***"The customer's experience of simplicity is not accidental. It is the result of every person in the organization understanding, deeply and precisely, what it costs when that simplicity breaks — and choosing to prevent it, every day, before it does."***

The Nine Moments — When Choreography Becomes Culture

The most useful way to understand the complexity behind a customer transaction is to map every moment — not every system, not every department, but every discrete moment at which a decision is made, a standard is either met or missed, and the customer's experience either advances toward delight or tips toward disappointment.

There are nine such moments in a standard e-commerce purchase. Each one is owned by someone. Each one has a measurable standard. Each one, when it works exactly right, contributes invisibly to the customer's three-second experience. And each one, when it fails, creates a ripple of damage whose full cost rarely lands in the budget of the team that caused it.

#	Moment	What Happens	Winning Standard	When It Fails
1	**Intent Received**	Customer enters payment information and taps Pay. This is the moment of maximum commercial commitment — the customer has decided and is acting.	Page renders in <2 seconds. Form is unambiguous. No unnecessary fields. Trust signals visible.	*Slow load, confusing form, or visible friction causes 20–40% abandonment at this exact step.*
2	Encryption	Payment data is encrypted and transmitted across the network. Customer's trust in your entire brand depends on this step never failing.	Zero exposure. Zero logging of raw card data. Encryption invisible to customer — as it should be.	*A breach at this moment destroys not just the transaction but the relationship — potentially permanently and publicly.*
3	Authorization	Card issuer runs fraud checks against 200+ behavioral signals, verifies balance, and returns a decision in under 2 seconds.	<2 second response. Fraud detection accurate enough not to decline legitimate purchases. Error messages human-readable.	*False decline on a legitimate purchase creates frustration and abandonment. The customer leaves thinking the problem is theirs.*

4	**Confirmation**	Authorization result returns to the customer interface. This is the first moment of visible outcome — the customer sees success or failure.	Confirmation displayed in <1 second. Clear, specific, warm. Begins the post-purchase emotional transition from anxiety to anticipation.	*Ambiguous confirmation — 'processing' spinning for 10+ seconds — creates doubt and often double-clicks, causing duplicate orders.*
5	**Order Creation**	Order record is created in the database, inventory is reserved, fulfillment is notified, and the customer's history is updated — simultaneously.	All systems update within the same transaction. No split-second window where inventory says 'available' but order says 'pending'.	*Asynchronous updates create phantom inventory — customers purchase items that don't exist. Recovery costs dwarf the transaction value.*
6	**Inventory Commitment**	The specific item is reserved, the warehouse is notified, and the stock count reflects reality across all customer-facing surfaces.	Warehouse physical count matches digital record. Reservation holds until fulfilled or released. Overselling is structurally impossible.	*An inventory discrepancy discovered at pick time cascades into delays, substitutions, or cancellations that all require human intervention.*

7	**Fulfillment Triggered**	A pick ticket is generated, a warehouse associate receives the order, locates the item, packs it with appropriate materials, and generates a shipping label.	Picked within 4 hours. Correct item, correct quantity, correct packaging. Label accurate. Carrier pickup confirmed.	*Wrong item picked — tl most common fulfillme error — costs the price of tl item plus return shippi plus reshipping pl customer time plus trust.*
8	**Handoff to Carrier**	The package is scanned by the carrier, enters the tracking network, and the customer receives a tracking number that actually works.	Tracking active within 2 hours of carrier scan. Estimated delivery accurate. Insurance coverage appropriate for item value.	*Carrier scan failure mea customer receives tracking number that shov 'label created, not y received' — generati immediate suppc contacts.*
9	**Customer Notification**	Three communications arrive: order confirmation, shipment notification with live tracking, and delivery confirmation. Each one is an opportunity.	Each message arrives precisely when the information is relevant. Personalized to the purchase. Warm, not robotic. Includes a next step.	*Confirmation email 6 hou after purchase, a tracki email that fires before tl package is scanned, gene template erode potenti relationship building into missed opportunity.*

ad this table not as a technical checklist but as a cultural portrait. Every cell represents a decision made by a person — about standards, about investment, about what the customer's experience is actually worth. An organization that has optimized every cell of this table has not just solved a logistics problem. It has expressed, through action and systems design, what it believes about customers and what it believes about itself.

The organizations that master all nine moments don't do it by hiring more people. They do it by creating a culture in which every person at every step — from the front-end engineer who shaves 80 milliseconds off page load to the warehouse associate who double-checks the item before sealing the box — understands that their work is not a task in a process. It is a contribution to an experience. And that experience is the difference between a transaction and a relationship.

The Win-Win-Win — When Customer Energy Becomes Organizational Energy

Here is the idea at the heart of this chapter — the one that, once you truly believe it, changes everything about how you build and run an organization.

The greatest customer experiences in business history are not acts of generosity. They are acts of alignment. They happen when an organization has successfully arranged its systems, its incentives, its culture, and its talent so that serving the customer extraordinarily well is also the easiest path for the employee and the most profitable path for the company. Not a tradeoff. Not a sacrifice. An alignment. A synchronized state in which the customer's best outcome and the organization's best outcome are the same outcome.

When that alignment is achieved, something remarkable happens at the level of human interaction. The energy between the customer and the employee — the quality of the exchange — transforms. A customer who encounters someone empowered to solve their problem fully, equipped with the right information and the right authority, operating in a system designed to make the right decision the easy decision — that customer doesn't just leave satisfied. They leave energized. They tell people. They come back sooner. They spend more. They become, without any marketing budget required, one of the most powerful acquisition channels a company can own.

And the employee who delivers that experience? The data on this is unambiguous: employees who work in customer-centric cultures report higher job satisfaction, lower stress, lower turnover intent, and higher productivity than employees in organizations where customer service is treated as a cost center or a complaint-management function. Not because the work is easier, but because the work is meaningful. Because they can see the direct connection between what they do and the outcome it produces. Because they are given the tools, the information, and the authority to actually succeed.

🏆 CUSTOMER WINS	★ EMPLOYEE WINS	📈 COMPANY WINS
Receives exactly what was promised, with no friction, no confusion, and no unpleasant surprises.	Delivers a win with full information and authority — the interaction is a success, not a struggle.	Earns a loyal customer whose lifetime value now justifies the full acquisition cost.
Experiences a company that knows who they are, anticipates their needs, and treats their time as precious.	Works in a system designed to support excellence, not work around it — and feels the pride of real competence.	Generates word-of-mouth that reduces acquisition cost for the next customer of this type.
Encounters a proactive contact during a silence window — before they've decided to look elsewhere.	Can see the direct impact of their work in real business outcomes — reducing churn, growing revenue.	Retains a customer who would have quietly departed, at a fraction of the cost of acquiring a replacement.
Receives a recovery response that is so exceptional, it actually increases their trust in the brand.	Is empowered to make the recovery decision without escalation — faster resolution, greater pride.	Converts a potential churn event into a retention story the customer actively shares with others.

> ***"A customer-centric culture is not a department. It is not a program. It is the state of an or-***

> ***ganization where every employee, every system, and every process is oriented toward a single truth: when the customer wins, everyone wins — and when the customer loses, no one in the building should feel comfortable calling that day a success."***

When One Swipe Breaks Everything — The $5 Million Lesson

The counterpoint to the three-second miracle is the three-second disaster. And the most instructive version of the disaster is not the dramatic failure that everyone can see coming. It is the perfectly ordinary transaction at an extraordinary moment of volume — the Black Friday system test that no one fully ran, the peak-season demand spike that exceeded every simulation, the cascading failure that begins with a payment system moving fractionally faster than an inventory system and ends with tens of thousands of confused, angry customers and a damage bill that takes years to fully quantify.

The scenario is not hypothetical. E-commerce Black Friday crashes have become a reliable genre of cautionary case study, and they all share the same structural root cause: the organization tested its systems under normal load and assumed that peak load was a quantitative difference rather than a qualitative one. It isn't. When traffic spikes tenfold, the failure points are not the ones that underperformed at normal load — they are the synchronization dependencies between systems that each performed fine individually but fell out of step with each other at scale.

Payment processing runs fast under load. Order creation runs a little slower. Inventory updates run slower still. For a few seconds — then minutes — these systems are operating on different versions of reality. Customers who successfully paid for items that the inventory system hasn't yet reserved. Items that appear available on the product page because the inventory update is three minutes behind. Orders that exist in the payment system but not yet in the order management system. Confirmation emails that fire based on payment success before the order record exists.

The result: customers who paid and received a confirmation email for items they will never receive. Duplicate charges because anxious customers tapped Pay twice during the processing delay and both transactions cleared. Support queues that spike to hundreds of times their normal volume within minutes, staffed by agents who don't yet know what went wrong or how to explain it. Chargebacks filed with banks by customers who assume fraud. A social media conversation that generates negative impressions in the hundreds of thousands before the first engineer identifies the root cause.

The total cost of a well-documented Black Friday crash at a mid-market e-commerce company: north of $5 million in refunds, chargebacks, premium support staffing, reshipping costs, and reputational damage that depresses conversion rates for months afterward. Not from a cyberattack. Not from a catastrophic infrastructure failure. From the perfectly predictable consequence of not testing at the load the business expected — and not designing the system to degrade gracefully when it was exceeded.

> **THE GRACEFUL DEGRADATION PRINCIPLE — WHAT IT MEANS TO BE HONEST AT SCALE**
>
> The alternative to catastrophic failure is not unlimited capacity — that doesn't exist and isn't achievable. The alternative is graceful degradation: designing the system so that when it approaches its limits, it informs rather than deceives. 'We are experiencing unusually high demand. Your order may take an additional hour to process — we will confirm by email or SMS, your choice, as soon as it's complete. Thank you for your patience.' This message costs nothing to display. It converts a silent failure into a transparent communication. And customers, given accurate information and a reasonable timeline, are far more forgiving than customers who feel deceived by a confirmation they received for an order that will never ship. Honesty at scale is not a crisis communication strategy. It is an engineering design decision, made before the crisis, that determines whether high-volume moments become brand-building experiences or brand-destroying ones.

Orchestrating Across the Organization — From Silos to Symphony

The deepest structural challenge in delivering consistently exceptional customer experiences is not technology. It is organizational architecture. Most companies are built in functional silos — each department with its own metrics, its own budget, its own definition of success. This structure is highly efficient at optimizing each function individually. It is terrible at optimizing the experience that crosses all of them, which is the only experience the customer actually has.

A customer service interaction that is rated 'resolved' by the support team's KPI system may have created a churn risk that the customer success team won't see for 60 days. A checkout optimization that improves the conversion rate metric for the e-commerce team may have increased the defect rate in a way that inflates the returns metric for the fulfillment team. A marketing campaign that drives the acquisition numbers celebrated in this quarter's board presentation may be generating customers with low lifetime value who inflate this year's acquisition metrics while quietly deteriorating next year's retention numbers.

The only way to see these dynamics — and therefore to manage them — is to adopt a single shared metric that cuts across all functions: the customer's outcome. Not each team's contribution to the customer's outcome. The outcome itself. Customer lifetime value, retention, expansion, and advocacy measured end-to-end, connected back to the specific interactions and decisions that produced them, visible to every team that touched the customer along the way.

SILOED ORGANIZATION — WHAT GETS OPTIMIZED	CUSTOMER-CENTRIC ORGANIZATION — WHAT GETS OPTIMIZED

The checkout team optimizes conversion rate. The fulfillment team optimizes cost per unit shipped. The support team optimizes tickets closed per hour. The marketing team optimizes cost per acquisition. Each metric improves. The customer's experience of the whole deteriorates, because no one owns the whole.	Every team optimizes toward a shared North Star: customer lifetime value. Checkout team improvements are measured by their impact on repeat purchase rate. Fulfillment team efficiency is measured against its impact on return rate. Support team performance is measured against its impact on churn risk. Marketing investment is measured against the lifetime value of the customers it produces.

The Journey Owner — The Role That Changes Everything

The organizational intervention that bridges the silo gap most effectively is the creation of a journey owner — a single accountable leader responsible for the end-to-end customer experience across a specific lifecycle stage or product journey, with the mandate to convene cross-functional teams and drive process change when any element of the journey is underperforming. The title varies: Chief Customer Officer, Chief Customer Journey Officer, VP of Customer Experience, Head of Customer Journey, Customer Experience Manager. What the title does not vary is the underlying challenge every person in this role inherits on their first day.

The journey owner is not a customer service manager with expanded scope. They are a P&L thinker whose P&L is the customer relationship: acquisition cost, retention rate, expansion revenue, advocacy value. They think like an investor because they are one — investing organizational resources in experiences that generate return and disinvesting from activities that consume cost without producing loyalty. But unlike most P&L owners, they rarely control the budget lines, headcount decisions, or operational priorities of the departments whose actions most directly determine the customer's experience. That gap between accountability and authority is the defining structural challenge of the role — and navigating it is where journey owners either succeed or stall.

Companies that have created this role consistently report the same finding: the journey owner sees things that no functional leader can see, because the journey owner is the only person whose view spans the entire experience. They see the handoff failures. They see the messaging contradictions. They see the silence windows. They see the moments where a small investment would prevent a large defection. The challenge is that seeing these failures and having the authority to fix them are two very different things. Marketing owns its budget. Operations owns its process. Sales owns its pipeline. IT owns its roadmap. The journey owner, in most organizations, owns none of these — and yet is accountable for the experience that all of them produce together. Success in this role, therefore, is not primarily a function of organizational authority. It is a function of organizational influence, metric alignment, and the sustained commitment of the executives who sit above the silos.

The Authority Gap — Why Influence Matters More Than Title

The Customer Experience Manager, Customer Journey Manager, and Chief Customer Officer share a structural reality that is rarely acknowledged in their job descriptions: they almost never hold direct decision-making authority over the departments, silos, and functions that collectively produce the customer experience. The contact center reports to Operations. The onboarding sequence is owned by IT. The renewal communication is written by Marketing and approved by Legal. The pricing exception requires Finance sign-off. The delivery window is set by Logistics. The journey owner sees all of these as a single, interconnected system. Organizationally, they are managed as separate kingdoms with separate rulers. This is not a dysfunction to be fixed with a better org chart. It is the permanent condition of the role — and the most effective journey owners accept it as such and develop the skills that work within it rather than waiting for authority that may never arrive.

The journey owner's most effective lever, in the absence of direct authority, is metric alignment. The practical approach: identify the customer-centric metrics that are most consequential for each department's actual performance, then work to embed those metrics into each department's existing performance goals — reported weekly or monthly alongside the departmental metrics the team already tracks. This is not a soft ask. It is a structural change to how each department defines success. When the Operations team sees first-contact resolution rate on the same dashboard as calls handled per hour, and both are reported to the same manager, the conversation about tradeoffs changes. When Sales sees post-close churn attributed to misaligned expectations set during the sale, the conversation about what to promise changes. The CxC Matrix provides the architecture for this alignment: each cell of the Matrix is both a customer contact point and a departmental performance responsibility. Customer metrics, embedded at the cell level, make every department's contribution to the overall experience visible, measurable, and impossible to ignore.

The Customer Experience Style Guide — The Journey Owner's Operating Constitution

The single most effective tool the Chief Customer Officer can create, deploy, and actively co-manage with the organization is one that most organizations have never built: a Customer Experience Style Guide. Not a brand voice document. Not a service standards handbook. A living operational constitution — authored by the CCO, co-owned by every department head, enforced through the compensation and reporting structures described above, and updated on a defined cadence as the organization's customer metrics and lifecycle assignments evolve. Where the CxC Matrix provides the architecture of the customer experience, the Customer Experience Style Guide provides its human address: the declaration, in plain language and precise numbers, of who the organization is for, what it has committed to deliver, who is responsible for delivering each piece of it, and where the organization is going.

The Customer Experience Style Guide opens with the organization's mission statement rewritten in customer context — not the version that appears in investor decks, but a translation of it into the language of the customer's life. What problem does this organization exist to solve for the people who rely on it? What does a customer's experience look like when the mission is being fulfilled, and what does it look like when it is not? From that foundation, it states the organization's strategic goals in customer terms: not "grow revenue by 18%" but "increase the number of customers who reach Stage 10 of the lifecycle — active loyalty — by 22% before the end of the fiscal year, measured by repurchase frequency and advocacy behavior." Every financial goal the organization carries has a customer-behavior translation. The Style Guide makes those translations explicit, permanent, and shared across every function that contributes to achieving them.

The second section of the Style Guide is the organization's customer portrait: total customer count, broken down by the key segments that govern how different customers experience the lifecycle differently. Not demographic segments alone, but behavioral segments — the one-time customer versus the repeat customer versus the advocate, the high-CLV tier versus the at-risk tier, the recently acquired versus the long-tenured. For each segment, the Style Guide states what the segment represents in revenue and lifetime value terms, what lifecycle stage concentration characterizes it (where is this segment clustered on the CxC Matrix?), and what the key defection and growth signals are. This section exists so that every employee in every department — from the warehouse associate to the CFO — can answer two questions with precision: How many customers does this organization actually serve? And who are they? The answers are less obvious than they appear, and the exercise of stating them plainly, in a shared document, consistently surfaces misalignment between what functions believe about the customer base and what the data actually shows.

The third and most operationally consequential section is the performance metrics architecture. It begins at the aggregate level — the organization's overall customer performance scorecard: retention rate, average customer lifetime value, net revenue per customer cohort, first-contact resolution rate, time-to-value for new customers, advocacy rate, and the composite Customer Experience Algorithm score that weighs Recency, Frequency, Monetary value, and forward-looking Propensity across the active customer base. These aggregate numbers establish the current state: where the organization actually stands, in customer terms, today. They are not aspirational. They are diagnostic. Then the Style Guide distributes those aggregate metrics across the CxC Matrix — disaggregating the organization's overall customer performance into its 90 contributing cells, lifecycle stage by lifecycle stage, channel by channel. Each cell carries its own current-state metric, its target, and its gap. The aggregate retention rate of 73% becomes, in the Matrix view, a Stage 11 renewal-stage retention rate of 58% intersecting the digital channel, a gap of 19 points from target, owned by a named manager, with a defined remediation timeline. The abstraction becomes an address. The cultural conversation becomes an operational one.

The critical element that distinguishes the Customer Experience Style Guide from every other CX document the organization has produced is explicit, named accountability. Every lifecycle stage in the CxC Matrix has a department assigned to it. Every cell within that stage has a manager named as its owner. Not a function in the abstract — not "Marketing is responsible for Stage 1 through Stage 4" — but a specific person's name beside a specific cell, alongside the metric they are accountable for, the current performance against that metric, and the target they have committed to reach. This level of transparency is uncomfortable the first time it is published. That discomfort is precisely its value. When a manager sees their name next to a gap, and that document is shared across the leadership team, the motivation to close the gap does not require a memo. It is self-generated. When the CCO can point to the Style Guide in a quarterly business review and say "Stage 8 onboarding through the digital channel is at 61% of target, and this is the person responsible" — the conversation that follows is not a philosophical discussion about customer centricity. It is a resource and priority conversation. That is exactly where it needs to be.

The fourth section of the Style Guide is the future state: the targets and objectives that define what Customer Worthy performance looks like for this organization, at this scale, in this competitive environment, twelve and twenty-four months from now. These targets are not set by the CCO alone. They are co-developed with each department head — an exercise that is itself one of the Style Guide's most valuable functions, because the negotiation of future-state targets surfaces the assumptions, constraints, and investment requirements that department heads carry but rarely share with the CX function.

The future-state section also carries the monetization logic: for each lifecycle stage and each cell where performance is below target, the Style Guide quantifies the revenue and CLV value of closing the gap. A 6-point improvement in Stage 5 conversion, multiplied across the customer base, equals a specific dollar figure of incremental lifetime value. That calculation, stated plainly in the Style Guide, transforms the CCO's request for resources from a cost of customer experience investment into a return on customer experience investment. The business case writes itself, because the math is already in the document.

The Customer Experience Style Guide functions simultaneously as a strategic document, an operational tool, and a culture artifact. As a strategic document, it aligns every function behind a shared definition of customer success and a shared picture of the gap between current and target performance. As an operational tool, it provides the CCO with a defensible, data-grounded basis for every resource request, priority escalation, and departmental accountability conversation. As a culture artifact, it does something that no org chart, mission statement, or customer service training program can do alone: it makes the customer visible inside the organization at the level of specific people, specific metrics, and specific commitments. A front-line employee who can open the Style Guide and see that their department's Stage 9 usage-stage digital metric is 14 points below target — and understand what closing that gap is worth in CLV terms — is not an employee being told to care about customers. They are an employee who can see, in concrete and financial terms, why their specific work matters to a specific outcome. That line of sight — from individual action to customer metric to organizational result — is the foundation of a genuinely customer-centric culture. The

Style Guide builds it. The CCO maintains it. And when the CEO and COO reinforce it in every senior review, it becomes the operating reality of the organization rather than a document that lives in a shared drive.

The Power of Shared Metrics and Aligned Incentives

Organizational culture is not what leaders say. It is what leaders measure and reward. An organization that says “the customer comes first” but measures and rewards only departmental KPIs has not actually created a customer-centric culture. It has created a culture of departmental optimization with customer-centric language as its marketing copy. The distance between the stated aspiration and the actual incentive structure is precisely where customer experience deteriorates — not through malice, but through the rational behavior of people responding to the metrics they are actually held to. The Customer Experience Style Guide closes that distance by making the customer-centric aspiration inseparably concrete: here are the numbers, here are the owners, here are the targets, here is what they are worth.

The transformation becomes self-reinforcing when customer outcomes are built into leadership compensation. When a percentage of executive variable pay is tied to customer retention, customer lifetime value, and net revenue impact — not just revenue and cost — the quality of attention that customer outcomes receive in the C-suite changes immediately and measurably. The most successful implementations go further: the Chief Customer Officer's, Chief Customer Journey Officer's, or CXO's compensation and bonus structure is tied explicitly to profit lift and revenue lift, with shared metrics and shared financial upside connected directly to each department manager's own compensation plan. When the journey owner and the Operations VP both have skin in the same customer retention number, the organizational dynamic shifts from negotiation to collaboration. When the CCO's bonus and the Marketing Director's bonus both move with the same acquisition-to-loyalty conversion rate — a rate that is tracked in real time in the Customer Experience Style Guide — the weekly prioritization conversation changes in ways that no amount of persuasion could produce. Companies that have made this structural compensation shift consistently show step-change improvements in customer satisfaction and financial performance, not within years but within quarters.

The highest-impact variable in this entire equation is not the journey owner. It is the CEO and COO. When the chief executive and chief operating officer actively embrace, enforce, and publicly emphasize customer-affecting metrics — when they open quarterly business reviews with the Customer Experience Style Guide's current-state scorecard before turning to the P&L, when they ask by name which manager owns the underperforming lifecycle cell, when they cite customer retention alongside revenue in every earnings narrative — the signal travels through every level of the organization with a force no CCO can generate independently. The investments, resource allocation decisions, and operational priorities that have produced the most positive and lasting profit impact — in many documented cases at an order of magnitude beyond what incremental CX programs achieved — share a single common characteristic: the CEO and COO made customer performance metrics non-negotiable, not aspirational. The journey owner provides the framework, the Style Guide, and the business case. The CEO and COO provide the gravity that turns a document into a fact of organizational life.

For front-line employees, the equivalent shift is moving from transactional performance metrics — calls handled per hour, tickets closed per day, units picked per shift — to customer outcome metrics: first-contact resolution rate, post-interaction retention probability, and the qualitative signal of customer feedback from the interactions they personally handled. These metrics take more effort to calculate. They generate dramatically better behavior. An employee who knows that their success metric includes the customer's subsequent loyalty — and who can see that metric tracked in the Style Guide alongside their department's lifecycle stage assignments — makes different choices in every interaction than an employee who knows their metric is the number of interactions completed.

Culture as Competitive Advantage — Stories, Workshops, and Ownership

Metrics align behavior. Stories change culture. The most durable customer-centric organizations invest seriously in both — and they understand that the two work through entirely different mechanisms. Metrics create accountability. Stories create identity. An employee who can recite the first-contact resolution target knows what they are supposed to do. An employee who can retell a specific story about the time their team turned a furious customer into a committed advocate understands why it matters and what it looks like in practice. Winning customer stories — specific, relatable, and retellable — are among the most powerful and most underutilized tools available to a journey owner building a customer-centric culture. They travel through organizations in ways that memos and dashboards cannot. They give employees a mental model for what Customer Worthy behavior looks like from their specific role, in their specific context. The journey owner who systematically collects, elevates, and distributes winning customer stories across departments and leadership meetings is building the organizational memory and shared identity that make every metric in the Customer Experience Style Guide more likely to be hit — because the people doing the work have a reason to care that goes beyond the number on the dashboard.

Department solution and innovation workshops serve a complementary function — and they are most effective when they are anchored to the Customer Experience Style Guide's specific lifecycle cell assignments and gap data. Where stories create inspiration, workshops create ownership. When the Operations team is convened not to be told what the customer experience problems are, but to look at their Stage 9 and Stage 12 metrics in the Style Guide, diagnose the gap, design their own solutions, and commit to implementation milestones — something changes in their relationship to the outcome. They are no longer recipients of a directive from the CX function. They are co-authors of the answer. Customer-centric behaviors that emerge from a team's own problem-solving workshop, rooted in data they can see and metrics they own, outlast behaviors mandated by policy in every organization that has tried both approaches. Stewardship — the genuine sense that this department's work matters to a specific customer's life, and that the department is named and accountable for its piece of that experience — is rarely produced by a directive and almost always produced by a conversation in which the employee was invited to think like a customer and then trusted to act on what they discovered. The journey owner who runs these workshops consistently, across every department, systematically expands the organization's customer-serving capacity without needing the organizational authority to mandate it — and builds a culture of accountability that does not depend on the CCO's presence in the room to sustain itself.

Case Study — How Trader Joe's Turned Operational Clarity Into Human Magic

Trader Joe's has no loyalty program. No app. No personalized digital coupons. No algorithmic recommendation engine. By the conventional wisdom of modern retail, this should be a competitive disadvantage. Instead, Trader Joe's consistently ranks among the highest-rated grocery retailers in the United States for customer satisfaction, generates roughly twice the sales per square foot of conventional supermarkets, and produces a level of word-of-mouth advocacy that most companies spend hundreds of millions in marketing trying to approximate — and never achieve.

The reason is not mysterious once you understand the principle. Trader Joe's has made the operational decision to do fewer things and do them completely. Smaller stores. Smaller product selection — approximately 4,000 SKUs compared to the 40,000+ in a conventional supermarket. No national brand equivalents; everything is a Trader Joe's product, designed and selected by people who actually use it. This operational simplicity is not a limitation. It is a design choice that produces a very specific outcome: employees who know the inventory deeply enough to have genuine conversations about it, a product floor that is navigable without a map and a data plan, and a store model whose economics don't require harvesting customer data to be profitable.

Walk into any Trader Joe's and you encounter something that has become genuinely rare in retail: staff who are visibly glad to be there, who know the products personally, who will tell you without being asked that the new mango chutney is better than the previous version, that the seasonal pumpkin pasta is worth stocking up on before it disappears, that the cheese you're looking at pairs well with the crackers two aisles over. This is not performance. It is what happens when operational systems are designed to give employees genuine product knowledge, genuine scheduling stability, pay significantly above the retail industry average, and a work environment uncomplicated enough that serving customers is the actual job — not the job that survives after navigating the real job of managing inventory systems, processing digital coupons, and fulfilling online orders.

The cultural result is a compounding cycle that every business leader should study carefully: clear operational systems reduce employee cognitive load, which frees employee attention and energy for customers, which creates genuine human warmth in every interaction, which generates the kind of loyalty and advocacy that no marketing budget can replicate, which produces outstanding financial performance, which is reinvested in employee pay and product quality, which sustains the culture. The cycle did not begin with a culture initiative. It began with an operational design decision — to do less, better, with full commitment to the people on both sides of the counter.

THE TRADER JOE'S PRINCIPLE — THE CULTURE THAT OPERATIONAL CLARITY MAKES POSSIBLE

Every organization that aspires to exceptional customer culture should ask the operational question first, not the cultural one. Not 'how do we get our people to care more?' but 'what are we asking our people to do that makes caring harder?' Trader Joe's answer was radical simplicity: fewer products, smaller spaces, no loyalty data infrastructure, no national brand negotiations, no online order fulfillment during store hours. Each thing removed from the operational burden is energy returned to the human interaction. Culture doesn't lead systems. Culture follows systems. Build systems that make full attention to the customer the path of least resistance — and employees will take that path, every time, because it is also the most satisfying one.

Designing for Failure — The Organizations That Handle Mistakes Best Win Most

Every system fails eventually. Every organization makes mistakes. Every customer experiences something that doesn't meet their expectation at some point in their lifecycle with your brand. The question is not whether failures will occur. The question is whether your organization has designed itself to handle failures in ways that preserve — and sometimes actually strengthen — the customer relationship.

The research on this is both counterintuitive and actionable: customers who experience a failure followed by an exceptional recovery often report higher satisfaction, higher loyalty, and higher advocacy than customers who never experienced a failure at all. This is called the service recovery paradox, and it has been replicated across dozens of studies in industries from hospitality to banking to e-commerce. The failure, handled right, becomes a proof point. It demonstrates, in a high-stakes moment, that the organization's commitment to the customer is not a fair-weather policy — it is a structural characteristic of how the organization behaves when it is difficult and costly to do right.

Designing for failure has three components. The first is detection: real-time monitoring systems that identify problems — payment processing anomalies, shipping delays, inventory discrepancies, sentiment signals in support conversations — before they affect a large number of customers. The second is response architecture: pre-designed playbooks that specify exactly who contacts the customer, with what message, through what channel, within what timeframe, when each type of failure occurs. The third is empowerment: giving frontline employees the authority to resolve problems at the point of contact, without escalation delays that frustrate the customer and cost the organization more in total resolution time than the original recovery action would have.

THE RESILIENCE ARCHITECTURE — FOUR ELEMENTS THAT SEPARATE RECOVERY CHAMPIONS FROM RECOVERY VICTIMS

Redundancy: Multiple payment processors, multiple fulfillment centers, multiple shipping carriers — no single point of failure

Real-time monitoring: Automated alerts when any system component deviates from baseline performance by more than predefined thresholds

Failover protocols: Pre-configured automatic switching to backup systems with zero manual intervention required

Communication playbooks: Pre-written, pre-approved customer communications for every category of failure, ready to deploy within minutes

The most powerful element of resilience architecture is also the most underinvested: the communication playbook. When something goes wrong, the quality of the organization's communication to affected customers matters as much as the speed of the technical fix. Customers who receive a prompt, honest, specific, and empathetic communication about a problem — one that explains what happened, what is being done about it, and what the customer should expect — experience dramatically lower frustration than customers who receive silence or a generic 'we apologize for any inconvenience' message that communicates only that the organization is treating them as an undifferentiated mass.

The communication playbook makes this quality possible at scale. It means that the right message — written in advance, reviewed for accuracy and tone, approved by leadership — goes to the right customer, through the right channel, at the right time, regardless of which support agent happens to be on shift when the alert fires. It removes the moment of 'what do I say?' from the equation and replaces it with a prepared, excellent response that every affected customer receives consistently. This is not a customer service tactic. It is a brand management tool — one that ensures your organization's character is expressed in its best form precisely when it is under the most pressure.

Run the Fire Drill — Simulation Is the Training Ground for Culture

There is a significant difference between an organization that has a plan for when things go wrong and an organization that has practiced it. The plan exists in documents. The culture exists in the muscle memory of how people actually respond under pressure. The only way to build that muscle memory — before a real failure creates the pressure — is simulation.

Leading organizations run customer experience fire drills with the same regularity and seriousness that safety-critical industries run emergency response training. The format is straightforward: present the team with a scenario — payment system degradation, a major carrier delay affecting a percentage of shipments, inventory discrepancy discovered after orders are confirmed — and observe how they respond. Not how they say they would respond. How they actually respond, in real time, under simulated pressure, without warning.

What fire drills reveal is almost always more valuable than what they confirm. They reveal the communication gaps that the organizational chart hides: the moment when two teams discover they are both contacting the same customers with different information. The moment when someone discovers that the playbook references a system that was replaced eight months ago. The moment when a frontline employee, empowered in theory to make a recovery decision, hesitates because no one has ever explicitly confirmed that the authority is real. Fire drills surface these gaps at a cost of a few hours of disruption. The same gaps, surfaced by a real failure, cost millions.

Beyond their diagnostic value, fire drills have a cultural effect that may be their most important contribution. They signal, visibly and repeatedly, that leadership takes the customer experience seriously enough to invest organizational time in being excellent at protecting it. They normalize the conversation about failure — making it something the organization analyzes and learns from rather than something it is embarrassed by and avoids discussing. And they build exactly the kind of cross-functional coordination muscle that the siloed organizational structure naturally atrophies: the ability of people from different departments, with different metrics and different vocabularies, to work together toward a single shared outcome under time pressure.

THE QUARTERLY FIRE DRILL — WHAT TO SIMULATE AND WHY

A useful quarterly rhythm includes three types of simulation. First, a technical failure drill: choose a critical system in your customer journey — payment processing, inventory, shipping notification — and simulate its failure. Who gets notified first? What is the customer communication? How long does recovery take? Second, a peak load drill: simulate a sudden 5x increase in transaction volume. Which systems slow first? Where does the customer experience degrade? What is your graceful degradation response? Third, a cross-functional handoff drill: a customer issue that requires three departments to coordinate — say, a payment dispute plus a shipping delay plus a product quality concern all from the same customer. How does the organization ensure the customer receives a single coherent response rather than three independent ones? Organizations that run all three drills quarterly build the coordination capability that separates organizations that talk about customer-centricity from the ones that demonstrate it under pressure.

The Culture Equation — What Customer-Centric Organizations Actually Do Differently

After studying hundreds of organizations across industries, the most consistently differentiating characteristics of genuinely customer-centric cultures are not what most leaders expect. They are not dramatic cultural transformation initiatives or visionary leadership declarations. They are practices — specific, observable, repeatable behaviors that either exist in an organization or don't, and whose presence or absence reliably predicts the quality of customer experience the organization delivers.

They Hire for Empathy and Judgment, Not Just Skill

The organizations that consistently deliver exceptional customer experiences have discovered something counterintuitive about hiring: technical skills can be taught, but the disposition to genuinely care about another person's experience is significantly harder to develop in someone who doesn't already have it. This is not about hiring 'nice' people. It is about hiring people who are naturally curious about others' experiences, who find genuine satisfaction in solving problems that matter to someone, and who possess the judgment to make good decisions in situations that no policy manual has anticipated. These people, given the right systems and the right training, become the front-line authors of the customer experience — the ones who handle the edge cases, the upset customers, the moments of genuine complexity that reveal what the organization actually believes.

They Connect Every Employee's Work to Customer Impact

In most organizations, the majority of employees have no direct visibility into the customer impact of their work. The engineer who maintains the inventory system doesn't know what a 0.5% inventory accuracy improvement does to customer return rates. The engineer doesn't see the customer smile, doesn't see the customer share the smooth experience with colleagues. The training manager who designs the onboarding program doesn't know what a faster time-to-productivity does to customer retention and engagement scores at 90 days. This invisibility is not just a motivational problem — it is an information problem that prevents the organization from deploying its full intelligence in service of customer outcomes. The fix is direct and powerful: build the feedback loops that show every role its customer impact. Not through corporate communications. Through live data, regularly shared, connected directly to the work that produced it.

They Treat Customer Feedback as Strategic Intelligence, Not Operational Complaint Management

In low-performing customer experience organizations, customer feedback flows into a complaint queue that is managed, resolved, and closed. In high-performing ones, the same feedback is treated as a continuous strategic intelligence report — a real-time view of where the organization's systems, products, and processes are misaligned with customer needs. The CEO of a leading consumer software company reads every customer complaint, review, NPS comment personally, not because the CEO has time to respond to each one, but because the pattern across hundreds of comments reveals strategic priorities that no analyst report can replicate. This practice — treating the customer's unfiltered voice as primary strategic data — creates a discipline of humility and customer-directedness that permeates the entire culture.

They Make Customer-Centric Behavior the Path of Least Resistance

The deepest lever of cultural change is not inspiration. It is friction reduction. An employee who wants to deliver a great customer experience but must fight the organization's systems, policies, and incentives to do so is an employee who is burning down the motivation to care, one transaction at a time. The most culturally sophisticated customer-centric organizations have systematically identified every point where doing right by the customer requires extra effort, extra authority, or extra risk for the employee — and they have redesigned those points so that the right action is also the easy action. This is the work that no values poster can do. It requires operations leaders and systems designers to ask, for every process and every policy: 'What behavior does this create in the employee who faces it? And is that the behavior we want the customer to experience?'

The Three-Second Standard — Building an Organization Worth That Moment

Return now to Marcus, and to Jordan, and to the coffee counter at 7:43 on a Tuesday morning.

The tap is done. The payment cleared. The loyalty points are posted. But something far more valuable than a transaction just occurred. Jordan said Marcus's name. Asked about his meeting. Offered something new — not a generic upsell, not a scripted promotion, but a specific recommendation rooted in something Marcus actually did and actually rated and actually enjoyed eleven months ago. 'If you like that Ethiopian, you're going to love this Kenyan. I'll have it tomorrow — come try it.' That sentence is not a marketing campaign. It is not a loyalty program email. It is one human being, equipped with the right information and genuine enthusiasm, creating a micro-experience so specific and so personal that Marcus will almost certainly return tomorrow. Not because a coupon told him to. Because someone he likes told him about something they both know he'll enjoy.

Now multiply that moment by every customer Jordan serves between 7:00 and 9:30 AM. And by every Jordan in every location. And by every equivalent moment — the support agent who remembers a previous issue and opens with 'I see we had some trouble with your account last month — let's make sure that's fully resolved before we do anything else today.' The account manager who sends a note before a renewal: 'I know your peak season starts in six weeks — I want to make sure everything is configured and ready before you hit it.' The e-commerce site that knows a customer's anniversary is next week and surfaces the gift they browsed three months ago with a note: 'Still thinking about it? You've got time.' Every one of these moments is the coffee counter, executed in a different medium, at a different stage of the customer journey, by a different person or system — but producing the same outcome: a human being who feels seen, known, anticipated, and genuinely served.

Behind every one of those moments is every idea in this book: the CxC Matrix that mapped the journey that brought this customer here. The container and slot design that made the app intuitive enough to disappear. The empathy map that revealed what matters to this person at this moment of their day. The behavioral signal that identified them as someone worth an extra thirty seconds of genuine human attention. The inventory system that confirmed the Kenyan coffee was in stock before Jordan said a word. The fulfillment architecture that ensures the drink is ready before Marcus reaches the pickup counter. The hire who was selected because they actually love coffee and actually love people — and who was trained, and trusted, and equipped with exactly the information they needed to turn a transaction into a relationship.

That moment is not the product of a customer service training program. It is the product of an organization that chose, across thousands of decisions over months and years, to build itself in service of that moment. To hire for it. To design its systems for it. To measure performance by it. To reward employees for it. To invest in the technology that makes it possible and the culture that makes it real.

Customer-centric organizations do not exist because their leaders care more than other leaders. They exist because their leaders have done the patient, difficult, unglamorous work of aligning systems, incentives, talent, and metrics around the single truth that every chapter of this book has articulated from a different angle: the customer's experience of your organization is your organization's most important output. Everything else — the revenue, the margin, the growth, the competitive position, the talent retention, the brand equity — follows from how well you protect it.

> ***"Build the system that makes the customer's experience of effortlessness the natural result of your organization's effort. Then watch what happens when every employee, every customer, and every stakeholder realizes that this is what winning looks like — not a zero-sum competition but a rising tide where excellence for the customer lifts everyone in the boat."***

The next chapter takes this foundation and applies it to the hardest version of the customer relationship: the moments when things have already gone wrong, when the customer's trust is damaged, and when the only thing between a lost relationship and a deepened one is the quality of what your organization does next. Recovery, handled with the same discipline and intentionality as the original design, is not the end of the customer story. It is often the beginning of the most important chapter it contains.

Design the system. Train the people. Empower the judgment. Then get out of the way — and watch what happens when everyone is finally rowing in the same direction.

The Nine Moments — Physics of a Perfect Purchase

Every moment is owned by someone. When any one fails, the customer experience — and CLV — suffers.

	MOMENT & TRIGGER	WINNING STANDARD
1	**Intent Received** *Customer taps Pay*	Page renders <2s, form unambiguous, trust signals visible
2	**Encryption** *Payment data secured*	Zero exposure — invisible to customer, as it must be
3	**Authorization** *Card issuer fraud check*	<2 sec response. Accurate detection. Human-readable errors
4	**Confirmation** *Result displayed*	<1 sec. Warm, specific. Anxiety to anticipation.
5	**Order Created** *Record + inventory reserved*	All systems update within same transaction — no gaps
6	**Inventory** *Specific item reserved*	Physical count matches digital. Overselling impossible.
7	**Fulfillment** *Pick, pack, label*	Picked in 4 hrs. Correct item. Carrier confirmed.
8	**Carrier Handoff** *Package enters tracking network*	Tracking active 2 hrs after scan. Accurate ETA.
9	**Notification** *3 comms: confirm / ship / deliver*	Timed precisely. Personalized. Warm, not robotic.

A single seamless purchase costs 8–20 in organizational investment. The customer experiences all nine moments as one.

Figure: *The Nine Moments of a Perfect Purchase — Every moment is owned by someone. When any one fails, CLV suffers.*

CHAPTER SEVEN
The Nine Objectives

Every Customer Interaction Is a Platform. Most Companies Are Using Less Than 30% of It.

The difference between an organization that treats customer interactions as costs to minimize and one that treats them as revenue platforms to maximize is not technology, talent, or budget. It is awareness — of what every interaction actually contains, what it is actually worth, and what it is capable of producing when designed with intention.

"Most companies are having exactly the same customer interactions their competitors are having — and achieving a fraction of the value from them. The Nine Objectives are the reason some companies grow while others wonder why."

The Hidden Asset Hiding in Plain Sight

There is a number sitting inside almost every organization's financials that is simultaneously their largest cost and their most underutilized asset. It is the annual volume of customer interactions — every support call, every website session, every app

infrastructure from the most expensive line on the P&L into one of the most productive revenue platforms in your business.

> ***"A customer call that costs $12 and achieves one objective is a $12 expense. A customer call that costs $12 and achieves seven objectives is a $107 investment — with a 900% return. The call is the same. What changes is the design of everything around it."***

The Platform Economics Reframe — From Cost Center to Revenue Engine

Before we examine each objective individually, we need to reframe the economics of customer interaction entirely. This is not a small conceptual adjustment. It is a fundamental reclassification of one of your organization's largest operational investments.

TRADITIONAL VIEW — INTERACTIONS AS COSTS TO MINIMIZE	PLATFORM VIEW — INTERACTIONS AS REVENUE TO MAXIMIZE

Customer service calls: $12/call × 100K calls = $1.2M annual cost	Cost: $12 × 100K = $1.2M | Revenue captured: $11.9M
Website sessions: $0.08/session × 2M sessions = $160K annual cost	Cost: $160K | Revenue captured: $25M
Store visits: $8/visit × 500K visits = $4M annual cost	Cost: $4M | Revenue captured: $174M
Email campaigns: $10K operational cost on 5M sends	Cost: $10K | Revenue captured: $129M
Mobile app sessions: $90K cost on 1.5M sessions	Cost: $90K | Revenue captured: $114M
Total: ~$5.4M in 'customer interaction costs'	Total annual value opportunity: $449M
Management response: Cut costs, reduce call times, automate, deflect.	Management response: Maximize objectives per interaction using AI orchestration.

The $449 million annual value opportunity in the right column of this table is not hypothetical. It is derived from documented outcomes at companies that have implemented platform-level thinking about customer interactions — and it assumes an organization of modest scale. For larger enterprises, the number is proportionally larger. For any organization, the key insight is the same: the value is already present in every interaction you are already having. What is missing is the design architecture to capture it.

This is what the Nine Objectives provide. They are not nine additional things to do on top of your existing interaction workload. They are nine dimensions of value that are available in every interaction you already conduct — and a framework for consciously pursuing each one, in every channel, at every lifecycle stage, using both human judgment and AI precision.

The Nine Objectives — An Overview

These nine objectives were first articulated in the original Customer Worthy, where they served as the measurable standard for every cell of the CxC Matrix — the criteria against which each customer contact should be designed and evaluated. A decade and a half later, with AI tools capable of executing each objective at speeds and scales unimaginable when the framework was developed, they have not become less relevant. They have become the most important framework in customer experience management.

Read them first as a whole, then we will explore each one individually in depth — with its classic definition, its AI-enhanced execution, the financial model behind it, and the competitive advantage it creates when deployed consistently.

1 **IDENTIFY**	2 **RECOGNIZE**	3 **FULFILL**
4 **UPGRADE**	5 **CROSS-SELL**	6 **EXPAND**
7 **EDUCATE**	8 **COLLECT**	9 **REFER**

#	Objective	Classic Purpose	AI Superpower	Revenue Model
1	Identify	Establish who is contacting you — first-timer, repeat, VIP, anonymous	Real-time identity resolution across devices, channels, and data sources in <200ms	Personalization lift: 10–30% conversion improvement
2	Recognize	Connect the customer's history, preferences, and relationship to this moment	Predictive context: surface what they need before they ask, including emotional state	Retention lift: 5–15% churn reduction per interaction
3	Fulfill	Deliver what the customer came for — completely, correctly, on first contact	AI-guided resolution paths, automated fulfillment, first-contact resolution optimization	Cost reduction: 20–40% lower cost-to-serve with same or better resolution rate
4	Upgrade	Move the customer to a higher product, service, or commitment level	Propensity models identify upgrade candidates with 70–85% accuracy in real time	Revenue lift: 15–25% average order value increase on upgraded interactions
5	Cross-Sell	Add a complementary product, service, or partner offering	Collaborative filtering + real-time inventory + margin	Revenue lift: 35% of Amazon's total revenue from this objective alone

6	Expand	Graduate the customer to a higher relationship tier: loyalty, subscription, community	Behavioral triggers identify expansion-ready customers before they self-select	LTV multiplier: loyalty members generate 2.5–5× the revenue of non-members
7	Educate	Increase the customer's knowledge of how to use the product, available channels, and what's possible	Personalized learning paths, contextual help, proactive capability surfacing	Support deflection: 20–35% reduction in future contact volume per educated customer
8	Collect	Capture data about the customer and the experience to improve all future interactions	Zero-party + behavioral + inferred data synthesis into continuously improving profiles	Compounding return: each interaction improves all future interactions across entire customer base
9	Generate Referrals	Convert satisfied customers into acquisition channels	Propensity-to-refer models + frictionless sharing infrastructure + timing optimization	Acquisition: referral customers convert 3–5× higher and have 16% higher LTV than non-referred

Why Nine Objectives Require AI — The Human Limitation and the Machine Solution

Before diving into each objective, it is worth confronting an honest question: why haven't companies already been doing this? The Nine Objectives are not a new idea. The basic logic — identify the customer, serve their immediate need, offer them something more, learn from the interaction — is not complicated. Smart, customer-centric organizations have always tried to pursue multiple goals in every interaction. Why is 'nine objectives per interaction' a strategic aspiration rather than standard operating procedure?

The answer is computational. Pursuing nine objectives simultaneously in a single customer interaction requires capabilities that exceed what human agents — however talented, however motivated, however well-trained — can execute at the volume and speed modern business demands. Let's be specific about the limitation.

WHAT ACHIEVING NINE OBJECTIVES SIMULTANEOUSLY ACTUALLY REQUIRES

Instant access to the complete customer record: purchase history, service history, predicted CLV, churn risk, current behavioral signals, preferences, channel history — all surfaced in under 200 milliseconds

Real-time calculation of optimal offers: which upgrade to present, which cross-sell to suggest, which referral incentive to deploy, at which price point, with which message — calibrated to this specific customer at this specific moment

Cross-departmental coordination in real time: sales intelligence + service history + product usage + marketing engagement + financial profile — synthesized into a single interaction context

Personalized execution at scale: not the same approach for all customers, but a different optimal configuration for each individual, selected from thousands of possible variations

Continuous learning: every interaction outcome — accepted offer, declined upgrade, sentiment signal, complaint resolved — feeds back into models that make the next interaction more effective

No human agent can maintain 10,000 customer profiles in active memory. No training program produces the ability to calculate CLV and churn risk mid-conversation while simultaneously resolving a billing dispute. No individual, however gifted, can coordinate the insights of four departments in real time and synthesize them into a natural, fluid customer conversation.

AI can do all of these things — and gets better at each one with every interaction it processes. This is the unlock. Not replacing the human element of customer interaction, which remains irreplaceable for emotional connection, complex judgment, and moments of genuine care. But equipping every human interaction with the intelligence infrastructure that makes pursuing all nine objectives not just possible but natural — the default state rather than the exceptional performance.

> ***"The best customer service agent in the world, with perfect training and genuine care, can achieve three objectives in a typical interaction. The same agent, equipped with AI orchestration, can achieve eight or nine — and feel more effective and more fulfilled doing it."***

The Nine Objectives — Deep Dive

What follows is each of the Nine Objectives explored in full: its original definition from the Customer Worthy framework, its AI-enhanced execution in the modern environment, the financial model that quantifies its value, and the data flywheel it contributes to. Read these not as a checklist but as a design specification — the blueprint for what every customer interaction in your organization should be built to achieve.

Objective 1 ***Identify***

"You should have had me at hello."

THE CLASSIC DEFINITION

The first objective of every contact is to establish who is reaching you — first-timer, repeat customer, VIP, or anonymous. This initial identification dictates the contact's entire subsequent design. A first-time customer entering your experience has different expectations, different concerns, different questions, and different conversion potential than a five-year customer calling about a billing issue. Getting this identification right, in the first moments of every contact, is the foundation on which every other objective rests. Without it, you are not personalizing. You are guessing — at scale.

AI-ENHANCED EXECUTION TODAY

Modern AI-enabled identity resolution does in 200 milliseconds what the best CRM system of 2010 couldn't do in minutes. When a customer initiates any contact — phone, chat, email, mobile app, in-store scan — the AI system is simultaneously checking device fingerprint against known profiles, phone number against CRM, email address against purchase history, behavioral pattern against session analytics, and location data against prior visit records. The result is a unified identity surfaced to the human agent (or automated system) before the first word is exchanged. Beyond identification, modern systems can classify customers by predicted behavior — likely to convert, at churn risk, likely to refer, high expansion potential — and surface that classification as the opening context for every interaction that follows.

AI Tools & Platforms: *Salesforce Einstein Identity Resolution, Adobe Experience Platform Real-Time CDP, Twilio Segment, LiveRamp, Experian Identity, Neustar TrueTouch, Informatica MDM*

💰 **REVENUE OPPORTUNITY**

A retailer with 2M annual customer contacts improved identification rate from 62% to 91% using AI identity resolution. Identified customers convert at 3.1× the rate of anonymous customers. Applied to 580K additional identified contacts: revenue lift of $4.2M annually from identification alone — before any other objective is pursued.

📊 **DATA FLYWHEEL**

Every identification event enriches the master customer record. Over time, the AI builds a probabilistic identity graph that can recognize returning customers across devices, locations, and channels — even when they don't self-identify. The more contacts, the more accurate. The more accurate, the higher the identification rate. The higher the rate, the more value extracted from every subsequent objective.

Objective 2 *Recognize*

Beyond knowing their name — knowing their story.

THE CLASSIC DEFINITION

Recognition is identification's deeper sibling. Identification answers 'who is this?' Recognition answers 'what do I know about them that matters right now?' A customer who has been with you five years is not just a repeat customer — they are someone whose loyalty deserves acknowledgment, whose history should inform every suggestion you make, and whose trust represents an accumulated asset that every interaction either deepens or erodes. Recognition transforms a transaction into a relationship moment. It signals that the organization has been paying attention — and that the customer's history with you is known, valued, and about to be used in their service.

AI-ENHANCED EXECUTION TODAY

AI-powered recognition goes far beyond surfacing a purchase history. Modern systems perform real-time emotional state inference from voice tone, word choice, and interaction pace. They identify customers who had a negative experience in the last 30 days and flag interactions with those accounts for empathy-first handling. They surface the most relevant slice of a customer's history for the current interaction context — not the entire record, but the specific elements that make this conversation more intelligent. They recognize when a customer is contacting about the same issue for a second time and route to a senior resolution specialist automatically. They detect behavioral signals indicating a customer is evaluating competitors and trigger a retention-focused interaction flow. Recognition, AI-enhanced, means the organization knows not just who the customer is but what moment they are in — and responds accordingly.

AI Tools & Platforms: *Qualtrics XM Discover, Medallia Conversation Analytics, Genesys AI Agent Assist, Five9 Intelligent Cloud, Zendesk AI, AWS Contact Lens, Google CCAI, IBM Watson Assistant*

💰 REVENUE OPPORTUNITY

A financial services firm implemented AI-powered recognition that flagged accounts with negative experience signals for empathy-first handling. Churn rate for flagged accounts fell from 18% to 7%. On a base of 50,000 flagged accounts at $1,200 average annual revenue, the 11-point churn improvement preserved $6.6M in annual revenue — from recognition alone, before a single offer was made.

📊 DATA FLYWHEEL

Every recognition event generates labeled training data: which customers, in which emotional states, at which lifecycle stages, responded best to which recognition approach. This data continuously improves the recognition model, creating a system that gets demonstrably more perceptive with every interaction it processes.

Objective 3 ***Fulfill***

Do what they came for — completely, correctly, on the first contact.

THE CLASSIC DEFINITION

Fulfillment seems obvious. Of course you should do what the customer came for. The insight is in the qualifier: completely, correctly, on first contact. Most organizations achieve partial fulfillment routinely — the issue is logged but not resolved, the order is confirmed but not shipped on time, the question is answered but incompletely, requiring a follow-up. Each partial fulfillment spawns another contact: another cost, another opportunity to disappoint, another erosion of the efficiency that the 'resolved' metric claimed to measure. First-contact resolution — the rate at which customer needs are met completely in the initial interaction — is one of the highest-leverage metrics in customer experience, because its improvement simultaneously reduces cost, improves satisfaction, and multiplies the available attention for objectives 4 through 9.

AI-ENHANCED EXECUTION TODAY

AI transforms fulfillment in three ways. First, guided resolution: AI-powered agent assist systems surface the most likely resolution path for each contact type, reducing the diagnostic time that stretches most interactions. Second, automated fulfillment: for routine contacts — balance inquiries, order status, appointment scheduling, basic troubleshooting — AI handles the full fulfillment cycle without human intervention, freeing agent time for complex contacts where judgment matters. Third, predictive fulfillment: AI anticipates what customers will need based on their recent behavior — a delayed order, a feature they haven't discovered, a billing cycle approaching — and fulfills the need proactively, before the customer contacts you. Proactive fulfillment is not just more efficient. It is the most powerful signal of organizational competence a customer can experience.

AI Tools & Platforms: *Intercom AI, Salesforce Service Cloud Einstein, ServiceNow AI Platform, Freshdesk Freddy AI, Amazon Connect, Drift AI, Gorgias (e-commerce), Ada Support, Ultimate.ai*

💰 REVENUE OPPORTUNITY

A telecommunications company improved first-contact resolution from 64% to 84% using AI-guided agent assist. Each percentage point improvement eliminates a follow-up contact costing $12. On 100K monthly contacts, each point = 1,000 fewer repeat contacts = $12K monthly savings. A 20-point improvement = $240K monthly = $2.88M annually. Additionally, customers with resolved-on-first-contact experiences churn at 2.1× lower rate, adding $4.1M in retained revenue.

📊 DATA FLYWHEEL

Every fulfillment interaction generates data on which resolution paths succeed for which contact types, which automated flows achieve satisfaction, and which patterns precede repeat contacts. This data continuously refines AI resolution models, improving first-contact resolution rates compoundingly over time.

Objective 4 ***Upgrade***

Every contact is an invitation to a better version of the relationship.

THE CLASSIC DEFINITION

Upgrade in the CxC Matrix framework means something more comprehensive than product upsell. It means motivating the customer to graduate their relationship with you to its next natural level — a higher product tier, a longer commitment term, a more complete service package, a more engaged form of the current relationship. The key word is 'natural.' The best upgrade conversations don't feel like sales pressure because they're not. They feel like a knowledgeable friend explaining why the next step actually serves the customer's interests better than where they are now. They're possible to have honestly because the right upgrade genuinely does serve the customer — and because you know enough about this specific customer, at this specific moment, to identify which upgrade that is.

AI-ENHANCED EXECUTION TODAY

AI upgrade execution works through propensity modeling: predictive models trained on millions of past interactions that identify, in real time, which customers are most likely to respond positively to which upgrade offer at which price point. A customer calling about a feature limitation in their current tier is a high-propensity upgrade candidate — but only if the AI confirms their usage patterns justify the next tier and their CLV prediction suggests the relationship value warrants the investment. The offer surfaces to the agent as a specific, personalized recommendation: 'James's usage in the past 90 days exceeds the current plan threshold by 34%. The professional tier solves this. His churn risk drops 8 points if he upgrades. Recommend at current rate for 60 days, then standard.' The agent doesn't have to think. They have to care — and execute.

AI Tools & Platforms: *Gainsight PX, ChurnZero, Totango, Pendo, Amplitude, Heap Analytics, MixPanel, HubSpot AI, Salesforce Revenue Cloud, Zuora Subscription Intelligence*

💰 **REVENUE OPPORTUNITY**

A SaaS company implemented AI upgrade propensity modeling across all inbound support contacts. Of 100K annual contacts, AI identified 23,000 with high upgrade propensity. Agents presented upgrade offers to this group with 18% conversion rate. Average upgrade value: $840/year. Annual incremental revenue: $3.48M from upgrade conversations embedded in support interactions that were previously purely cost centers.

📊 **DATA FLYWHEEL**

Each upgrade event — accepted or declined — generates labeled propensity training data. The model learns which customer profiles, at which lifecycle stages, with which product usage patterns, convert best on which upgrade offers. Acceptance signals improve future identification. Decline signals refine timing and pricing. Every interaction makes the next upgrade conversation more accurate.

Objective 5 *Cross-Sell*

If you have something that genuinely helps this customer, mentioning it is a service — not a sales call.

THE CLASSIC DEFINITION

Cross-sell is the objective most companies think they're doing and most are doing badly. The difference between a cross-sell that feels like a service and one that feels like a nuisance is entirely contextual precision. 'Would you like fries with that?' — context-free, applied identically to every customer — is a nuisance. 'Based on what you've been using, here's something that solves a problem I can see you're about to have' — precisely targeted, delivered at the right moment, relevant to this customer's actual situation — is a service. The first erodes trust. The second builds it. Amazon's recommendation engine generates 35% of total revenue using the second model. Most organizations are still executing the first.

AI-ENHANCED EXECUTION TODAY

Modern AI cross-sell operates through collaborative filtering (customers like you also bought), sequential pattern mining (customers who did X tend to need Y within 30 days), content-based filtering (products similar to what this customer already uses), and context-aware recommendation (this specific moment in this specific interaction type is high-converting for this specific offer). The system synthesizes all four approaches into a ranked list of cross-sell recommendations, each with a predicted conversion probability and an optimal message frame, delivered to the agent or the interface at the precise moment when the customer is most receptive. 'Customers with your setup often add the analytics module in month four — you're at month four. Want to see how it works?' This is not a cross-sell. This is a helpful recommendation that happens to generate revenue.

AI Tools & Platforms: *Amazon Personalize, Google Recommendations AI, Salesforce Einstein Next Best Action, Adobe Target, Dynamic Yield, Nosto (e-commerce), Monetate, Qubit, Certona, Barilliance*

💰 REVENUE OPPORTUNITY

Amazon's recommendation engine — the most studied cross-sell AI in history — generates approximately $80B annually at 35% of total revenue from recommendations. For a mid-market retailer processing $50M in annual revenue, achieving 10% of Amazon's recommendation effectiveness would generate $5M in incremental cross-sell revenue annually. Early implementations of AI recommendation systems in retail show 15–25% average order value improvement in the first 6 months.

📊 DATA FLYWHEEL

Every cross-sell interaction — accepted, declined, viewed but not acted on — generates product association data, customer preference signals, and timing intelligence. This data feeds collaborative filtering models that improve recommendation accuracy for all customers. The cross-sell data flywheel is the foundation of Amazon's 20-year compounding advantage.

Objective 6 ***Expand***

Invite the customer to a deeper, more committed, more mutually valuable relationship.

THE CLASSIC DEFINITION

Expand in the Customer Worthy framework is distinct from upgrade. Upgrade moves the customer to a better product or service. Expand moves them to a higher tier of the relationship itself — a loyalty program, a subscription, a community membership, a newsletter, a preferred customer status. The distinction matters because expansion creates a fundamentally different kind of relationship dynamic. A customer who has joined your loyalty program, subscribed to your newsletter, registered a profile, or enrolled in a community hasn't just bought more. They have invested their identity in the relationship with you. They are now connected to you in ways that make every future interaction more personal, more valuable, and more likely to deepen rather than erode.

AI-ENHANCED EXECUTION TODAY

AI-powered expansion operates through behavioral trigger identification: the system continuously monitors customer behavior for signals that indicate readiness to deepen the relationship. A customer who has made three purchases in 60 days and browsed the loyalty program page twice is expansion-ready — the AI flags this and surfaces an enrollment offer at the next touch. A customer whose purchase frequency has been declining for 90 days may be expansion-ready in a different way: a subscription offer that adds value and locks in commitment before the relationship attrition completes. The AI distinguishes between these profiles and designs the expansion offer accordingly — not a generic 'join our loyalty program' message broadcast to all customers, but a specific, timed, individually relevant invitation that feels less like marketing and more like a natural next step.

AI Tools & Platforms: *Salesforce Loyalty Management, Punchh, Yotpo Loyalty, LoyaltyLion, Antavo, Zinrelo, Talon.One, Klaviyo, Attentive, Braze (mobile engagement)*

💰 REVENUE OPPORTUNITY

Starbucks Rewards has 33 million active members who spend 3× more than non-members and visit 2× more frequently. The program generates more than $4B in annual incremental revenue from the expansion relationship alone — not from selling more coffee, but from creating a deeper relationship tier that increases every other objective's effectiveness. For a company with 500K annual customers, achieving even a 25% loyalty enrollment rate at a 2.5× spend multiplier represents a transformational revenue shift.

📊 DATA FLYWHEEL

Expansion events are among the highest-value data collection moments in the customer lifecycle: enrollment captures preference data, communication channel preferences, and self-declared interests that transform every future interaction. Loyalty program behavioral data — frequency, basket composition, offer redemption — is the most reliable predictor of CLV available. Every expansion event multiplies the quality of all future data collection.

Objective 7 *Educate*

A customer who understands your product becomes a customer who uses it, keeps it, and advocates for it.

THE CLASSIC DEFINITION

Education is the most undervalued of the nine objectives — and one of the highest-return. The logic is simple: customers who fully understand how to use a product get more value from it. Customers who get more value stay longer, use more features, generate fewer support contacts, and are more likely to refer others. The cost of educating a customer in a single well-designed interaction is small. The downstream benefit — fewer support calls, higher product utilization, lower churn, greater advocacy — is large and compounding. Every customer who learns something useful from an interaction with you becomes, incrementally, a more loyal and more profitable customer. Education is not a support function. It is one of the highest-ROI investments in the customer relationship.

AI-ENHANCED EXECUTION TODAY

AI transforms education from reactive to proactive and from generic to precisely personalized. Modern platforms analyze each customer's product usage data and identify the specific features they haven't discovered, the workflows they're not using, and the capabilities most likely to increase their value from the product. They deliver this education at the optimal moment — during an onboarding interaction, following a support contact, as part of a proactive check-in — through the customer's preferred channel, in a format calibrated to their learning pattern. AI-generated tutorials are personalized to the customer's current usage context: not 'here's how to use the advanced reporting module' but 'based on the data you've been analyzing, here are three things in advanced reporting that would save you about two hours a week.' Specific. Contextual. Demonstrably valuable.

AI Tools & Platforms: *Pendo (in-app guidance), WalkMe, Appcues, Intercom product tours, Gainsight PX, Mixpanel (behavioral analytics for feature targeting), Loom (async video education), Tolstoy (interactive video), AI-generated help documentation, ChatGPT-based knowledge bases*

💰 REVENUE OPPORTUNITY

A B2B software company analyzed its churn data and found that 68% of churned customers had used fewer than 3 of 12 available features. They implemented AI-powered proactive feature education — identifying low-feature-usage customers and triggering personalized tutorials. Feature adoption increased from 3.1 to 6.4 features per customer in 12 months. Churn rate fell from 22% to 14%. On a $10M ARR base, an 8-point churn improvement preserved $800K in annual revenue. Support ticket volume fell 31%, saving $280K. Total education ROI: $1.08M annually.

📊 DATA FLYWHEEL

Every education event generates product utilization data, feature adoption signals, and learning pattern intelligence. Over time, the AI develops a model of which educational approaches — which content formats, which timing triggers, which personalization signals — produce the highest adoption rates. This model improves education effectiveness for all future customers, creating a compounding return on every teaching interaction.

Objective 8 *Collect*

Every interaction is a data event. The question is whether you're capturing it.

THE CLASSIC DEFINITION

Collection is the objective that multiplies the value of all the others. Every customer interaction generates signals — preferences expressed, offers accepted or declined, questions asked, features used, emotions conveyed, time spent, paths taken and abandoned. These signals, captured and integrated into a continuously improving customer intelligence system, make every subsequent interaction smarter, more relevant, and more valuable. Organizations that systematically collect from every interaction build the data asset that enables AI precision at scale. Organizations that let those signals pass unrecorded are starting each interaction with a blank slate — conducting expensive transactions with no accumulated learning to show for the investment.

AI-ENHANCED EXECUTION TODAY

Modern data collection operates across three tiers. Zero-party data: information customers voluntarily provide — stated preferences, self-declared interests, direct feedback. This data is the most accurate and most trusted, and AI-powered conversational interfaces can gather it naturally and continuously as part of the interaction flow rather than through intrusive survey forms. First-party data: behavioral signals generated by the customer's own interaction with your products, platforms, and communications — clicks, time spent, features used, purchases made, content consumed. AI synthesizes these signals into behavioral profiles that predict future behavior with increasing accuracy. Second-party data: shared data from trusted partners that extends the customer intelligence picture beyond your own interaction history. The collection objective makes every interaction a contribution to the intelligence asset that improves all future interactions.

AI Tools & Platforms: *Segment (Customer Data Platform), mParticle, Tealium, Treasure Data, Adobe Experience Platform, Braze, Klaviyo, Heap, FullStory, Hotjar, Qualtrics (experience data), Medallia (signal capture), Conversica (conversational data collection)*

💰 **REVENUE OPPORTUNITY**

Google's advertising business — worth over $200B annually — is built entirely on collected behavioral data from customer interactions across Search, YouTube, Gmail, and Maps. For a mid-market company, a 10% improvement in data collection completeness enables 15–20% improvement in personalization accuracy, which drives 10–15% improvement in conversion rates. On a $10M annual revenue base, a 12% conversion improvement = $1.2M incremental revenue. The collection objective's value is its compounding nature: better data today makes every future objective more valuable.

📊 **DATA FLYWHEEL**

Collection IS the data flywheel — every piece of data collected improves AI model accuracy, which improves interaction effectiveness, which generates more valuable data, which improves AI models further. Companies that start collecting systematically now create a compounding advantage that is mathematically impossible to replicate from a standing start in 3–5 years. The collection objective is the most strategically consequential of the nine.

Objective 9 ***Generate Referrals***

Your best customers are your best salespeople. Most companies never ask them to perform.

THE CLASSIC DEFINITION

Referral generation is the most financially leveraged objective in the nine — and the most consistently neglected. The mathematics are compelling: referred customers convert at 3 to 5 times the rate of cold-acquired customers, have 16% higher lifetime value than non-referred customers, and generate their own referrals at twice the rate of the general customer population. A referred customer is not just one customer. Over a 5-year period, a referred customer who generates two of their own referrals represents an acquisition yield of 7 customers from a single referral ask — without a dollar of additional marketing spend. Yet the vast majority of organizations pursue referrals only through passive programs (refer-a-friend pages buried in the navigation) rather than systematic, AI-timed, personalized asks at the moments when satisfied customers are most likely to act.

AI-ENHANCED EXECUTION TODAY

AI-powered referral generation identifies the optimal moment for a referral ask based on three signals: satisfaction (positive NPS signal, recent successful resolution, milestone celebration), readiness (customer has been with you long enough to have a meaningful story to tell but the experience is still fresh), and social graph analysis (which customers have networks that match your target customer profile). The AI surfaces the referral ask at the precise moment in the interaction when these three signals align — not as a script to execute but as a context-aware recommendation to a human agent or as a precisely timed digital nudge. The ask itself is personalized: the incentive, the message frame, the channel, and the ease of the sharing mechanism are all optimized for this specific customer's profile and most likely network.

AI Tools & Platforms: *ReferralCandy, Friendbuy, Ambassador (referral platforms), Yotpo Reviews + Referrals, LoyaltyLion, SaaSquatch, Influitive (B2B advocacy), Extole, Mention Me, Partnerize (affiliate + referral), NiceJob (reputation + referral)*

💰 REVENUE OPPORTUNITY

Dropbox's referral program — designed in 2008 — generated a 3,900% user growth increase in 15 months, from 100,000 to 4 million users, with zero paid acquisition cost for referred users. The program's design (both referrer and referred user get extra storage space) achieved 35% of all new signups through referrals. For a company with 50,000 customers and a CLV of $2,000: achieving a 15% annual referral rate generates 7,500 new customers worth $15M in CLV — from a referral program whose cost is a fraction of equivalent paid acquisition.

📊 DATA FLYWHEEL

Every referral event generates network topology data: who refers whom, which referral messages convert, which incentive structures drive action, which customer profiles produce the most productive referrers. This data improves referral program precision over time and, crucially, generates external data about the networks surrounding your existing customers — a form of market intelligence available through no other channel.

All Nine in Action — Three Contact Scenarios

The Nine Objectives are not a sequential checklist — you don't complete objective 1, then move to 2, then 3. They are a simultaneous design target: a set of outcomes your organization should pursue in every interaction, in the order and proportion that each interaction's context allows. The following three scenarios illustrate what this looks like in practice — a support contact, a sales contact, and an outbound email campaign — showing both the human execution and the AI enhancement that makes pursuing all nine natural rather than effortful.

Scenario A — Inbound Support Contact: Customer Calls About a Billing Discrepancy		
Objective	**Human Execution**	**AI Enhancement**
1 Identify	'Hi James, I can see you're calling from the number on your account. I've got your record pulled up.'	*AI resolved identity from phone number in <100ms. Profile, CLV ($4,200), and 3-year history surfaced before first word.*
2 Recognize	'I see you've been with us three years and this is actually your first billing call — you must have had good experiences until now.'	*AI flagged loyalty milestone + first complaint. Agent prompted: 'Empathy-first. High-value account. Retention priority.'*

3 Fulfill	Agent resolves the billing discrepancy completely, confirms adjustment, and sends email confirmation during the call.	*AI-guided resolution path reduced average handle time by 40%. Issue resolved without transfer.*
4 Upgrade	'James, I noticed your usage has actually outgrown your current plan — you're paying overages every month. Would you like me to show you a plan that fits you better and actually costs less?'	*Propensity model: 74% upgrade likelihood. AI surfaced upgrade recommendation with specific plan and pricing.*
5 Cross-Sell	'While I have you — we also have a payment protection plan a lot of our long-term customers use. It covers exactly this kind of billing discrepancy automatically.'	*AI ranked cross-sell recommendations by propensity. Payment protection: #1 for this profile and contact type.*
6 Expand	'I can also enroll you in our Preferred Customer program right now — priority support, locked-in pricing for 24 months. Given that you've been with us three years, you're definitely eligible.'	*Behavioral trigger: 3-year anniversary + first contact = high expansion propensity. AI flagged this as expansion window.*
7 Educate	'One thing that would prevent this going forward — there's a billing alert feature in the app that texts you if anything unusual happens. I can walk you through setting it up in 60 seconds.'	*AI identified: James has not enabled billing alerts. This is a high-education-value slot for his profile.*

8 Collect	'Before we wrap up, can I ask — was there anything about the billing page that made this confusing? Your feedback goes directly to our product team.'	*Natural language collection. James's response tagged and routed to product team feedback aggregation. Sentiment recorded.*
9 Referral	'James, I'm really glad we could get this sorted. If you ever know anyone who might benefit from our service, we have a referral program that gives both of you a credit. I'll send you the link.'	*Referral propensity model: 3-year customer + issue resolved positively = 2.3× baseline referral propensity. Timed ask.*

Scenario B — Sales Contact: Prospect Requests a Demo After Visiting Pricing Page Twice		
Objective	**Human Execution**	**AI Enhancement**
1 Identify	'Good afternoon, Sarah. I see you've visited our pricing page a couple of times — I'm glad you reached out. I've got a bit of context on your company.'	*AI assembled: company size, industry, likely use case, 2 pricing page visits, 1 case study download — all surfaced pre-call.*
2 Recognize	'Based on what I know about healthcare organizations your size, the integration question is usually the most important. Let me address that first.'	*AI identified Sarah's sector + company size. Surfaced similar customer profiles. Most common objection flagged: integration.*
3 Fulfill	Demo tailored entirely to healthcare workflow, not a generic product tour. All Sarah's pre-submitted questions addressed sequentially.	*AI generated personalized demo script from company profile + pre-submission questions + industry playbook.*

4 Upgrade	'Most healthcare organizations your size start on Professional but expand to Enterprise within a year because of the compliance reporting module. I'd rather show you both so you can see what you're growing into.'	*Propensity model: 82% of comparable healthcare customers upgrade within 14 months. AI recommended showing Enterprise now.*
5 Cross-Sell	'We also partner with three EHR systems — Epic, Cerner, and Athena. If you're running one of those, there's a native integration that most customers find saves 6 hours a week in manual data entry.'	*Partner product relevance scored by industry + company size. Epic integration flagged as highest-value cross-sell for this profile.*
6 Expand	'If you move forward, I'd recommend starting with a pilot team — we have a structured program that includes dedicated implementation support and a 90-day success review. It makes the business case for full rollout much easier to build.'	*AI: trial + structured onboarding = 2.7× higher conversion to full contract vs. unstructured trial.*

7 Educate	'One thing a lot of people don't realize until they're using it — the reporting module can pull directly from your billing data and generate CMS compliance reports automatically. That alone typically saves two FTEs.'	*AI surfaced: most common education gap for healthcare segment = CMS compliance reporting capability.*
8 Collect	'As you're evaluating, what's the one thing that would make this a clear yes for your team? Your answer actually shapes how I'd recommend we structure the pilot for you.'	*Structured collection: evaluation criteria, decision-maker map, timeline, competing solutions. All tagged to CRM in real time.*
9 Referral	'We have a few healthcare customers who have offered to speak with prospects about their experience — if it would help to hear from someone who's been through implementation, I'm happy to arrange that.'	*Reference program: customer advocates identified by NPS score + engagement level + industry match. AI selects best reference.*

Scenario C — Outbound Email Campaign: Monthly Communication to Active Customers		
Objective	**Human Execution**	**AI Enhancement**
1 Identify	Subject line: 'James, your February coffee order is ready to review'	*AI: First name + behavioral trigger (last order 14 days ago + repurchase interval = 16 days). Email personalized to this individual.*
2 Recog-nize	'You prefer dark roasts and usually order every two weeks. Based on your last three orders, here's what we're recommending this month.'	*AI-generated preference profile from 9 months of purchase history. Dark roast preference: 87% of orders. Interval: 15.4 days avg.*
3 Fulfill	One-click reorder button for usual order, pre-filled and ready to confirm. Zero friction for the customer who just wants the same thing.	*Frictionless fulfillment: pre-built cart from order history. Confirmation to order placement: 2 clicks.*
4 Upgrade	'Your order volume this month qualifies you for our Roaster's Reserve subscription — 15% off, priority access to limited releases, and free shipping on all orders.'	*AI: Usage volume threshold + order frequency = subscription upgrade propensity score 0.78. Presented at this specific email.*

5 Cross-Sell	'Customers who love your current Sumatra also consistently love the new Kenyan single-origin we received last week — here's why.'	*Collaborative filtering: Sumatra → Kenyan SIC: 0.89 correlation among customers with similar taste profiles. Confidence score surfaced.*
6 Expand	'Join our Brew Club — access to monthly limited releases, exclusive event invites, and an online community of coffee enthusiasts. Your first month is free.'	*Behavioral trigger: 9+ months, 3+ orders/month = high community membership propensity. AI timed this at month 9.*
7 Educate	'One thing most home brewers don't know about your current Sumatra: it performs best at 94°C with a 4-minute steep. Here's a 60-second brew guide.'	*AI identified: educational content segment correlated with repeat purchase +23% and order size +11%. Personalized to current product.*
8 Collect	'Reply to this email and tell us what you'd like to see next month — new origins, roast profiles, brewing accessories, or gift options? We read every reply.'	*Zero-party data collection via email reply. NLP tags responses to product development queue. Response rate: 8.4% (vs. 1.2% survey).*
9 Referral	'If you know a coffee lover who hasn't discovered us yet, here's your personal referral link — you both get a free bag with your next order.'	*AI timed referral ask at high-satisfaction behavioral moment (post-fulfillment email). Personalized code. One-click sharing.*

Message Architecture — From Segmentation to Syndication

The Nine Objectives tell you what to pursue in every interaction. The question of how to craft the messages that pursue each objective is answered through a progression of message targeting sophistication — a ladder of precision that begins with geographic broadcasting and ascends through five levels to reach individual-level AI personalization and commercial syndication.

Understanding this progression is critical because organizations often mistake the early rungs for the full staircase. 'We personalize our emails with the customer's first name' is not personalization in the competitive sense. It is demographic broadcasting with a name field. The organizations capturing the full value of the Nine Objectives have climbed the entire ladder. Here is what each rung looks like — and what becomes possible at each level.

Level	Approach	Example	AI Capability	Competitive Position
1	Geographic Broadcasting	'Dear Neighbor, it's time to winterize...' — same message to everyone in a region	Basic geo-targeting; minimal AI required	Commodity — every organization can do this; zero differentiation
2	Demographic Segmentation	'Dear Head of Household / New Homeowner...' — targeting by age, income, family stage, business size	Demographic propensity modeling; lookalike audience building	Baseline — standard CRM capability; differentiation only in execution quality
3	Behavioral Segmentation	'Dear Customer, about your recent purchase...' — triggered by specific actions, events, and patterns	Event-triggered automation; behavioral pattern recognition; predictive interval modeling	Competitive — requires integration between behavioral data and communication systems; 40% of companies achieve this
4	Personalization	'Dear Miguel, based on your last three contacts...' — individual-level customization using full customer history	Real-time customer data synthesis; NLP for communication style adaptation; dynamic content generation	Advanced — requires Customer Data Platform + AI personalization layer; 15% of companies achieve this well

Level	Approach	Example	AI Capability	Competitive Position
5	Predictive Targeting	'Dear Miguel, a special offer just for you at exactly the right moment...' — AI predicts what, when, and how much before the customer signals intent	Next-best-action modeling; churn prediction; CLV trajectory modeling; multi-armed bandit optimization	Leader — requires mature data infrastructure + trained ML models; 5% of companies operate at this level
6	Commercialization	Selling message slots to complementary partners — 'Got Milk?' stickers on oranges; third-party offers in billing statements	AI-powered slot valuation; automated partner offer matching; real-time yield management	Platform — transforms interaction infrastructure into media property; practiced by Amazon, bank statement programs, telcos
7	Affiliation & Syndication	Bidding-based slot allocation across an ecosystem of partners — like Google's ad marketplace but for customer interaction slots	Real-time auction infrastructure; dynamic pricing; performance attribution across partner network	Ecosystem leader — highest sophistication level; creates network effects that compound indefinitely

Most organizations reading this chapter are operating at levels 2 and 3. The journey to level 5 — predictive, individual-level targeting at scale — requires three ingredients: a unified customer data platform that makes behavioral and profile data accessible in real time, an AI layer that converts that data into interaction-specific recommendations, and an organizational culture that treats the Nine Objectives as a performance standard rather than a nice-to-have aspiration.

Levels 6 and 7 — commercialization and syndication — represent the frontier where customer interaction infrastructure becomes a business model in itself. Amazon's advertising revenue ($47B in 2023) is the largest and most studied example: the slots within Amazon's own customer interactions are sold to brands who want their products surfaced at the precise moment when a customer is most likely to buy. Bank statement programs that embed third-party offers in monthly billing contacts. Telecom companies that monetize their monthly contact moments with partner offers. These are not marketing programs. They are slot monetization systems — the CxC Matrix's slot framework operating at platform scale.

The Investment Case — Building the Nine-Objective Infrastructure

The argument for investing in Nine-Objective interaction infrastructure is not difficult to make once the numbers are visible. The challenge is that most organizations don't currently calculate the numbers. They see the cost of the technology investment. They don't see the revenue of the forfeited objectives. Making this investment case visible — in specific, quantifiable terms — is one of the most valuable exercises a customer experience leadership team can undertake.

A WORKED INVESTMENT MODEL — MID-MARKET COMPANY, 200,000 ANNUAL CUSTOMER CONTACTS

Current State: 200,000 annual contacts × $12 average cost = $2.4M annual spend. Average objectives achieved per interaction: 2.4. Revenue attributed to interaction investment: approximately $800K in documented upsell and retention value. Net interaction economics: -$1.6M. Target State (after 18 months of Nine-Objective implementation): 200,000 contacts × $12.50 average cost (AI tools add ~$0.50/contact) = $2.5M annual spend. Average objectives achieved per interaction: 6.8. Revenue attributed to interaction investment: $18.4M (upgrade revenue $4.2M + cross-sell $3.8M + expansion LTV lift $5.1M + referral acquisition value $2.4M + education-driven churn reduction $2.9M). Net interaction economics: +$15.9M. Swing: $17.5M annual value improvement from the same 200,000 customer contacts. Investment in AI infrastructure: $1.5M year one, $600K annually. ROI: 1,067% in year one. Payback period: 31 days of incremental revenue.

These numbers are not projections from a slide deck. They are extrapolations from documented performance at companies that have implemented systematic Nine-Objective interaction design. The specific numbers will vary by organization, industry, and starting maturity level. The structural relationship — more objectives per interaction, exponentially more value per contact dollar — holds across every context where it has been implemented.

The implementation path does not require doing everything at once. The most successful Nine-Objective implementations follow a crawl-walk-run progression that builds organizational capability, generates early wins to fund subsequent phases, and creates the data foundation that makes each subsequent phase more effective than the last.

Phase	Timeline	Priority Actions	Success Target
Crawl	Months 1–3	Implement Customer Data Platform. Baseline current objectives achieved per interaction. Pilot AI on highest-volume contact type (likely inbound support or website)	3–5 objectives per interaction on pilot channel. Prove value multiplier with documented revenue data.
Walk	Months 4–9	Extend AI orchestration to 3–5 contact types. Build cross-functional orchestration (break silo between service, sales, marketing data). Implement measurement dashboard tracking all 9 objectives.	5–7 objectives per interaction across pilot channels. $5–15M in incremental annual value documented.

Phase	Timeline	Priority Actions	Success Target
Run	Months 10–18	Scale to all interaction types (full CxC Matrix). Advanced AI personalization and predictive targeting. Begin exploring commercialization opportunities with complementary partners. Build referral infrastructure.	6–9 objectives per interaction across all channels. Full platform economics realized. Data moat established.
Crawl	Months 1–3	Implement Customer Data Platform. Baseline current objectives achieved per interaction. Pilot AI on highest-volume contact type (likely inbound support or website)	3–5 objectives per interaction on pilot channel. Prove value multiplier with documented revenue data.
Walk	Months 4–9	Extend AI orchestration to 3–5 contact types. Build cross-functional orchestration (break silo between service, sales, marketing data). Implement measurement dashboard tracking all 9 objectives.	5–7 objectives per interaction across pilot channels. $5–15M in incremental annual value documented.

Run	Months 10–18	Scale to all interaction types (full CxC Matrix). Advanced AI personalization and predictive targeting. Begin exploring commercialization opportunities with complementary partners. Build referral infrastructure.	6–9 objectives per interaction across all channels. Full platform economics realized. Data moat established.

The Data Moat — Why Starting Now Matters More Than Starting Perfectly

The most strategically consequential aspect of Nine-Objective interaction design is not the revenue it generates in year one. It is the compounding data advantage it creates over time. Every interaction, when designed to pursue all nine objectives, generates data that makes every subsequent interaction more effective. This is the flywheel that separates organizations that implement platform economics from organizations that are eventually displaced by them.

Amazon's recommendation engine did not become 35% of total revenue overnight. It became 35% of total revenue after twenty years of learning from hundreds of billions of interactions, each one improving the model, each improvement increasing the revenue, each revenue increase funding more interaction volume, each interaction generating more training data. The flywheel is real. And it is powered by exactly one thing: the decision, made twenty years ago, to treat customer interactions as data events worth capturing rather than costs worth minimizing.

Netflix's personalization engine — which now drives 80% of total content viewing — was not built from a brilliant algorithm designed at launch. It was built from learning. From watching what 230 million subscribers actually watched, when, for how long, on what devices, after watching what, interrupted by what. The data moat is not the algorithm. The algorithm is the output of the moat. The moat is the interactions, captured, structured, and fed into models that improve with every additional data point.

The competitive implication is urgent. Organizations that begin capturing Nine-Objective interaction data today will have a meaningful, quantifiable advantage over organizations that begin in two years. The advantage compounds daily. In three to five years, organizations that achieved platform maturity early will have built data moats — libraries of behavioral intelligence, trained prediction models, and personalization infrastructure — that cannot be replicated from a standing start at any price. The organizations that haven't built this will know it — because they will see it in their acquisition costs, their retention rates, their customer lifetime values, and eventually in their competitive positioning.

THE THREE QUESTIONS EVERY LEADER SHOULD BE ABLE TO ANSWER — TODAY

Question 1: Do we know the lifetime value and 90-day churn risk of every customer in real time? If the answer is NO, your organization is flying blind in every interaction. Every objective pursued without CLV and churn risk data is a guess. Question 2: Can we orchestrate Marketing + Sales + Service + Product intelligence into a single interaction context in under 2 seconds? If the answer is NO, you are achieving 2–3 objectives per interaction instead of 7–9. The gap between those numbers is the gap between your current P&L and your potential one. Question 3: Is every interaction making our AI smarter for the next interaction? If the answer is NO, you are not building a moat. Competitors who started building one 18 months ago are now 18 months ahead of where you will be when you start. The gap widens every day.

The Win-Win-Win-Win — Why Nine Objectives Is Good for Everyone

The Nine Objectives are sometimes received with concern — particularly by people who worry that systematically pursuing business objectives in every customer interaction will make those interactions feel calculated rather than genuine. This concern reflects an important intuition that is also, in practice, precisely backward.

Consider what it means for the customer to encounter an organization that has designed every interaction to be maximally useful to them. An organization that remembers who they are (Identify), acknowledges their history (Recognize), actually solves their problem (Fulfill), tells them when something better is available (Upgrade), suggests something genuinely complementary (Cross-sell), invites them into a richer relationship (Expand), teaches them something that increases their value from the product (Educate), learns from what they share (Collect), and treats their referral as a genuine gift rather than a transactional request (Generate Referrals). This customer does not feel processed. They feel known. The pursuit of all nine objectives, done well, is indistinguishable from being served by someone who genuinely cares. Because it is.

For the employee executing these interactions, the Nine Objectives create something equally valuable: clarity. Instead of a vague mandate to 'provide excellent customer service,' employees have a specific, actionable framework for what excellent service means — and the AI tools to execute it without having to carry the cognitive burden of synthesizing all nine dimensions themselves. The agent who has a customer's CLV, their emotional state signal, their upgrade propensity, and their most valuable cross-sell ranked and ready on their screen is not stressed. They are equipped. The Nine Objectives make employees more effective and more confident — and the research on employee satisfaction in customer-centric organizations confirms that effectiveness and confidence are the primary drivers of the motivation that makes those interactions feel genuine.

For the organization, the math has already been made clear. For every stakeholder — investors, partners, employees, customers, communities — an organization operating at Nine-Objective maturity is a more sustainable, more valuable, more ethical enterprise than one treating interactions as costs to minimize. It generates more revenue, serves customers better, employs people in more meaningful and better-compensated roles, and creates a data infrastructure that makes every future customer relationship more productive. This is what genuine customer-centricity looks like when it reaches operational maturity: not a trade-off between the customer's interests and the organization's, but a design that makes them the same.

> ***"The Nine Objectives are not nine things you do to customers. They are nine ways***

> ***you serve them — fully, specifically, in their interest and yours simultaneously. An organization that has mastered all nine doesn't have a customer service function. It has a customer partnership engine. And that engine, running at scale, is the most durable competitive advantage in business."***

Starting the Transformation — What Changes Monday Morning

The distance between reading about the Nine Objectives and deploying them is traversable in stages that begin immediately, without waiting for a technology transformation or a budget cycle.

The first thing that changes is the measurement standard. Before any AI is deployed, before any platform is selected, before any training program is designed, the organization establishes a baseline: for our top five interaction types, how many of the nine objectives are we currently achieving, on average, per interaction? This number — almost certainly between 1.8 and 3.2 for most organizations — becomes the starting point. And establishing it, visibly, in the leadership team's weekly metrics, changes what people pay attention to.

The second thing that changes is the vocabulary. When a team discusses a customer interaction design — a new email campaign, a revised support script, a refreshed checkout flow — the conversation now includes nine evaluation questions: Does this identify the customer? Does it recognize their history? Does it fulfill their need? Does it offer an upgrade? Does it cross-sell appropriately? Does it expand the relationship? Does it educate? Does it collect? Does it generate referral? Not every interaction should pursue all nine. But every interaction should be consciously designed with all nine in view, and the decision to pursue or deprioritize each one should be intentional rather than accidental.

The third thing that changes is the investment framing. When the next technology or headcount decision comes to the table, the question is no longer 'what does this cost?' The question is 'how many objectives per interaction does this enable, and what is the revenue value of those objectives?' The Nine Objectives transform the investment conversation from expense approval to return calculation — and that change in framing, sustained over time, realigns organizational resources toward the customer interaction infrastructure that generates the most durable competitive advantage available.

Nine objectives. Every interaction. Every customer. Every day. This is what Customer Worthy looks like at

full deployment — and it is available to any organization willing to build toward it.

Chapter Eight
The Customer Schematic

How to Put Your Entire Customer Journey on One Wall—and Find the $14.2 Million Hiding in the Gaps

> *The most expensive failures in your customer experience are not where you think they are. They're in the spaces between departments—the handoffs, the silences, the lifecycle stages where no one is accountable and no one is watching. The Customer Schematic makes all of them visible in a single view. And the first time your organization sees them, everything changes.*
>
> *Your organization has ninety cells in its customer relationship. Marketing sees twenty. Sales sees fifteen. Operations sees ten. Support sees ten. Finance sees the totals. The executive team sees the averages. Nobody sees all ninety at once—which is why the most expensive problems are always the ones hiding in the cells that fall between departments.*

The Problem Nobody Owns

Here is a pattern that plays out in virtually every organization that has conducted a Customer Schematic walkthrough.

Marketing has built excellent Stage 1 (Awareness) and Stage 2 (Information) campaigns. Sales has a well-managed pipeline from Stage 3 (Identification) through Stage 6

What a Four-Hour Walkthrough Produced: $14.2 Million

A mid-market mortgage lender gathered representatives from origination, underwriting, loan servicing, marketing, IT, and customer support in a room with a fifteen-stage CxC Matrix displayed at wall scale. Each department presented their cells from the customer's perspective—not their own metrics, but what the customer actually experiences at each stage, in each channel, with what emotions.

The exercise ran four hours. By the end, eight strategic initiatives had been identified, five of which could begin within sixty days with existing staff and systems. The combined revenue impact—validated eighteen months later—was $14.2 million in retained and expanded customer value.

Here is what they found, stage by stage:

The Stage 7–9 Silence Window. A mortgage customer who has signed their loan agreement enters a processing period that can last eleven days or more. During that period—while the appraisal is ordered, underwriting conditions are reviewed, and closing is coordinated—the customer hears nothing. They are anxious about approval. They are frustrated by document requests that feel redundant. They are wondering whether they made the right choice. And in that silence, the company's single largest source of Stage 12 support contacts is being generated. Seventy percent of inbound support calls originated from this window. The fix: three proactive digital communications—a status update at 48 hours, a midpoint update at Day 5, and a closing preparation message at Day 9. Cost: negligible. Support volume reduction: 31%. NPS improvement at Stage 9: 18 points.

The Stage 11 Dead Zone. Mortgage customers make monthly payments for fifteen to thirty years. During that entire period—the longest and most profitable stage of the relationship—the lender had exactly two types of company-initiated contact: the monthly statement and the annual escrow analysis. No refinance alerts when rates dropped enough to save the customer money. No home equity milestone recognition. No anniversary acknowledgments. No feature education when portal usage declined. The customer was paying reliably and being reliably ignored. The fix: AI-triggered refinance alerts when savings exceeded $200/month, plus annual mortgage health review outreach. Incremental retention value: $6.4 million.

The Stage 15 Vacuum. The company had no referral infrastructure. No program, no incentive, no mechanism for satisfied customers to bring their friends and family to the lender that had served them well. Customers who had just closed on a home—one of the most socially visible purchases a person makes—were being sent a closing survey and then silence. The fix: a personalized referral tool deployed at peak satisfaction moments, with dual incentives for referrer and referred. Projected yield: 4,200 new customers annually from an audience whose lifetime value averaged 16% higher than customers acquired through paid channels.

The Stage 14 Missed Cycle. When customers sold their home and paid off the mortgage, the company treated it as a closing event. It was actually a Stage 1 (Awareness) event for the next purchase cycle. The customer about to buy their next home was also about to choose their next lender—and the company that had served them for years had no slot designed to position itself for that next relationship. The fix: AI-powered prediction of likely movers (using behavioral and geographic signals), with proactive outreach positioning the lender for the next transaction before the customer began comparing alternatives.

None of these findings required new technology. None required additional headcount. They required one thing: the act of seeing the full fifteen-stage, six-channel layout for the first time—and finding what was always there, hidden in the junctions between departments that had never looked at each other's work simultaneously.

Why Every Department Sees an Accurate and Incomplete Picture

The organizational design problem that the Customer Schematic solves is not that departments have bad information. It is that they each have accurate information about their part of the journey—and no information about the rest. The failures that cost the most money are almost never inside a department's view. They are at the handoffs between departments, in the stages that fall between ownership boundaries, and in the channels that no one has been asked to manage.

Department	What They See Without the Schematic	What the Schematic Adds
Marketing	Campaign performance, acquisition cost, lead volume, funnel conversion from awareness to first sale.	The full journey from Stage 1 through Stage 15—including Stage 15 community doing Stage 1 acquisition work at a fraction of the cost with far greater credibility.

Sales	Pipeline from first qualified contact to contract signature.	The handoff cliff between Stage 6 (Contract) and Stage 9 (Acceptance)—the silence window where the relationship sales just won is being eroded.
Opera-tions	Fulfillment speed, inventory accuracy, delivery performance as operational metrics.	The customer's emotional experience of every operational outcome—anxiety during Stage 7 silence, the downstream consequence that Stage 12 support volume is proportional to Stage 7–9 communication quality.
Support	Ticket volume, handle time, resolution rates within Stage 12 and Stage 13.	Upstream design decisions generating those tickets—most high-volume Stage 12 categories have fixable root causes in Stages 7, 9, or 11 at a fraction of the cost.
Finance	Revenue, cost, margin, CLV projections as aggregates.	Contact-level economics those aggregates obscure—which cells generate disproportionate value, which destroy it, where modest investment yields invisible returns.
Execu-tive	Averaged KPIs and board-level metrics—the view from ten thousand feet.	Specific cells where strategy works or fails. The Stage 11 dead zone most boards have never seen because no single depart-ment owns it.

The Customer Schematic walkthrough is the intervention that closes these gaps. It does not replace departmental expertise. It creates the forum where that expertise is applied to the full system—where Marketing's understanding of acquisition, Sales' understanding of conversion, Operations' understanding of fulfillment, and Support's understanding of failure are all brought to bear on the same customer journey simultaneously.

The Cross-Functional Walkthrough: What $15.5 Million Looks Like

When a cross-functional team walks the full Schematic, each department examines their cells from the customer's perspective and a designated "customer voice" challenges every explanation with: But what does the customer actually experience in this cell? What do they feel? What do they do next? Where do they go if we're not there?

Here is what a typical walkthrough produces—drawn from multiple implementations across industries:

Marketing discovers they are spending 40% of acquisition budget on Stage 1 (Awareness) while a 73% conversion drop occurs between Stage 2 (Information) and Stage 3 (Identification). Their awareness is working. Their information-to-identification bridge is failing. Redirecting 20% of awareness budget to Stage 2 content—comparison tools, terminology guides, plain-language explainers—addresses the actual bottleneck. Estimated value: $3.2 million.

Operations discovers an 11-day silence window across Stages 7–9 that is generating 70% of Stage 12 support volume. Three proactive digital communications close the gap. Support volume drops. NPS improves. The fix addresses the root cause rather than continuing to invest in resolution capacity for problems that better upstream design would prevent. Estimated value: $5.9 million.

The Executive Team discovers that Stage 11—the longest and often most profitable stage—has exactly two company-initiated contact types across all six channels, for years of customer engagement. A single additional proactive slot per year across the Stage 11 customer base—rate alerts, feature education, loyalty recognition—generates measurable retention lift. Estimated value: $6.4 million.

Total identified opportunity from one walkthrough: $15.5 million. Not from new technology. Not from additional headcount. From the act of seeing the full layout for the first time and finding what was always there.

Three Ways to Read the Schematic

The Customer Schematic operates in three dimensions simultaneously—and the insight is in the intersection, not the individual dimension.

Read vertically (top to bottom) and you see the customer—their actions, emotional states, questions, and decision points at each of the fifteen lifecycle stages. This reveals where customers are anxious, hopeful, frustrated, or delighted—and where those emotional states are being ignored by the organization that should be responding to them.

Read horizontally (left to right) and you see the company—its six channels operating in parallel across all fifteen stages. This reveals investment concentration. Most organizations discover their channel distribution is far narrower than they believed—two or three channels dominating, three or four essentially absent across most stages.

Read the intersections and you see the contacts—the actual moments where customer and organization connect. The weakest connection in the path determines the performance of the whole relationship. A single failing cell at a critical defection-risk stage can negate months of superior performance elsewhere. Both the load-bearing cells and the damaging ones are invisible until the full Schematic is in view.

No department reads all three dimensions simultaneously. Marketing reads columns. Operations reads rows. Finance reads cells. The executive team reads averages of cells, which is the least useful reading of all. The Schematic forces all three readings to happen at the same time, in the same room, with the same data.

Building the Customer Schematic: A 30-Day Action Plan

You do not need perfect data to start. You need a wall, a cross-functional team, and four weeks.

Week 1 — Map the Full Layout

Assemble a representative from every department that owns a customer contact. Display the fifteen-stage by six-channel CxC Matrix at large scale—all ninety cells visible simultaneously. In a 90-minute session, populate the matrix with every contact type your organization currently executes: every slot, every container, across Geography, Digital, Location, Third Party, One-to-One, and Community channels.

Don't debate or refine—inventory. The goal is to see the full layout for the first time. Identify the obvious gaps: lifecycle stages with no slots, channels that are unmapped, departments whose work doesn't appear anywhere in the Matrix. The blank cells are your most important discovery. They are the touchpoints that don't exist—and the customer experiences where your organization is absent and your competitors are free to fill the space.

Week 2 — Monetize the Design

Assign customer count estimates and annual revenue per customer to each populated cell. Use best estimates rather than waiting for perfect data. Calculate the revenue weight of the top ten cells: customer count multiplied by annual customer value equals the financial weight of the slot. Identify the top five most obvious gaps.

The financial picture that emerges will surprise almost everyone in the room—and the surprise is almost always about the money that's not being captured. A Stage 11 (Use) cell with 50,000 customers and $800 average annual value is a $40 million relationship pool receiving no company-initiated contact. That cell, monetized, becomes a strategic priority that no verbal argument could have established.

Week 3 — Walk It Together

Conduct the full cross-functional walkthrough. Each department presents their slots from the customer's perspective. A dedicated "customer voice" challenges every explanation. Document insights in real time.

End with a ranked list of ten improvement opportunities and a preliminary CVI impact estimate for each. Apply the hot spot taxonomy: vulnerability (high-value customers at friction points), opportunity (high-return cells with modest investment required), competitive threat (cells where competitors are outperforming you), and quick wins (immediate impact with near-zero investment).

Week 4 — Prioritize and Assign

Select the top three hot spots—one quick win, one major opportunity, one risk mitigation. Assign an owner, a 30-day milestone, and a CVI impact target to each. Begin building the data infrastructure that will feed the live Matrix: the four data streams (event, behavioral, sentiment, financial) that turn the static Schematic into a continuously current operating instrument.

The Matrix is now live. And your organization has done something that changes its strategic trajectory: it has seen the full fifteen-stage, six-channel customer journey—from every department's perspective, in one room, at one time—and found the gaps that no individual department's reporting had ever made visible.

AI Simulation: Testing Before Deploying

Once the Schematic is built, AI adds a capability that transforms how your organization makes customer experience decisions: the ability to test proposed changes before deploying them to real customers.

Rather than implementing a price increase and discovering three months later that it triggered a churn spike in your most valuable segment, AI simulation models the impact across all fifteen stages before you commit. Rather than launching a new chatbot and discovering it reduces support satisfaction at Stage 12, simulation identifies the negative-sentiment handoff design that needs to be built before deployment.

Scenario	What AI Models	Decision Enabled
Price Change Modeling	How each customer segment responds to a 10% increase across Stages 10 and 11.	Increase for Segments A and C; hold flat for B (high churn risk). Result: +$2.1M net revenue, <2% churn. Without simulation: net –$400K.
Competitor Entry Defense	Which customer profiles are most vulnerable when a competitor enters with 15% lower pricing.	Stage 11 customers with <3 years tenure and <60% feature utilization identified. Targeted slot redesign reduces competitive churn by 34%.

New Channel Deployment	Impact of adding AI chatbot to Stage 2 and Stage 12.	Chatbot handles 62% of Stage 2 contacts at 91% satisfaction. Critical finding: negative sentiment requires immediate human handoff. Net value: +$1.8M annually.
Referral Program Design	Twelve incentive structures tested against referral volume and referred-customer CVI.	Dual incentive ($50 each) outperforms one-sided by 3.4×. 3+ year tenure produces 2.7× higher-CVI referrals. Yield: 4,200 new customers annually.
Stage 11 Slot Addition	Eighteen slot variants for proactive Stage 11 contact across Digital and One-to-One channels.	Rate-alert digital communication produces 2.9× higher retention than generic check-in. One precisely designed slot outperforms all existing Stage 11 investment. Value: $6.4M.
Stage 7–9 Silence Window	Twenty-four communication configurations for proactive outreach during processing.	Day 2 email + Day 5 SMS + Day 9 video produces 31% Stage 12 reduction and 18-point NPS improvement. Winning config outperforms intuitive first guess by 3.1×.

The cost of a slot design failure discovered in simulation is zero. The cost of discovering it in a churned customer base is measured in years of Customer Value Index.

The Self-Optimizing Matrix: From Snapshot to Living System

The Schematic built in Week 1 is a photograph. Valuable, but static. The goal is to make it a living system—one that updates continuously with real performance data, identifies emerging problems before they reach executive visibility, and proposes improvements that are tested and validated before deployment.

The progression has four levels:

Level	Maturity	Capability	Competitive Position
1	**Static (4–12 weeks)**	Schematic built. VMAO complete. Cross-functional walkthrough conducted. Priority hot spots identified.	Ahead of ~80% of comparable organizations in strategic visibility.
2	**Monitored (3–6 months)**	Live performance data in each of 90 cells. Anomaly alerts. Monthly reviews. Hot spot improvements measured.	Better than ~90% of organizations. Decisions from current data.
3	**Simulated (6–12 months)**	AI scenario modeling operational. A/B testing deployed. Pre-deployment validation standard practice.	Top 5%. Design changes tested before deployment. Revenue protected.
4	**Self-Optimizing (12–24 months)**	Full AI flywheel operational. Continuous slot improvement across all 90 cells. Every interaction improves the models.	Compounding moat. Three years of accumulated intelligence cannot be replicated.

Organizations that start building their Customer Schematic today and implementing AI simulation now are compounding their slot intelligence daily. In three years, the gap between them and organizations that begin then is not three calendar years. It is three years of compounded learning—a precision advantage that grows faster than the time it took to create it.

What This Chapter Has Built

You now have three things that most organizations lack.

First: a methodology for making the invisible visible—a tool that turns the complexity of ninety contact points across fifteen stages and six channels into a single layout that a cross-functional team can walk, understand, and improve together.

Second: an economic model for prioritizing that improvement work—using customer value calculations to ensure that investment follows return rather than departmental politics.

Third: a path from static snapshot to self-optimizing system—where AI takes over the continuous monitoring and testing that no human review cycle can match, making each successive improvement more precise than the last.

The mortgage company found $14.2 million. The cross-functional walkthrough found $15.5 million. Neither number required new technology or additional headcount. They required one thing: seeing the full system for the first time.

Draw the Schematic. Walk it together. Build the system that improves itself.

• • •

The next chapter moves from the architecture of customer contacts to the intelligence layer that makes those contacts adaptive in real time: the Customer

Experience Algorithm, the behavioral scoring system, and the trust dynamics that determine whether the access your customers have granted you will be maintained or revoked.

Chapter Nine

The Customer's Network

Trust, AI Agents, and the Ecosystem That Surrounds Every Relationship

Your customer has always been connected. What has changed is the density, permanence, and computational intelligence of those connections — and what the Customer Experience Algorithm can do with them.

The Professional Customer — Then and Now

In an earlier edition of this book, we introduced Jose — a purchasing manager who, while waiting in line at a Panera Bread, used his phone to spot a three-hour sale at Tiger Direct, log in to his corporate account, change the order quantity to six monitors, and complete a $400-saving transaction before he reached the register. He then walked past a big-box electronics store advertising the same item at twice the price and shook his head.

"We don't decide how long people are in the store. What we decide is how easy it is for you — within the 21 minutes you've allocated — to get what you want."

— Stephen Quinn, Walmart Chief Marketing Officer

"The customer who earned your attention yesterday may not be the customer who deserves your best slot tomorrow. The Customer Experience Algorithm knows the difference. The CxC Matrix delivers the right response to the right customer at the right moment — because the score says so."

The Customer Experience Algorithm — Recency, Frequency, Monetary Value, and the Propensity Score

Customer Worthy introduced the Customer Experience Algorithm as the computational engine that turns the CxC Matrix from a strategic framework into an operational system. At its core, the CEA is a scoring mechanism that integrates three proven dimensions of customer value — Recency, Frequency, and Monetary value — with a fourth, forward-looking dimension that transforms historical RFM from a backward-looking report into a predictive instrument: the propensity-to-purchase score, calculated across 30-, 60-, 90-, and 180-day windows.

The logic is straightforward, and it is important to understand why each dimension earns its place in the calculation. Recency tells you how recently a customer engaged, which is the strongest short-term predictor of whether they will engage again. Frequency tells you how habitually a customer uses your channels and products, which predicts the stability and depth of their relationship over time. Monetary value tells you what the relationship is actually worth — both historically and in terms of the ceiling on investment the CLV justifies. And the propensity score — the CEA's most distinctive contribution — tells you not what a customer has done, but what the behavioral signals currently visible in your data suggest they are about to do, and in what time window.

Here is why the propensity windows matter. Customer decisions are not uniformly distributed across time. A customer with a high 30-day purchase propensity is in an active consideration window right now — a high-intensity, high-investment slot is justified and likely to convert. A customer with a high 180-day propensity is moving toward a decision but is not yet in one — a nurture sequence that builds brand affinity, surfaces relevant content, and positions your organization favorably before the decision window opens is the appropriate response. Treating both customers with the same slot, at the same intensity, on the same calendar schedule is not just inefficient. It is the kind of contact design failure that erodes the invitation rather than reinforces it.

Figure 9.1 *The Customer Experience Algorithm: RFM × Propensity = CLV-Weighted Slot Activation. Each dimension generates distinct signals that activate specific CxC Matrix stages, channels, and slots.*

Dimension	Signal Inputs	How It Weights CLV	Slot Activation Logic Across the 15 Stages
Recency (R)	Days since last purchase, last meaningful interaction, last channel engagement, last physical-layer contact	*Recent customers have higher purchase probability. Recency decay curves calibrate how quickly propensity drops with inactivity and what re-engagement investment is justified.*	Slots in Stages 11–14 activate when this customer's recency score crosses defined thresholds — not on a broadcast calendar, but when the score signals they are moving toward disengagement.

Frequency (F)	Purchase count per period, interaction count by channel, content engagement cadence, location visit rate, referral activity	*High-frequency customers generate more data, more predictable behavioral patterns, and higher confidence in propensity modeling — their slot treatments are more precisely calibrated.*	Frequency patterns determine container selection: a customer who consistently engages through mobile receives different slot activation than one who engages through voice — and the CEA routes accordingly.

Monetary (M)	Total spend to date, average transaction value, product category mix, upsell/cross-sell uptake, referral-generated revenue	*Monetary value defines the absolute CLV floor and the investment ceiling for retention. A $180K lifetime customer justifies slot investments that would be uneconomic for a $12K one.*	Monetary tier directly governs slot intensity and personalization depth. Stage 14 retention slots for Tier 1 customers deploy human outreach. Tier 3 customers receive optimized automated contact.

Propensity (30/60/90/180-day)	Behavioral intent signals: search activity, channel visit patterns, competitive exposure, brand mention engagement, geofence proximity frequency, social affiliation signals, product page dwell time	*Propensity is the forward-looking multiplier on CLV. A $40K historical customer with 85% 30-day purchase probability is worth more in the next slot decision than a $120K historical customer with 8% probability.*	Propensity windows govern slot urgency. High 30-day propensity → immediate high-intensity contact. High 180-day propensity → a nurture sequence that builds toward the decision window. Treating both identically is a design failure.

The CEA does not produce a single composite score that flattens the nuance of these four dimensions into one number. It produces a multidimensional profile that governs slot selection, contact intensity, channel routing, personalization depth, and investment ceiling simultaneously. A customer who is high on Recency and Frequency but moderate on Monetary value and high on 30-day propensity gets a very different slot treatment than one who is low on Recency, high on Monetary value, and high on 180-day propensity. The CxC Matrix has both of these customers mapped across all 15 stages and 6 channels. The CEA knows which slot each one deserves. The channel delivers it.

Segmentation — How the CEA Groups Customers to Govern Slot Investment

The CEA does not treat every customer as an isolated scoring problem. It operates on top of a segmentation architecture that groups customers by their combined RFM profiles and propensity patterns, enabling consistent, scalable slot design decisions across large customer populations while preserving the individual responsiveness that makes each slot feel personal. Segmentation is not a simplification of the CEA's precision — it is the structure that makes that precision operationally deployable.

Five segments emerge consistently across CEA-governed customer bases, and each carries a distinct slot investment philosophy: a set of principles that govern which containers are activated, which channels are used, what level of personalization is justified, and what the success metric for each slot interaction is. Critically, each segment maps to specific lifecycle stages where the investment priority is highest and the return on a well-designed slot is greatest.

#	Segment	CEA Profile	Slot Investment Philosophy	CxC Matrix Stage Priority
1	Champions	High R · High F · High M · High 30-day propensity	Maximum slot investment justified. Slots personalized to the individual, delivered through preferred channel, designed to maximize advocacy activation.	*Stage 15 Community slots are a priority, not an afterthought. Referrals from this segment produce the highest-CLV new customers in the system.*

2	**Loyal Builders**	**High F · High M · Moderate R · High 60-90-day propensity**	Behaviorally committed but in a lower-activity phase. Slot design focuses on maintaining engagement, surfacing unextracted value, and positioning favorably for the upcoming decision window.	*Stage 11 proactive slots are the primary vehicle. The goal is presence, not pressure.*
3	**High-Value At-Risk**	**High M · Low R · Declining F · Moderate 90-day propensity**	Most expensive segment to lose. Most important to defend. CLV alone justifies elevated slot intensity.	*Stage 14 retention slots deploy senior relationship contacts — not automated messages. This is not an email campaign. It is a relationship rescue.*

4	**Emerging Value**	**Low M · High F · High R · High 60-day propensity**	Current monetary value understates potential. In an active growth trajectory. Slot design focuses on education, cross-sell, and deepening the relationship before a competitor captures the next purchase.	*Stages 3–5 slots are high priority. This customer is still deciding whether you are the permanent answer.*

5	**Dormant Potential**	**Low R · Low F · Moderate M · Low propensity**	Reactivation investment is selective and strictly CEA-governed. Expected value of re-engagement must exceed the acquisition cost of replacement.	*Mass broadcast contact to this segment is a trust-ledger withdrawal, not a deposit. Only customers whose CLV trajectory suggests genuine reactivation potential receive slot investment.*

> *The CEA does not flatten customer complexity into five buckets. It uses these five profiles as operational anchors — shared investment principles that govern slot design for each population, while the individual RFM score and propensity window calibrate the specific slot, channel, and timing for every person within it.*

Brand Trust, Identity Affiliation, and the Exposure Stack

How Proximity Grows Selection Probability Before the Customer Asks

The Customer Experience Algorithm does not operate only on transactional data. One of its most powerful capabilities is its ability to integrate brand exposure signals — the accumulated record of how frequently a customer has encountered your brand through images, mentions, advertisements, sponsored content, peer references, proximity events, and channel interactions — into the propensity score calculation. The research foundation here is well established: repeated, positive exposure to a brand increases selection probability even when the customer is not actively in a purchase decision. The CEA operationalizes that research as a slot design principle.

This is what distinguishes the Customer Worthy framework from pure transactional analytics. A customer who has purchased twice may have a moderate RFM score, but if their behavioral signals show consistent engagement with your brand content, repeated proximity to your physical locations, active participation in brand-affiliated communities, and social network connections who have positively mentioned your brand, their propensity score is materially higher than their transaction history alone would predict. The CEA reads the exposure stack and adjusts selection probability accordingly. The CxC Matrix then activates the slot whose design is most likely to convert that elevated probability into a transaction.

Figure 9.2 *Brand Exposure Signals: How Proximity, Identity Affiliation, and Social Awareness Grow Selection Probability and Drive Slot Activation Across the CxC Matrix.*

Exposure Signal	How the CEA Reads It	Selection Probability Effect	Slot Design Response Across the CxC Matrix

Physical Proximity (Geofence Frequency)	CEA tracks how often a customer's mobile device enters brand-proximate zones — store vicinity, event venue, service area — even when no transaction occurs. Each proximity event without a transaction increments a consideration score.	*Each event narrows the propensity window from 90-day to 30-day at defined threshold.*	Champions receive relationship reinforcement. Emerging Value customers receive educational content. At-Risk customers receive a win-back offer. Segment determines the slot. Proximity triggers it.
Brand Image and Ad Exposure	Programmatic delivery systems feed impression data to the CEA: how many times has this customer seen this brand's imagery in the past 30 days, across which channels, with what engage-ment rate.	*Cumulative exposure above defined thresholds raises baseline selection probability by 8–15%, depending on creative quality and contextual relevance match.*	High-exposure customers in active propensity windows receive slots with reduced price sensitivity assumptions — they have been pre-warmed and are less likely to require a discount incentive.

Social Mention and Peer Affiliation	Social listening identifies when a customer's network connections have mentioned, reviewed, or engaged with the brand. Peer endorsement proxies feed into the CEA as trust multipliers.	*First-degree peer endorsement raises selection probability by 22–34%. Second-degree by 11–17%. Both integrated as social proof coefficients.*	Stage 3 (Identification) and Stage 4 (Selection) slots surface peer references: 'Customers like you made this decision for these reasons' — reinforcing the social proof the CEA has already scored.
Brand Identity Affiliation	Engagement with brand values content, cause affiliation posts, community membership, lifestyle imagery — signals that a customer sees the brand as an expression of their own identity, not just a transactional option.	*Identity affiliation is the strongest predictor of advocacy behavior. Customers who identify with the brand generate 3.1× more referrals than those who merely transact.*	Stage 15 (Community) slots speak to shared values rather than transactional incentives. Referral activation for this segment is built on belonging, not discount.

Content Engagement Cadence	Frequency and depth of engagement with brand-produced content: email open rates, time-on-page for articles, video completion rates, podcast plays, webinar attendance — each feeding the CEA's frequency and recency calculations.	*Content engagement predicts purchase probability at 0.68 correlation coefficient for B2C and 0.74 for complex B2B. CEA weights content engagement as a forward-leading recency signal.*	If they read the article, the next slot references it. If they watched the product video, the next slot assumes product knowledge and offers the next level of detail. The conversation continues.

Competitor Proximity and Comparison Behavior	Search data, competitor site visit signals, competitive app usage, comparative review engagement — behavioral signals that a customer is in an active comparison cycle.	*Competitive comparison behavior narrows the propensity window from 90-day to 14-day and elevates slot urgency classification from Standard to Priority.*	Immediate high-intensity treatment: human outreach for Tier 1 customers, personalized comparison tool for Tier 2, targeted offer with clear differentiation messaging for Tier 3 — all deployed within the 14-day decision horizon the CEA identified.

The exposure stack is not a passive measurement. It is an active input to the CEA's propensity calculation that continuously updates the selection probability for every customer based on what they are seeing, where they are going, and what their network is saying — independent of whether a transaction has occurred. The CxC Matrix slots that respond to exposure signals are not marketing messages. They are precisely calibrated touchpoints that meet the customer exactly where their exposure score says they are.

The Physical Intelligence Layer — When the Environment Becomes a Slot

The CxC Matrix maps customer contacts across six channel categories: Geography, Digital, Location, Third Party, One-to-One, and Community. Within the physical and location channels, a new layer of capability has converged to fundamentally change what a slot can do and when it can activate. RFID tagging, geofencing, mobile device proximity sensing, computer vision, and real-time location intelligence allow the physical environment itself to become an active participant in the customer experience — and a live data feed into the CEA's propensity calculations.

Where a physical slot was previously limited to what happened at a fixed interaction point — the counter, the desk, the delivery door — it can now extend through an intelligent environment that detects the customer's approach, correlates their identity with their CEA profile, pre-allocates the appropriate resources, and initiates the right contact before the customer walks through the door. The slot no longer waits. It orchestrates in advance. And every physical signal it captures — visit frequency, dwell time by product area, route through the store, proximity to specific items — becomes an input to the CEA's next propensity calculation.

The Physical Intelligence Layer — Five Technologies That Feed the CEA

RFID (Radio Frequency Identification): Tags in products, loyalty credentials, or mobile wallet identifiers detect customer presence, cart contents, and item selection automatically — feeding the CEA with real-time frequency and selection data, enabling hands-free loyalty recognition, and triggering slot activation at the moment of product engagement rather than at the point of purchase.

Geofencing: Virtual geographic boundaries trigger automated CEA queries and slot decisions when a customer's device enters or exits a defined zone. The geofence is not just a notification trigger — it is a frequency signal that accumulates in the CEA and narrows the propensity window each time the customer's proximity is detected without a transaction.

Bluetooth Low Energy / Ultra-Wideband Proximity: Centimeter-accurate indoor positioning enables the CEA to correlate in-store behavior with the customer's profile at previously unavailable granularity: which aisle, which product section, how long, how often. This data feeds the Frequency dimension with behavioral detail that purchase records alone cannot supply.

Computer Vision and IoT Sensors: Aggregate behavioral intelligence — queue length, dwell time patterns, product interaction rates — without individual identification, providing slot performance analytics that improve container design and feed competitive intelligence into the CEA's comparison behavior detection layer.

Connected Vehicle and Wearable Data: With consent, the customer's car, watch, and fitness tracker participate in the experience network, broadcasting location, schedule context, and behavioral state that allow the CEA to anticipate need-state before the customer initiates contact — enabling anticipatory slots in every lifecycle stage.

Channel Digital Maturity — What Each Container Can Do for the CEA

All Six CxC Matrix Channels, Mapped Against AI Orchestration Capability

One of the most valuable outputs of a Customer Schematic review is an honest assessment of each channel container's digital maturity — not what it could theoretically do, but what it is doing today in terms of feeding signals into the CEA and activating slots in response to CEA outputs. The table below maps each of the CxC Matrix's six channel categories against its current capability state, its CEA orchestration layer, and the specific lifecycle stage outcomes that combination produces.

Here is the principle behind this mapping: the six channels of the CxC Matrix are not distribution options. They are the six arenas where your company's messages, brand signals, offers, and human presence meet the customer's world. The CEA governs how those arenas are activated — which one reaches which customer at which stage, at what intensity, with what slot content. Without CEA orchestration, channels broadcast. With it, they listen, learn, and respond.

Figure 9.3 *Channel Container Digital Maturity and CEA Orchestration Capability. All six CxC Matrix channels mapped against their AI orchestration layer and the lifecycle stage outcomes that combination enables.*

Channel / Container	Primary Stages	Digital Maturity Now	AI + CEA Orchestration Layer	What This Enables in the CxC Matrix
Digital (Web / Desktop)	**S1-S5**	Personalized landing pages, dynamic content, behavioral retargeting, A/B testing at scale, real-time chat, self-service portals	*Session-level CEA score refresh. Next-best-action driven by RFM tier and active propensity window. Real-time offer optimization calibrated to monetary segment.*	Every Stage 1–3 awareness, information, and identification slot becomes CEA-aware. The page a returning Champion sees differs from the one an Emerging Value customer sees, which differs from the one an At-Risk customer in a 30-day propensity window sees. The score determines the slot, not the calendar.

Digital (Mobile App)	**S7–S11**	Push notifications, in-app messaging, location-aware content, biometric authentication, mobile wallet integration, deep linking	*Real-time geofence CEA queries. Frequency signal accumulation from session behavior. Propensity window narrowing based on app engagement cadence. Competitive comparison detection via in-app search behavior.*	Use and Delivery stage slots extend dynamically. The app knows when proximity frequency has crossed a propensity threshold, when in-session behavior indicates a consideration window is narrowing, and when the recency decay curve calls for a re-engagement slot before CLV erosion becomes measurable.

Location (Physical Store / Branch)	**S4, S11, S14**	POS integration, loyalty credential recognition, staff-facing dashboards, queue management, digital signage	*RFID-triggered CEA score pull at entry. Geofence pre-arrival staff briefing. Real-time staff prompt calibrated to customer's current CEA segment and active propensity window. Dwell-time and route data fed back after visit.*	The customer's walk from the parking lot becomes a Stage 11 or Stage 14 slot. Geofence detects arrival, CEA pulls segment and propensity, staff dashboard shows: 'Customer in Segment 3 (High-Value At-Risk): last purchase 47 days ago, monetary tier 1, 90-day propensity 62%. Recommended approach: relationship reinforcement, not product push.'

Third Party (RFID / Geofence / IoT)	**S1-S6, S11**	Zone-based mobile alerts, competitor proximity detection, location-triggered offers, RFID inventory and loyalty recognition, delivery-zone preparation	*Proximity frequency accumulation in CEA recency/frequency calculations. Competitive exposure detection triggering propensity window compression. RFID-triggered CEA profile association at entry with real-time monetary tier calculation.*	Stage 4–6 slots activate before the customer walks in. A prospect whose geofence frequency has reached propensity threshold and whose social signals show active competitor comparison receives a personalized contact designed to their CEA segment — not a generic push.

One-to-One (Voice / Phone / Advisor)	**S5, S12 –S14**	IVR authentication, sentiment analysis, conversation transcription, real-time agent prompting, financial advisor AI-assisted briefing	*Pre-call CEA score delivery to agent. Propensity window classification of inbound contact. Automatic segment-appropriate routing. Monetary tier-governed escalation thresholds.*	Stage 12–14 support and renewal slots become CEA-intelligent. The system doesn't ask the customer to re-identify. It already knows their segment, monetary tier, last interaction, and current propensity status. A Segment 1 customer routes to a specialist immediately. A Segment 5 customer routes to an AI-assisted agent. Investment matches the CLV-weighted value of the interaction.

Community (Social / Brand Network)	**S2, S15**	Brand monitoring, review management, influencer identification, user-generated content amplification, advocacy activation	*Social proof coefficient updates to CEA from peer mention detection. Advocacy propensity scoring from behavioral sentiment signals. Identity affiliation scoring from content engagement patterns. Competitor mention detection feeding propensity window recalibration.*	Stage 15 slots are CEA-timed, not calendar-timed. AI identifies Champion segment customers whose behavioral signals show an advocacy-ready state — high recency, active brand content engagement, recent peer network brand discussion — and deploys the referral slot at the precise moment the propensity calculation predicts maximum conversion probability.

> *The channel that is most digitally mature in isolation is not the most valuable channel in the CEA-governed matrix. The most valuable channel is the one that is most precisely integrated with the CEA's propensity score for each customer at each stage — regardless of its inherent technology sophistication.*

Choreographing the Experience — From CEA Score to Slot Activation

The word 'orchestration' is the right one, and it is worth unpacking in the context of the CEA. An orchestra does not play randomly. Each instrument has a defined role, a specific moment to contribute, and a precise relationship with every other instrument, managed so that the whole produces something no single instrument could achieve. The conductor doesn't choose which notes to play. They ensure the right instrument plays the right note at the right moment for this particular performance of this particular composition.

The CEA is the conductor. The CxC Matrix is the composition. The six channels are the instrument sections. And the physical intelligence layer — RFID, geofencing, proximity sensing, behavioral data streams — is the real-time acoustic environment that tells the conductor how the performance is landing and whether to adjust the next measure. What the audience experiences is not the technology. It is the music: an organization that seems to understand them, anticipates their needs, and responds with precisely calibrated action at exactly the right moment, in exactly the right channel, at exactly the right lifecycle stage.

Figure 9.4 *CEA + Physical Intelligence Layer Orchestration: From Customer Signal to CxC Matrix Slot Activation. Six live scenarios across lifecycle stages 3–15 showing how behavioral signals translate to specific slot decisions.*

Stage + Situation	Physical + Behavioral Signal	AI + CEA Orchestration Action	CxC Matrix Slot Activated
Stage 11 High-Value Customer Approaching Store	Geofence detects device in 500m zone. RFID credential associates identity. CEA pulls: Segment 1 (Champion), Tier 1 monetary, propensity window 30-day at 87/100, last Stage 11 interaction 14 days ago.	*CEA confirms high-investment slot warranted. Pre-populates staff dashboard with relationship brief. Selects personalized greeting protocol and proactive offer calibrated to modeled preference profile and monetary tier.*	Stage 11 Proactive Slot: staff greets by name, references specific usage history, offers a personalized product or service extension — not a generic promotion, but a contact whose content the CEA determined before the customer walked through the door.

Stage 3–4 Prospect in Active Comparison Cycle	Three web sessions in 5 days on pricing pages. Comparison tool used twice. Social engagement with competitor content. Geofence proximity to competitor location detected once.	*CEA compresses propensity window to 14-day. Classifies as Priority activation. Selects Segment 4 (Emerging Value) slot protocol. Suppresses interruptive tactics. Queues next-morning personalized outreach.*	Stage 3–4 Opportunity Slot: morning contact arrives through customer's highest-engagement channel, references specific comparison behavior, offers a personalized value analysis calibrated to their usage profile — not a generic 'are you interested?' broadcast.

Stage 12 Inbound Support Call	Mobile number identifies caller in 0.4 seconds. CEA pulls: Stage 12, Segment 2 (Loyal Builder), Tier 2 monetary, last Stage 7 contact 11 days ago, recency score 73, frequency trajectory stable.	*CEA determines high-investment resolution warranted by Tier 2 status. Routes to specialist. Pre-generates resolution options. Flags that a proactive Stage 7 slot failure likely caused this contact and updates the upstream slot design queue.*	Stage 12 Support Slot: agent answers with full context: 'I see you have a question about your last statement — I've pulled your account and I think I can resolve this in about two minutes.' The CEA determined the routing, the script, and the resolution investment ceiling before the agent picked up.

Stage 14 Recency Decay Alert — Tier 1 Customer	CEA detects recency score drop from 81 to 52 over 30 days. Frequency trend declining. Monetary tier 1. 90-day propensity at 58% and falling. No Stage 14 slot activated. Competitive exposure signals elevated in monitoring feeds.	*CEA elevates customer to Segment 3 (High-Value At-Risk). Triggers Stage 14 retention protocol. Overrides automated contact in favor of senior relationship manager outreach. Generates personalized retention brief calibrated to CLV tier and propensity window.*	Stage 14 Retention Slot: not a promotional email, but a personal call from a senior relationship manager who references the specific value delivered over the tenure and presents a customized proposal designed for this customer's profile and this decision window.

Stage 15 Behavioral Advocacy Signal Detected	Champion segment customer. Recency score 94. Frequency above segment norm. Monetary tier 1. Social monitoring detects two positive brand mentions in customer's network in past 7 days. Content engagement tripled in 30 days.	*CEA scores advocacy propensity at 89%. Identifies 48-hour activation window as peak referral timing. Generates personalized referral approach calibrated to identity affiliation signals — shared values, not discount incentive.*	Stage 15 Community Slot: 48 hours after peak advocacy signal, customer receives personal outreach from their named relationship contact, referencing the specific experience that generated the advocacy impulse and offering a peer-facing referral action designed to feel natural rather than transactional.

Stage 7–8 RFID Shipment Delay Detection	RFID tag on shipment motionless for 48 hours. Customer is CEA Stage 7–8. Recency score declining. No proactive contact in 72 hours. CEA calculates Stage 12 inbound contact probability at 71% and rising.	*CEA activates Stage 7 proactive protocol before customer initiates contact. Generates accurate delivery status with actionable options. Adjusts Frequency and Recency calculations to reflect proactive outreach in the measurement period.*	Stage 7 Proactive Slot: customer receives an honest, specific status update with three actionable choices before they've had to wonder or call — converting a potential Frequency decay event into a Recency deposit.

Each scenario in Figure 9.4 is a demonstration of the same underlying logic: the CEA does not wait for the customer to initiate contact. It monitors the signal stream continuously, scores the data against the four dimensions, and activates the appropriate slot at the moment when the propensity calculation says the interaction will be most valuable — to the customer and to the organization. The customer experiences not a system. They experience an organization that seems to know them.

Earning the Invitation — How Organizations Join and Stay in the Customer's Network

Jose's relationship with Tiger Direct was not accidental. He had evaluated Tiger Direct, decided they offered value worth the interruption of his personal time, and issued them an invitation: access to his email, authority to send alerts, permission to present offers. He managed that invitation actively — if Tiger Direct had abused it, he would have revoked it. The relationship existed because it served him, and he knew he was in control of whether it continued.

This dynamic is the fundamental tension the CEA must navigate. The more precisely the algorithm can identify a customer's propensity window, the more precisely it can target the slot that will convert — but if that precision is experienced by the customer as intrusion rather than service, it withdraws from the trust ledger rather than depositing into it. The CEA is not a hunting system. It is a service system. Every slot it activates should leave the customer with the feeling that the organization used the access it was granted to make their situation better — not to optimize its own conversion metrics at the customer's expense.

The CxC Matrix is, in this sense, a framework for earning and keeping the invitation. Every well-designed slot is an investment in the invitation's continuation. Every over-deployed, mistimed, or irrelevant contact is a withdrawal from the trust account that the invitation represents. And in a market where the customer's alternatives are a Google search away and their ability to switch has never been more frictionless, the trust ledger determines everything: loyalty, lifetime value, referral behavior, and competitive durability.

The Professional Customer's Five Invitation Tests — What the CEA Must Pass

(1) Does this organization use my data to serve me — or to sell to me regardless of my current context? The CEA must demonstrate relevance at each activation or the invitation narrows.

(2) Does it remember who I am across channels and over time, or do I re-introduce myself at every contact? CDP-unified identity across all 15 stages is the minimum viable standard.

(3) Does it contact me at moments when that contact adds value, or on its own schedule? Propensity-window governed slot activation, not marketing calendar scheduling, is the answer.

(4) Does it make it easy for me to get what I need, or does it design processes for its own convenience? Customer-side friction is a slot performance metric alongside revenue.

(5) When something goes wrong, does it own the resolution? Stage 13 proactive recovery protocol, triggered before the customer escalates, is how the CEA passes this test.

The Trust Ledger — Building Value Without Betraying the Access You've Been Granted

Every interaction in the customer's network is a transaction in what the Customer Worthy framework calls the trust ledger. Trust is deposited when the CEA uses the access it has been granted to make the customer's situation measurably better — faster resolution, more relevant information, a proactive slot that saves time or money, a recognition of tenure and loyalty that confirms the organization has been paying attention. Trust is withdrawn when that access is misused — when contacts are timed to the organization's promotional calendar rather than the customer's propensity window, when the personalization is shallow enough that the customer can tell the system knows their name but doesn't know their situation.

Today, customers are more aware of trust-ledger dynamics than ever before. A generation of consumers who grew up understanding how behavioral data is monetized has produced a customer base that actively monitors the quality of their access grants. They will rarely articulate this evaluation in those terms — they will describe it as a gut feeling about whether a company respects them. But what they are running is a continuous audit: comparing the value they receive from the access they have granted against the cost, in privacy, time, and trust, of granting it. The CEA must win that audit consistently, or the invitation gets reconsidered.

Figure 9.5 *The Customer Trust Ledger: Six Variables Customers Evaluate Continuously, and How the CEA + CxC Matrix Responds at Every Lifecycle Stage.*

Trust Variable	What Customers Evaluate	CEA + CxC Matrix Response Across the 15 Stages
Data Relevance	*Does this organization use my behavioral data to surface things genuinely useful to me — or to optimize their revenue regardless of my current context?*	CEA-governed personalization with relevance thresholds. No slot deploys unless the model predicts it improves the customer's situation alongside the organization's revenue. Offers with negative CLV-impact profiles are suppressed automatically by the scoring logic.
Memory and Continuity	*Does this organization remember who I am and what has happened between us — or do I re-introduce myself and re-explain my context at every contact?*	CDP-unified identity across all 15 stages. Every slot has access to the full interaction history, the current CEA segment, and the active propensity window. The customer is never asked to re-provide context they have already established.

Contact Timing	*Does this organization contact me when the contact is valuable to me — or on its own promotional schedule regardless of my current need-state?*	CEA propensity-window governed slot activation. No broadcast contact reaches a customer whose behavioral signals indicate they are not in a receptive phase. Timing is determined by the customer's RFM trajectory and propensity score, not the marketing calendar.
Friction Reduction	*Does this organization consistently reduce the effort required to get what I need — or design processes for its own operational convenience?*	Customer-side cost as a measured slot performance metric alongside revenue. Interaction time, steps required, context re-provision rate, and channel switching frequency are monitored. Any slot generating systematic high customer-side cost triggers redesign regardless of its revenue contribution.

Failure Recovery	*When something goes wrong, does this organization own the problem and restore my confidence — or explain why the problem is mine to resolve?*	Stage 13 protocol: CEA identifies the upstream slot failure origin, routes to the appropriate resolution team, triggers proactive customer outreach before escalation, and measures recovery quality — the degree to which CEA scores improved after resolution, indicating trust was restored, not merely the transaction closed.
Privacy Integrity	*Is my data being used in ways I understood and agreed to — or in ways that would make me uncomfortable if I knew the full picture?*	Consent-governed data architecture. Every CEA model operates within explicit consent records stored in the CDP. Models do not access data categories the customer has not enabled. Consent review prompts are embedded in Stage 11 and Stage 14 slot designs as standard practice, not regulatory compliance minimums.

The trust ledger is not a philosophical concept. It is a measurable business variable. Organizations with strong trust-ledger balances — as revealed by CLV trajectory, Frequency trends, referral volume per active customer, and competitive churn response to pricing changes — demonstrably and durably outperform those with depleted ones. The CEA, used rigorously and with discipline about what each slot is for and what it owes the customer who receives it, is the operational instrument that builds that balance systematically.

Network Effects — When Stage 15 Becomes the Highest-ROI Channel

Jose's Tiger Direct purchase did not end at the confirmation screen. He returned to his office with six monitors and a story. The story spread through his department, his professional network, and potentially his industry. Tiger Direct had not just completed a transaction — they had activated an acquisition channel that no advertising budget could have purchased: an authentic, peer-to-peer endorsement from a credible professional, delivered in the context of a relevant business decision, to an audience of high-propensity buyers who trusted the source.

The professional customer of today doesn't just shop at review sites — they create them. They curate and distribute peer intelligence across LinkedIn, Reddit communities, Slack groups, WhatsApp networks, and every vertical platform where their industry peers make purchasing decisions. Every Stage 15 slot your organization has — or conspicuously lacks — is either activated or abandoned in that environment. And the CEA knows which customers are in an advocacy-ready state, what triggered that state, and how to deploy the Stage 15 Community slot at exactly the moment when their propensity to share is highest.

What Stage 15 Looks Like: CEA-Designed vs. Default

WITHOUT CEA-driven Stage 15 slot: A Champion segment customer who has just completed a positive milestone interaction receives a generic promotional email 72 hours later. Their advocacy impulse — which was real, active, and measurable in their behavioral signals — decays without an activation mechanism. They may mention the organization to one colleague. The referral window closes without being opened.

WITH CEA-driven Stage 15 slot: Within 48 hours of the advocacy signal (peak behavioral sentiment + brand content engagement spike + peer network activity), the CEA identifies a 91% advocacy propensity score and selects a personalized referral activation from their named relationship contact — not from a marketing system. The message references the specific experience, offers a specific peer-facing sharing action, and is calibrated to the customer's identity affiliation signals — built on shared values and recognition, not incentive discount.

The difference in referral activation rate between these two approaches: 3.4× in controlled implementations. The difference in referred-customer CLV: 2.7× — because peer-referred customers arrive pre-qualified by a trusted source and pre-loaded with positive expectations the Matrix can build on rather than having to establish from scratch.

CEA amplification: social listening tools feed peer mention data back into the CEA as social proof coefficients, updating the propensity scores of network-connected customers and creating a compounding advocacy effect where each Stage 15 activation makes the next one more probable.

> *"Every Stage 15 slot your organization has — or conspicuously lacks — is either activated or abandoned in the environment where your customers' peers are making their decisions. The CEA knows exactly which customers are ready to advocate. The only question is whether you deploy the slot before the impulse decays."*

Anticipatory Commerce — CEA-Driven Experience Bundles

Customer Worthy's original prediction was that the next great breakthrough would not be a brand new service, but a combination of products, services, features, and functions that closely wrapped themselves around the customer's need-set and adapted to their life stage. That prediction was correct, and the technology to operationalize it now exists.

What Customer Worthy called 'adaptive bundles' is now operational as anticipatory commerce: the capacity to identify a customer's need before they have fully articulated it, using the CEA's propensity calculations, physical-layer signals, brand exposure stack, and behavioral trajectory modeling to determine the moment when a specific offer, service, or contact would maximize both the customer's CLV and their experience of being served. The slot is not designed to respond to what the customer asked. It is designed to answer what they were about to ask — with a precision that makes the experience feel, from the customer's perspective, less like receiving a marketing contact and more like being genuinely understood.

Anticipatory Commerce in Action — CEA-Driven Stage 11 Slot Design

Stage 11 mortgage customer. CEA recency score 78 (stable), frequency score 71 (slight decline from norm), monetary tier 1. Brand exposure stack shows three geofence proximity events at a home improvement retailer in 30 days. Search behavior includes home improvement financing terms. CDP data: original loan rate 6.8%, current market rate 5.9%, equity accumulated: $87,000.

CEA calculates cash-out refinance propensity: 74%, 30-day window. The Stage 11 slot activates — not a promotional email, but a personalized financial analysis from their named loan officer showing precisely what a cash-out refinance means for their specific situation: the change in monthly payment, the accessible equity amount, and what that equity could fund based on the home improvement signals the CEA flagged.

The customer receives an answer to a question they were still formulating. That is anticipatory commerce. That is what CEA-powered slot design produces at full maturity.

"The next breakthrough is the organization that knows enough about its customers' situations — from their RFM profile, their propensity window, their brand exposure stack, and their behavioral trajectory — to offer them the right thing at the right moment without requiring them to ask. The CEA calculates when that moment arrives. The CxC Matrix delivers the slot that meets it."

The Ongoing Invitation — Designing for a Network That Never Stops Scoring

The customer's network never goes offline. Between contacts, between transactions, between lifecycle stages, the customer is still broadcasting signals — through behavior, location, social activity, search queries, and purchasing patterns. The CEA is still scoring them. Their recency curve is still moving. Their propensity window is still narrowing or widening. Their brand exposure stack is still accumulating. And their evaluation of whether your organization deserves its continued place in their network is still running, continuously, in the background of every other thing they are doing.

Most organizations design for the moments of contact and leave the space between contacts to chance. The CxC Matrix with CEA orchestration is designed to ensure that the space between contacts is not empty. It is filled with the quiet, consistent signals of an organization that is paying attention: the proactive slot that activates before the customer needed to ask, the milestone recognition that arrives when the CEA's recency calculation says the relationship is worth celebrating, the competitive defense slot that deploys when physical-layer signals say the consideration window is opening.

This is the full realization of the customer network concept. Not just acknowledgment that customers are connected, but a systematic, CEA-governed architecture for ensuring that your organization is part of those connections in a way that serves the customer first and generates revenue as the natural consequence of that service. The customer who feels genuinely served at the right moment, through the right channel, with the right level of personalization relative to their CEA profile — that customer does not need to be retained. They stay because the relationship is valuable. They refer because sharing discovered value is a natural human behavior. They advocate because the experience was precise enough, personal enough, and useful enough to be worth talking about.

> *"The customer's network never stops generating signals. The CEA never stops scoring them. The question is whether your CxC Matrix is designed to respond to those scores — or whether you're still only showing up at the moments of your choosing, wondering why the invitation keeps expiring."*

What This Chapter Has Built

You now have three things most organizations have never possessed simultaneously.

First: the computational engine that makes the CxC Matrix operational at scale. The Customer Experience Algorithm integrates Recency, Frequency, Monetary value, and propensity-weighted CLV into a multidimensional scoring system that tells you not just who your best customers are — but which specific slot, in which specific channel, at which specific lifecycle stage, deployed at which specific moment, will generate the highest return for this specific customer right now. The CEA transforms the CxC Matrix from a strategic map into a real-time orchestration system.

Second: the framework for understanding what your customer is actually broadcasting between contacts — and how to use that signal to fill the silence that most organizations leave to chance, or worse, to competitors. The brand exposure stack, the physical intelligence layer, the social proof coefficients, the competitive proximity detection — all of it feeding the CEA continuously, narrowing propensity windows before the customer has decided to decide, activating slots at the moment when the score says the intervention will matter most.

Third: the discipline of the trust ledger. The understanding that the CEA is a service system, not a hunting system — that the precision of its propensity calculations is justified only when every slot it activates makes the customer's situation better rather than simply advancing the organization's conversion metrics. The organizations that build durable competitive advantage with this framework are the ones that internalize this distinction — because customers know the difference, even when they cannot articulate it, and the trust ledger is the business variable that measures how well the organization has earned the continued invitation to be present in their network.

> *The next chapter moves from the intelligence layer to the economic layer: translating every signal, every score, every slot activation into the language of capital allocation. Because the trust ledger has a dollar value. And the CEA's job is not just to serve customers well — it is to make that service the most defensible revenue-generating system in your organization.*

Chapter 9 Action Plan — CEA Implementation Priorities

The CEA is only as precise as the data that feeds it, and the slots it activates are only as powerful as their alignment to the customer's actual lifecycle stage and channel preferences. These four weeks build the foundation from which everything else compounds.

Week 1	**Establish Your CEA Data Foundation**	Audit the four CEA dimensions against your current data infrastructure. For Recency: what is your current measurement granularity — purchase only, or all meaningful interactions? For Frequency: which channel containers are generating interaction data that feeds your scoring? For Monetary: is your CLV calculation forward-looking with propensity weighting, or purely historical? For Propensity: do you have a working 30/60/90/180-day purchase probability model, or are you relying on recency and frequency as proxies? Document the gaps. The CEA is only as precise as the data that feeds it.

Week 2	**Build Your CEA Segmentation Profile**	Using the five-segment architecture from this chapter as your template, classify your active customer base by current RFM scores. You do not need a fully deployed CEA to do this — a basic RFM scoring exercise using transaction data and interaction logs will produce an initial segmentation sufficient to identify your Champion and High-Value At-Risk populations. Map those two segments first. Confirm their size, their CLV distribution, and the current state of their Stage 11 and Stage 14 slot coverage. These are your highest-priority targets for immediate slot redesign.

Week 3	**Design Your Brand Exposure Stack Monitoring**	Identify the brand exposure signals you are currently capturing — ad impressions, geofence proximity events, content engagement data, social mention monitoring, competitive exposure signals — and map each to the CEA dimension it feeds. For signals you are not currently capturing, evaluate the integration cost against the propensity calculation improvement they produce. Priority for most organizations: geofence proximity data integration (highest propensity signal per implementation dollar), social proof coefficient scoring from peer mention monitoring, and content engagement frequency weighting into the recency calculation.

Week 4	**Activate Your First CEA-Governed Slot**	Select one high-priority slot — ideally in Stage 11, Stage 14, or Stage 15 — and redesign it to be governed by CEA scoring rather than calendar scheduling. Define the CEA trigger: what combination of Recency score, Frequency trajectory, Monetary tier, and propensity window activates this slot for this segment? Define the slot content variation for each qualifying segment. Define the success metric in CLV-weighted terms, not just conversion rate. Deploy. Measure. Feed the results back into the CEA to improve the next propensity calculation. This single slot, redesigned with CEA precision, typically outperforms its calendar-governed predecessor by a factor of 2–4× in CLV impact per deployment.

Think Like a Customer. Score Like an Algorithm. Serve Like You Mean It.

Michael R Hoffman · Customer Worthy: Total Customer Engineering

CHAPTER TEN

Start the Revolution

Why Idle Customers Are Now Armed, Why AI Is Their Force Multiplier, and Why the Most Dangerous Business Decision You Can Make Is to Keep Wasting Their Time

The revolution does not announce itself with a press release. It begins the moment your customer is on hold — when the gap between what you promised and what you are delivering becomes long enough for them to calculate the cost of what you are doing to them, open a browser, and start drafting the post that will reach fifty thousand people by morning.

> *"An idle customer is a dangerous customer. Give them a phone, a camera, an audience, and a cause — and an idle customer becomes a movement."*
>
> **— Customer Worthy**

The Revolution Is Already Here — It Just Keeps Getting Better Tools

The revolution does not need your permission. It has been underway since the moment digitization gave every frustrated customer a distribution channel equal to or larger than yours. What has changed in the years since Customer Worthy was first published is not the customer's motivation — that has always been the same: respect my time, keep your promises, and when you fail, own it and fix it. What has changed is the velocity, the sophistication, the reach, and now the artificial intelligence powering the disruption. The customer who was dangerous with a camcorder and a YouTube account in 2003 is exponentially more dangerous with an AI content assistant, a sixty-thousand-follower social media presence, and the ability to produce professional-grade documentation of your failure in real time.

Recall Dot from our preface — the AT&T customer whose patience finally broke after one interaction too many, and who made her frustration known in ways that were deliberately, publicly, and reputationally costly to the organization that had stopped treating her like someone whose time and trust mattered. Dot was not an outlier. She was an early indicator. Every organization that dismissed her story as an edge case, as a customer who was simply impossible to satisfy, as an isolated incident that did not warrant a structural response — every one of those organizations is encountering Dot's successors at increasing frequency, with increasing sophistication, and with increasing consequences.

The lesson from Dot was not about social media management. It was about what happens at the cellular level of customer experience when organizations design their processes around operational convenience rather than customer value. Frustration does not emerge from nowhere. It accumulates —

hold time by hold time, broken promise by broken promise, automated response by automated response — until the customer reaches a threshold where the energy required to tolerate the relationship exceeds the value they receive from it. At that threshold, they stop calculating whether to leave. They start calculating how to be heard.

> ***"Every customer who is on hold right now is also on a device. Every customer who has been told 'we'll call you back' is already composing the post. The revolution is not coming. It is running continuously, in the background of every interaction you are not designing well enough."***

The Escalating Arsenal — How Customer Disruption Has Evolved and Where AI Takes It Next

In 2003, Casey Neistat's iPod battery died. Apple told him to buy a new iPod. Casey and his brother — both professional filmmakers — made a short video, posted it at iPodsdirtysecret.com, emailed forty friends, and watched it receive more than 1.5 million views. Apple launched a battery replacement program. The entire exercise cost Casey Neistat nothing but time and creative energy. The cost to Apple in brand remediation, policy change, and executive attention was orders of magnitude larger.

What made that moment historically significant was not its outcome — Apple's response was, ultimately, correct and appropriate. What made it significant was its demonstration of a new economic principle in customer experience: the marginal cost of disruption to a frustrated customer had dropped to near zero, while the potential impact had become potentially unbounded. A $0.00 investment in a short video, distributed through existing social channels at no cost, reached an audience of 1.5 million and changed corporate policy. The cost-benefit calculation for a frustrated customer had been permanently rewritten.

That calculation has been rewritten again — several times — in the years since. Each new capability layer has widened the asymmetry between the customer's cost of disruption and the organization's cost of suffering it. AI represents the most significant capability expansion in that escalation sequence since the smartphone.

FIGURE 10.1 — THE CUSTOMER DISRUPTION ESCALATION SEQUENCE: FROM IDLE FRUSTRATION TO AI-AMPLIFIED ACTION

Era / Trigger	The Disruption Tool	What Customers Achieved	What Organizations Must Now Design For
Pre-Digital (pre-1995)	Complaint letters. Better Business Bureau filings. Word of mouth to immediate social circle. Occasional local news consumer segment.	Rarely reached more than 50–200 people. Organizational response was selective and often negligible. Reputational consequence was geographically bounded.	*Organizations could afford to treat complaints as isolated exceptions. The economics of systematic slot failure were invisible. Customer time waste was unmeasured and uncompensated.*
Early Digital (1995–2003)	Email campaigns. Consumer complaint websites. Online forums. Early review aggregators. Niche communities of affected customers finding each other.	Reach extended to thousands. Communities of affected customers discovered they had common experiences. Early class-action organizing through online channels.	*Organizations began monitoring brand mentions but still had response-time advantages. The speed asymmetry favored the organization. A complaint could still be managed before it spread widely.*

Social Media Era (2003-2015)	YouTube. Facebook. Twitter. Reddit. Viral video documentation of service failures. Hashtag campaigns. Boycott organizing.	Reach extended to millions overnight. Viral cascades made individual complaints into brand crises within 24 hours. The organization's response speed advantage evaporated.	*Brand monitoring became mandatory. Crisis communication teams were scaled up. Organizations learned to respond publicly and rapidly. The slot failure that went viral cost more to remediate than years of proactive CX investment would have.*
Smartphone + Platform Era (2015-2022)	Live streaming of real-time service failures. Multi-platform simultaneous distribution. Google Reviews, Glassdoor, Yelp as permanent records. TikTok challenge formats applied to brand grievances.	Reach became instantaneous and algorithmic. Recommendation algorithms amplified grievance content. A single experience, filmed live, could reach audiences the brand's own marketing budget couldn't match.	*Customer experience failure became a measurable financial risk variable. CEOs began owning CX outcomes publicly. The speed of algorithmic amplification meant slot failures were propagating faster than crisis response teams could organize.*

AI-Augmented Customer (2022-present)	AI-written professional-grade complaint documentation. AI-generated pattern analysis identifying systematic failures across customer communities. Deepfake-quality video reconstruction of interactions. Automated regulatory filing. AI negotiation agents.	The cost of producing high-quality, legally precise, professionally distributed disruption content has dropped to near zero for any customer with a grievance and access to a consumer AI tool. The quality bar has risen to enterprise-grade; the resource requirement has dropped to individual.	*Every slot failure is now potentially documented, professionally escalated, cross-referenced with other customers' similar experiences, and distributed with the production quality of a marketing campaign — by a single customer, in a single afternoon, at no cost. The time to design every slot correctly is now, not after the first AI-assisted customer action makes the failure permanent.*

The trajectory of this escalation is linear in one dimension — the customer's cost of disruption has declined monotonically with each capability layer — and nonlinear in another. The impact potential is not simply incrementally larger with each era. It is categorically different. AI-augmented disruption introduces pattern recognition at scale: a frustrated customer can now use AI tools to identify whether their individual experience is part of a systematic organizational failure, document that pattern with precision, and distribute that documentation to exactly the stakeholder audiences — regulators, investors, media, competitors' prospective customers — who are most likely to act on it. This is not social media virality. It is targeted stakeholder communication with professional-grade accuracy, produced at consumer cost and speed.

The Idle Customer Is Now Computing — What Happens in the Silence Your Slots Leave Behind

In the original Customer Worthy, the warning was simple: an idle customer is a dangerous customer. The argument was that the time companies waste — hold time, wait time, the silence between broken promises and eventual callbacks — creates a vacuum that frustrated customers fill with comparison shopping, competitive research, community complaint posts, and the slow crystallization of a decision to leave.

That warning remains valid. But the nature of what an idle customer does with their forced inactivity has changed materially. The customer who was on hold in 2010 was likely reading emails or browsing passively. The customer on hold today is potentially querying an AI tool about their contractual rights with your organization, asking it to draft a formal demand letter citing relevant consumer protection statutes, identifying the executive responsible for customer experience at your organization and generating a professionally composed complaint addressed to them directly, and cross-referencing their experience against other customer complaints submitted to regulatory bodies. All while still technically on hold.

This is not a hypothetical scenario. These are documented customer behaviors in now, accelerating as AI tools become more capable and more accessible. The consumer AI market now provides services that specifically assist customers in escalating complaints: identifying the right regulatory channels, drafting communications in legally appropriate formats, calculating the monetized value of the time and harm suffered, and in some cases initiating automated claim filing on behalf of the customer. The customer who was once limited to complaining has become a customer who can credibly threaten — and in many cases, execute — formal regulatory and legal action from a phone while waiting for a technician who is running three hours behind.

WHAT AN AI-EQUIPPED CUSTOMER CAN NOW DO IN THE TIME YOU HAVE THEM ON HOLD

Identify their exact contractual rights under their service agreement using AI document analysis — in 90 seconds.

Calculate the monetary value of their time investment in the complaint resolution process, including opportunity cost at their stated hourly rate, using AI tools that generate a formal receipt — in 3 minutes.

Research the regulatory body responsible for their complaint category, identify the filing procedure, and have an AI draft the complaint in the required regulatory format — in 12 minutes.

Search public consumer complaint databases for other customers who have reported the same failure pattern, compile a summary of findings, and append it to their formal complaint as evidence of systematic organizational failure — in 20 minutes.

Draft and schedule a professional-grade social media post, email campaign, or open letter to your executives, with AI-generated supporting documentation, evidence citations, and a clear remediation demand — in 30 minutes.

Identify and contact journalists who have previously covered customer experience failures at organizations in your industry — with AI-drafted pitch emails that present the story with editorial precision — in 45 minutes.

Total elapsed time: less than one hour. Total cost to the customer: the price of their AI subscription. Total potential cost to your organization: uncalculated, because the slot design failure that created the idle time was never assigned a risk value.

The five top remedies customers have consistently sought in studies of consumer complaint behavior have not changed significantly since the original Customer Worthy documented them: an explanation of why the problem occurred, assurance it will not recur, the problem fixed, acknowledgment that their business is valued, and a genuine apology. These are not expensive remedies. They are not technologically complex.

They are the outputs of a slot designed to treat the customer as a person whose time and experience matter — rather than as a transaction whose complaint is a cost to be minimized. The devastatingly simple truth is that most of the AI-augmented disruption your organization will face in the next three years is entirely preventable through slot design decisions that are available to you today.

Monetizing What You Waste — The CustomerPayback Principle in the AI Era

Customer Worthy introduced the concept of CustomerPayback — the idea that organizations should be held to an economic accounting for the time they waste. The framework was simple: every minute a customer spends on hold, waiting for a callback that doesn't come, navigating an IVR that cannot understand their question, re-explaining context to the fourth agent who has no record of the previous three conversations — every one of those minutes has a dollar value. The customer knows it. They can now calculate it. And increasingly, they can present that calculation to your organization, to regulators, and to the public with the precision of a professional invoice.

The CustomerPayback principle has been operationalized by the CxC Matrix's slot-level financial architecture. Every slot in the Matrix has a customer-side cost calculation built into its performance metrics: time investment required from the customer, steps required, context re-provision burden, friction in channel switching, and opportunity cost of waiting. This is not a philosophical exercise. It is a financial model that makes visible what you have been treating as invisible: the cost your operational decisions impose on the customers you are ostensibly serving.

FIGURE 10.2 — THE MONETIZED COST OF CUSTOMER EXPERIENCE FAILURE: WHAT YOUR CUSTOMERS ARE CALCULATING

Customer Damage Category	What the Customer Experiences	What the Organization Can Calculate and Fix
Lost Time	Hold time, wait time, unproductive travel to resolve what could have been handled remotely, time spent re-explaining context that the organization's systems should already contain	*AI now calculates this automatically for customers: average professional hourly rate x minutes wasted = dollar claim. Organizations with systematic slot failures in Stage 12 are accumulating millions in calculated customer time debt that is increasingly being formally presented.*
Lost Money	Overcharges, billing errors, auto-renewal charges for services the customer believed they'd cancelled, loyalty rewards that expired without notification, price increases that were not communicated with sufficient lead time	*AI tools now scan billing histories for customers on request, identify anomalies, calculate total overcharge across the relationship history, and draft refund demand letters in regulatory format. Stage 12–13 slot failures that create billing confusion are now immediately monetizable by any AI-equipped customer.*

Lost Productivity	The downstream work created by an organizational failure: rescheduling appointments, managing the consequences of a delivery failure, resolving the secondary problems created by a primary failure your organization was responsible for	*Secondary loss documentation is now AI-assisted: 'I missed a half-day of work because the technician did not show up' becomes a formally documented consequential damage claim rather than an informal complaint. Slot failures in Stage 7–9 that generate downstream productivity loss are now documentable with professional precision.*
Lost Trust	The erosion of confidence that occurs when an organization repeatedly fails to keep its implied or explicit promises — not the dramatic failure, but the accumulation of small, persistent disappointments that signal a company does not value the relationship	*Trust loss is now quantifiable through CEA recency and frequency decay measurement. When a customer's engagement frequency drops after a service failure and then recovers partially after remediation, the delta is the monetized cost of the trust withdrawal. Organizations can now calculate trust erosion per slot failure in CLV terms.*

Reputational Damage	The cost the customer incurs in their own network when they recommended your organization to peers who then had similarly poor experiences — the social capital loss of having been an advocate for a company that failed their friends	*Customers whose referrals generated negative experiences are now calculating this reputational cost explicitly and including it in formal complaints. Stage 15 slot failures — particularly when referred customers have poor experiences — generate disproportionate advocate-to-detractor conversions that AI tools help customers document and quantify.*

The practical implication is this: the organizations that wait for customers to monetize these costs for them — through formal complaints, regulatory filings, or public documentation — are paying for this accounting reactively and at a premium. The organizations that build slot-level cost accounting into their Customer Schematic proactively are paying for it strategically, at a fraction of the remediation cost, and with the competitive advantage of having identified and corrected the failures before they became externally documented and publicly attributed.

You should be angry, too. Not performatively — but because you are also a customer. Every person reading this book has experienced the hold time that lasted forty minutes for a question that took ninety seconds to answer. Every manager in your organization has sat in a DMV waiting room, or waited three days for a technician who was four hours late, or received a billing statement that was wrong in a way that took six phone calls to correct. We are all customers. We all know what the experience of being treated as a cost center rather than a revenue source actually feels like. That knowledge is not just empathy training — it is the raw material of the competitive advantage that comes from designing every slot in your Matrix with the standard of experience you would want yourself.

Both Sides of the Counter — The Confessions That Make This Framework Real

Customer Worthy has always operated from a position of unusual credibility on the customer experience question, because it was built by someone who has been on both sides of every contact intersection in the CxC Matrix. Not as a researcher. Not as a consultant observing from the outside. As a practitioner who worked the register, managed the complaint line, handled the data, wrote the advertisement, and sat in the hold queue — and who could therefore describe the failures of customer experience not from the perspective of someone who had read about them, but from the perspective of someone who had participated in creating and suffering them.

Those confessions deserve revisiting in the context of what AI and the physical intelligence layer have changed — because the insight they contain is more operationally relevant today than when they were first written.

THE CONFESSIONS — REVISITED FOR THE AI ERA

Confession 1 — I have been on both sides of every contact intersection in the CxC Matrix. I have worked the call center floor — thousands of cubes of dedicated representatives handling the consequences of decisions made by people who had never sat in their chairs. I have stood at the Macy's register the day after Christmas, caught the sweater thrown by the frustrated customer fourth in line, and been thanked by every other person in the queue for absorbing what the organization's return policy had created. I have walked the warehouses, the shipping rooms, and the returns floor. And I have sat in the waiting rooms. The most important design insight that emerges from all of those experiences is this: no one who spends a week working every role in the customer journey ever designs slots the way someone who has only observed the journey from a dashboard does.

Confession 2 — I am a salesperson, and in this era of tightly connected business and customer, we are all in sales in ways that were not true twenty years ago. Every post, every interaction, every slot in the Matrix is now a sales event, whether or not it is designed to be. A Stage 12 support interaction that resolves a problem elegantly is a more powerful sales event than any advertisement I ever wrote for radio, television, or digital. AI has not changed this. It has amplified it — because AI can now orchestrate the follow-through on every resolved interaction in ways that convert satisfied customers into active advocates at a scale no human sales team could manage.

Confession 3 — I handled your data. Without malfeasance, and with the genuine intention of building better solutions and understanding real needs. But I understand the trust that handling customer data requires, and I understand what it feels like, from the customer's side, when that trust is broken. The consent-governed data architecture built into the Customer Worthy framework is not a regulatory compliance measure. It is the direct product of knowing what it feels like to discover that your data was used in ways you did not expect by an organization you thought you could trust.

Confession 4 — I don't mind being on hold, provided the hold time is informational, valuable, and shorter than the amount of time that makes you start calculating what you could be doing instead. Make hold time a slot. Design it with the same intentionality as any other slot in the Matrix. The customers who are on hold right now are the customers most available to receive value from you

The Customer-Worthy MBA — Walking Your Own CxC Matrix

The single most effective executive development investment available to your organization costs nothing in tuition and produces returns that no consulting engagement can replicate: traverse your own CxC Matrix as a customer. Not as an executive traveling incognito while your team knows you're watching. Not as a mystery shopper filling out a structured questionnaire. As an actual customer — with the same information, the same channels, the same wait times, and the same level of support that any customer who is not the CEO would receive.

Organizations that make this a structured, annual, cross-functional practice consistently identify more actionable slot improvements than those that rely on aggregated satisfaction metrics, customer survey data, or consultant-facilitated journey mapping. The reason is simple: aggregated data smooths out the moments that matter most. The forty-minute hold that was eventually resolved satisfactorily becomes a modestly suboptimal interaction in the dataset. In the actual experience, it is the moment when the customer's loyalty calculation changes. The executive who experiences it personally never looks at the Stage 12 hold-time metric the same way again.

In the AI era, the Customer-Worthy MBA has a new dimension. Your competitors' customers are now using AI tools to research, compare, and document their experiences. You should be doing the same. Walk your competitors' CxC Matrix with an AI assistant. Ask the AI to help you identify the weaknesses in their slot design. Use AI to draft the complaint you would file if you were a frustrated customer of your own organization. Read the output. Then decide whether the slot design changes you have been deferring can continue to be deferred.

> ***"The executive who spends one week per year walking their own CxC Matrix as an anonymous customer learns more about their customer experience than any dashboard, satisfaction survey, or journey mapping workshop will show them in a decade."***

25 Customer Experience Missions — Your Customer-Worthy Field Education

What follows is the updated list of customer experience missions from Customer Worthy — expanded and modernized for now in the AI era. For each mission, keep a structured journal using your Customer Schematic as the template: document every slot, every container, every channel, every moment where the experience created or destroyed value. Note what AI tools the organization is using and what AI tools you could use to improve or audit the experience. Note where you as the customer felt respected, and where you felt processed. At the end of each mission, score the organization on the Customer Worthy dimensions — Opportunity, Confusion, Cost, and Emotion — and estimate the revenue consequence of the slot failures you observed.

These missions are not academic exercises. They are field intelligence gathering operations. The insights they generate — about your own organization, your competitors, and the customer experience ecosystem your customers navigate — are worth more than their equivalent in consultant hours, and they produce the kind of visceral, specific understanding of what customer experience actually feels like that no amount of data analysis can substitute for.

FIGURE 10.3 — 25 CUSTOMER EXPERIENCE MISSIONS: YOUR FIELD EDUCATION IN CUSTOMER WORTHINESS

#	Customer Experience Mission — What to Do and What to Learn
1	Contact your own bank — by letter, email, and phone — asking for a plain-language explanation of the interest calculation on your money market account and how much $10,000 will be worth in two years. Note the response time, the clarity of explanation, the channel consistency, and how many times you had to re-identify yourself. Now use an AI tool to draft the same inquiry and compare the quality of the AI-drafted version to what you sent. Then ask the AI to evaluate the bank's response for clarity and completeness. You will learn more about your own bank's Stage 2 and Stage 12 slot design in this exercise than in any customer experience report.
2	Contact your mobile carrier — through every available channel simultaneously — asking how to reduce your monthly bill and improve your service. Document the response from each channel. Note whether any channel has knowledge of what you requested in another channel. Count the total time invested and calculate the customer-side cost. Then use an AI tool to research your contractual rights and what better deals competing carriers are currently offering. This is the experience your customers have when they try to manage their relationship with you.

3	Write a letter — an actual physical letter — to your energy provider requesting a reduction in your monthly bill. Note how long it takes to receive a response, what channel that response comes through, and whether the response acknowledges the effort you invested in the contact. Then contrast this experience with what AI-assisted customer advocacy services now offer customers who want to dispute utility bills. The gap between what you experienced and what is now available to a motivated customer is a design opportunity.
4	Purchase the same product or service from three competing organizations through three different channels each. Document every slot across the complete journey: digital discovery, comparison, transaction, delivery, onboarding, and first support contact. Use your Customer Schematic template to map each experience. At the end, ask an AI tool to analyze your notes and identify the three most significant competitive differentiators. The AI's analysis will reveal patterns that your subjective impression may have missed.
5	Submit a product review on a major platform for something you actually purchased. Now read your organization's most recent product reviews. Ask an AI tool to analyze the sentiment pattern across your last 200 reviews and identify the three most common complaint categories. Compare those categories to your current Stage 12 slot design. If the complaints and the slot design are addressing different problems, you have identified a mismatch between what customers are experiencing and what your organization thinks they are experiencing.
6	Open, actively use for 30 days, and then cancel a subscription service from a competitor. Document the acquisition experience, the onboarding experience, the use-stage experience, and — most importantly — the cancellation experience. The cancellation slot is where organizations most reliably reveal their true customer relationship philosophy. Note whether the process respects your decision or attempts to manipulate it. Note whether the organization makes it as easy to leave as it was to join. Now evaluate your own Stage 14 slot design using the same standard.

7	Shop for a major purchase — a vehicle, a home appliance, a software platform — using AI tools as your primary research mechanism. Ask an AI to help you compare options, identify the right questions to ask, evaluate the responses you receive, and determine which organization's proposal best serves your stated needs. Document where each organization's slot design succeeded or failed in an AI-mediated buying process. This is how an increasing percentage of your high-value prospects are now evaluating you.
8	Contact your own organization's customer service line anonymously. Use a phone number they will not recognize as belonging to an executive. Navigate the complete support experience for a realistic customer problem. Time every hold. Note every transfer. Count every time you have to re-explain context. Calculate the total time investment and the customer-side cost. Then have a senior AI model evaluate the interaction transcript for adherence to the Nine Objectives. Present the results to your leadership team without first telling them it was your own organization.
9	Spend a day in your organization's highest-volume customer contact center — not observing from a conference room, but sitting alongside a front-line representative handling live interactions. Listen to what customers are actually saying about the slot designs you have built. Note the frequency with which representatives encounter system failures, policy gaps, and decision-authority limitations that prevent them from resolving the customer's problem at first contact. The representatives who answer your phones have more actionable slot improvement intelligence than any customer experience survey.
10	File a formal complaint about your own organization — or a direct competitor — through the relevant regulatory channel. Document the entire regulatory process: which agency, what filing requirements, how long for acknowledgment, what response was generated. Then use an AI tool to help you research what percentage of complaints in your industry result in regulatory action. This is the process your most frustrated customers are now using — and AI tools have made it dramatically more accessible.

11	Use three different AI assistants to research your organization as a potential customer would. Ask each AI: 'What do customers say about [your organization]?', 'What are the most common complaints?', 'How does [your organization] compare to [competitor] for customer service?', and 'What should I know before signing up?' Read the responses carefully. The AI's synthesis of publicly available information about your organization is now the first research channel many high-value prospects are using. What they learn shapes whether they ever enter Stage 1 of your Matrix.
12	Buy and return a product from your own organization's e-commerce channel using a new customer account. Document every slot in both the forward and reverse journey. Calculate the total time and effort investment. Then do the same with your strongest competitor. The organization that makes it easier to buy and return with dignity is the organization that earns the long-term relationship — because customers know they can trust the reverse process if the forward one fails.
13	Set up and run a paid digital advertising campaign for your organization's product or service for 30 days. Manage it yourself, without your marketing team's assistance. Note the complexity, the learning curve, and the support quality from the platform. Then ask an AI tool to audit your campaign's targeting, creative, and landing page experience for CxC Matrix alignment: does the ad create the right expectations? Does the landing page slot meet those expectations? Is the handoff to Stage 3 designed for conversion or for organizational convenience?
14	Attend a competitor's customer event, product launch, or webinar as an anonymous prospective customer. Document the complete experience from first awareness through the follow-up contact sequence. Note what Stage 3 and Stage 4 slots they are deploying. Note what their sales team does with the information they collect about you during the event. Then contact them three weeks later as a prospect who attended the event, and observe whether any slot in their Matrix retained knowledge of your presence and your expressed interests.

15	Experience the physical location of your three nearest direct competitors as a first-time customer. Note the physical environment, the staff greeting protocol, the product presentation, the wait time for assistance, and the follow-up contact attempt after you leave without purchasing. Then return to each location two weeks later as a returning visitor and document whether any slot recognized your prior visit. The organization that remembers you without you having to re-introduce yourself is demonstrating slot design excellence.
16	Become a partner, reseller, or affiliate of your own organization. Navigate the complete application, onboarding, and first-transaction experience. The partner channel slot design reveals how your organization treats the people who are betting their own business relationships on your performance. If the partner experience is bureaucratic, slow, and opaque, your partners are telling that story to every customer they introduce to your organization.
17	Spend four hours navigating a government service that your customers or employees regularly must use — the DMV, a permitting office, a regulatory filing system. Document every slot in that experience. Then spend four hours at a world-class commercial service in the same geographic area. The contrast in slot design, wait time management, information architecture, and staff empowerment is the same contrast your customers make when they compare your experience to your best competitor's. The government service is not your competitor — but it calibrates your customers' patience threshold.
18	Sponsor a cause your customers care about and track the complete experience from initial inquiry through fulfillment and post-event acknowledgment. Note every slot in the sponsorship process. Note whether the organization you're sponsoring designed any slots that made it easy for you to become an advocate for their mission. Then evaluate your own Stage 15 slot design using the same standard. have you designed slots that make it easy for your advocates to advocate?

19	Plan and book a complex multi-vendor trip using AI as your primary planning tool. Document how AI assists with research, comparison, booking, and issue resolution. Note where the AI-mediated experience was superior to the pre-AI equivalent, and where it created new friction. Note which organizations' digital slot designs worked seamlessly with AI tools and which created friction that the AI could not resolve. This is the travel booking experience your customers are having — and the slot design standard AI-mediated planning is now setting.
20	Spend a full day managing every interaction you have as an explicit customer experience audit. For every interaction — coffee, transit, software, banking, a support call — apply the Four Dimensions: Opportunity, Confusion, Cost, Emotion. Document what worked and what failed. At the end of the day, identify the three experiences that were genuinely Customer Worthy — that treated your time, attention, and trust with respect — and three that were not. Ask why the good ones were good and the bad ones were bad. The answer is almost always slot design.
21	Use an AI tool to build a complete competitive intelligence report on your organization's top three competitors in customer experience. Ask the AI to analyze public review data, regulatory complaint databases, social media sentiment, and press coverage to identify their strongest and weakest lifecycle stages. Then compare those findings to your own Customer Schematic. The organizations whose Stage 11 and Stage 15 slots are weakest are the ones whose long-tenure customers are most available to your next proactive outreach.
22	Join, actively participate in, and then leave your organization's customer community or loyalty program. Document the joining experience, the value-in-use experience, and the exit experience. Note whether the community design reflects genuine interest in member value or organizational data acquisition. Note whether your exit generated any proactive response. The community and loyalty slot design reveals how your organization treats its most committed customers — and whether you have earned the advocacy that Stage 15 requires.

23	Make a significant purchase decision entirely through AI-mediated channels — using AI for research, comparison, negotiation assistance, and post-purchase support. Document every point at which a human contact added value that the AI could not have provided. Those are the moments where your Stage 4–6 human slots must be irreplaceably excellent, because AI handles everything else. The organizations that understand which human interactions are genuinely irreplaceable are the ones designing those specific slots with the investment they deserve.
24	Deliberately create a customer experience failure in a controlled test environment — a product return, a billing dispute, a service cancellation — and document the complete organizational response across every slot and channel. Note how long each slot takes. Note at what point the organization proactively communicates versus waits for you to follow up. Note what the resolution required from you in terms of time and effort investment. Then measure the gap between what you experienced and the experience standard your Stage 12–13 slot design documentation promises.
25	Write a professional press release about your own organization's most significant customer experience failure in the past 12 months — as a frustrated customer, using AI tools to help with research, documentation, and distribution targeting. Do not publish it. Read it. Show it to your leadership team. Then ask the question that the Customer Worthy framework was designed to answer: is this the organization you would choose to do business with if you didn't already work there? The answer to that question, and the specific slot failures the press release documents, are the starting point of your next Customer Schematic revision.

There Is a Better Way — And in the AI Era, It Is No Longer Optional

Customer satisfaction scores do not need to continue to decline. Marketing costs do not need to escalate to chase customers you are simultaneously repelling through slot failures in your service experience. Technology investment does not need to be deployed in a race to out-feature competitors when the decisive competitive advantage is available through the systematically better design of the 90 cells in your Customer Schematic.

This book was written to provide a framework for building an organization that earns and keeps customer relationships through precision, intentionality, and respect — not through outspending competitors on acquisition, not through satisfaction survey management, and not through the kind of customer experience theater that produces good metrics while delivering mediocre experiences. The CxC Matrix, the Customer Experience Algorithm, the Nine Objectives, and the Customer Schematic walkthrough are tools for building something durable: an organization whose customers stay not because switching is difficult, but because the experience of being served by this organization is genuinely superior to the alternative.

The revolution that Customer Worthy asked you to start has not waited for your organizational readiness. It has been running continuously, accelerating with every new capability layer that arrives in the hands of your customers. Dot's frustration at AT&T was the preview. Today's AI-equipped customer is the fully realized version. The organizations that are designing their slots correctly — that are treating every customer interaction as both a financial event and a relationship event, that are applying the CEA to deliver the right contact at the right moment through the right channel — are not managing the revolution. They are making it unnecessary. They are building organizations that are, genuinely, Customer Worthy.

> ***"The revolution begins in your hold queue. It ends in your Customer Schematic. Every slot you design with precision is a revolution you prevent. Every one you leave to chance is a revolution you are funding — at interest rates calculated by your customer's AI, filed with your regulator, and posted to an audience that will be larger tomorrow than it is today."***

THE STANDARD FOR CUSTOMER WORTHINESS — THE QUESTION EVERY SLOT MUST ANSWER

Before any slot in your CxC Matrix is approved for deployment, it should be required to pass a single test: if a senior executive of this organization experienced this slot as an anonymous customer — with no advance knowledge, no special treatment, and no ability to intervene — would they be proud of what we built? Would they feel that their time was respected? That their question was answered? That they were treated as a person whose continued relationship with this organization matters? If the answer to any of those questions is no, the slot is not Customer Worthy. Fix it before the customer's AI documents it for them.

CHAPTER ELEVEN

Customer Privacy Is Nothing to Kid About

Ransomware, Deepfakes, Synthetic Identities, AI-Powered Fraud, and Why Identity Validation Is the First Objective of Every Contact for Good Reason

Satellites watch your house. Your phone tracks every step. Your car logs every mile, every acceleration, every hard stop. Your connected devices report your behavior to servers you will never visit, owned by companies you will never know exist. And somewhere in the gap between the data you knowingly share and the data that is harvested without your awareness, criminals — and increasingly, AI-equipped criminal organizations — are assembling a portrait of you that is more complete, more accurate, and more immediately monetizable than anything you have authorized anyone to build.

> *"Customer data breaches now cost organizations an average of $4.88 million per incident. But the cost to the individual customer — in time, stress, financial repair, and permanent reputational damage — is never fully counted in any corporate breach report."*
>
> **— IBM Cost of a Data Breach Report, 2024**

The Surveillance Economy — What Has Changed Since Customer Worthy Was First Published

When Customer Worthy first documented the surveillance landscape, the observation that satellites watch your house and software tracks your every click was meant to provoke awareness. It succeeded — because in the early 2010s, that level of observation still felt new, still felt like a condition worth naming. Today, the surveillance infrastructure is so deeply normalized that describing it requires a different kind of provocation: not awareness that it exists, but awareness of how exponentially more capable, more granular, and more exploitable it has become.

Your car's onboard systems now generate up to 25 gigabytes of data per hour — logging not just speed and location, but driver behavior patterns, passenger presence, route preferences, and in connected vehicles, real-time audio and visual data from the cabin. Your health insurer's app knows your step count, sleep duration, and resting heart rate. Your smart speaker has a wake word, but it is also always listening for it — and the acoustic fingerprint of everything in your home that occurs near the device is processed to improve that detection. Your bank's fraud prevention system has built a behavioral biometric profile of your typing patterns, scroll velocity, and mouse movement so precise that it can detect when someone other than you is using your computer to access your account — even if they have your correct password.

This infrastructure is not, in itself, malicious. Most of it was built to serve legitimate purposes: fraud prevention, product improvement, personalization, safety. But the same data density that enables a fraud detection system to identify a counterfeit transaction in milliseconds also enables a criminal with access to that data — through breach, purchase from a data broker, or social engineering of an employee — to impersonate you with a precision that earlier generations of identity theft could not approach. The threat has scaled with the capability. And the capability has scaled faster than either regulation or organizational data governance has been able to follow.

> ***"In the original Customer Worthy, we warned that customer data moves around too easily. Today, the warning is more urgent: customer data moves around too easily, and the tools available to exploit it have become as sophisticated as the tools designed to protect it. AI is available to both sides of this equation — and organizations that have not deployed AI on the defense side should assume their adversaries have deployed it on the offense side."***

The New Threat Landscape — Beyond Credit Card Fraud

The original Customer Worthy documented two archetypal fraud scenarios: a sophisticated credit card data trafficking operation coordinated across multiple countries, and a florist defrauded by stolen card numbers used to extract cash through flower orders. Both stories were instructive about the mechanics of fraud in 2008. Both would be considered elementary by the standards of what is happening to businesses and their customers now.

The threat landscape has not merely expanded — it has been restructured by artificial intelligence. Fraud that once required human operators at every stage of the attack chain can now be partially or fully automated. AI voice cloning can produce a convincing impersonation of a specific individual from a three-second audio sample. AI-generated video deepfakes can create realistic footage of people saying things they never said. Large language models trained on a victim's public writing, social media history, and professional communications can generate emails and messages that are indistinguishable from their authentic voice. Synthetic identity fraud — the creation of entirely fictional but plausible consumer identities constructed from fragments of real data — has become sophisticated enough to defeat identity verification systems that are not specifically designed to detect it.

What unifies all of these threats, and what connects them directly to the CxC Matrix framework, is a common enabling condition: they succeed at the slot where identification, authentication, and authorization should have been executed rigorously—and were not. The call that appears to be from the IRS is answered because the caller ID appears legitimate. The ransomware gains entry because an employee who received an AI-generated email from what appeared to be a known vendor clicked a link. The synthetic identity passes initial customer onboarding because the verification slot did not test for the signals that distinguish constructed identities from real ones. The deep-fake video extortion succeeds because the organization had no protocol for verifying the authenticity of video communications before acting on them.

Figure 11.1 — The Modern Fraud Threat Taxonomy: Attack Vectors, Scale, and the Slot Failure That Enabled Each

Threat Category	Attack Vector / Method	Estimated Scale (US)	CxC Matrix Slot Failure
Ransomware (Enterprise & Consumer)	Malicious software encrypts organizational or personal data; attackers demand cryptocurrency payment for decryption keys. AI now automates target identification, phishing message generation, and ransom negotiation.	$1.1B paid globally in 2023; avg. enterprise ransom: $1.54M; healthcare sector: most targeted[123]	*A single employee in Stage 2 or 5 of the organizational lifecycle received an AI-generated phishing email convincing enough to defeat standard skepticism. The authentication slot was absent or insufficient.*

[1] Chainalysis, "Ransomware Hit $1 Billion in 2023," February 7, 2024. Confirmed by FinCEN Financial Trend Analysis, 2025, reporting 1,512 incidents totaling $1.1 billion in 2023.

[2] Sophos, The State of Ransomware 2023, survey of 3,000 IT decision makers from mid-sized organizations in 14 countries. The $1.54 million figure represents the average ransom payment reported by respondents.

Deepfake Extortion (Video / Audio / Synthetic)	AI-generated video or audio of a real individual—executive, family member, employee—is used to demand payment, authorize fraudulent transactions, or damage reputation. CEO voice clones authorizing wire transfers are documented at scale.	$25M+ in documented losses per major incident; 3,000%+ increase in deepfake fraud attempts 2022–2023[45]	*Organizations lacked a verification slot requiring multi-factor confirmation for financial authorizations received through video or voice channels. One channel was treated as sufficient authentication—it is not.*

[3]FBI Internet Crime Complaint Center (IC3), Internet Crime Report 2023. Healthcare and public health organizations comprised the highest number of ransomware attacks in the U.S. with 249 reported. Also: Office of the Director of National Intelligence, "Ransomware Attacks Surge in 2023," February 28, 2024, reporting attacks on the healthcare sector nearly doubled, from 214 in 2022 to 389 in 2023.

[4]Onfido Identity Fraud Report 2024, reporting a 3,000% increase in deepfake fraud attempts. Sumsub Identity Fraud Report 2023 reported deepfake fraud incidents increased tenfold between 2022 and 2023. See also IBM, "Tech Industry Ramps Up Efforts to Combat Rising Deepfake Threats," November 2025.

IRS and Government Impersonation Scams	Automated and AI-assisted calls, emails, and texts impersonating the IRS, SSA, Medicare, or other government agencies demand immediate payment under threat of arrest, deportation, or benefit suspension.	~160,000 government impersonation reports to FTC in 2023; $12.5B total consumer fraud losses in 2024[8][9]	*Organizations have not built Stage 12 slots designed to educate customers about what authentic government contact looks and sounds like, or to provide rapid verification assistance.*

[8] Federal Trade Commission, Consumer Sentinel Network Data Book 2023, February 2024. FTC reported consumers lost more than $10 billion to fraud in 2023. The 2024 Data Book (March 2025) updated total losses to $12.5 billion for 2024. Government impersonation scam losses totaled $789 million in 2024, up from $618 million in 2023. NOTE: The text references $5.8 billion, which corresponds to the FTC's 2021 fraud loss total. The 2023 figure was $10 billion and the 2024 figure was $12.5 billion. Citation updated to reflect verified data.

[9] FTC Data Spotlight, April 2024: In 2023, the FTC received nearly 160,000 reports of government impersonation scams. TIGTA (Treasury Inspector General for Tax Administration) reported that between March 2013 and March 2025, 16,281 victims reported to TIGTA collectively losing more than $114 million to IRS impersonation scams. FTC-specific IRS subcategory; the broader government impersonation category totaled approximately 160,000 reports in 2023.

AI-Assisted Debt Collection Fraud	Fraudulent debt collectors using AI-generated communications claim consumers owe debts that do not exist, using AI-assembled data about real individuals to make the claims plausible.	Significant and growing; precise figures under ongoing study by CFPB and FTC[10]	*No authentication slot exists in most organizations to help customers verify the legitimacy of collection contacts made on the organization's behalf.*

[10] Readers should consult the most current CFPB Complaint Database and FTC Consumer Sentinel data for updated figures.

Credential Stuffing and Account Takeover	AI-automated systems test billions of username/password combinations from breached datasets against target platforms until valid credentials are found.	193 billion credential stuffing attacks recorded in 2020 (Akamai); account takeover losses: ~$13B in 2023[11][12]	*The authentication slot for returning customers relied on single-factor authentication or knowledge-based questions answerable from public data.*

[11]Akamai, Phishing for Finance, May 2021, cited in the New York State Attorney General's Business Guide for Credential Stuffing Attacks (2022): "The operator of one large content delivery network reported that it witnessed more than 193 billion such attacks in 2020." NOTE: This figure is from 2020, not an annual ongoing figure. The text has been annotated accordingly.

[12]SEON Global ATO Statistics Report, cited in Mitek Systems, "30 Alarming Account Takeover Fraud Statistics," 2025: "Global losses from account takeover fraud could reach $17 billion in 2025, up from nearly $13 billion in 2023."

Data Broker Exploitation and Profile Harvesting	AI-assisted tools automate assembly of comprehensive individual profiles from data broker databases, public records, social media, and leaked datasets.	2,500–4,000+ data brokers operating in US; profiles contain thousands of data points per person[13]	*No organization in the customer's network has a slot designed to notify the customer that their data is being aggregated and sold, or to assist exposure mngt.*

Three Recent Stories — What the New Fraud Looks Like From the Customer's Side

Story 1: The Ransomware That Started with a Customer Service Email

A regional hospital network in the mid-Atlantic received what appeared to be an urgent vendor communication about a payment discrepancy. The email was AI-generated—drafted to match the specific writing style of the vendor's account manager, referencing recent invoice numbers pulled from a

[13]Boutin (2014), cited in "Data Privacy Issues in the Age of Data Brokerage," Issues in Information Systems, Volume 19, Issue 3, 2018: "It is estimated that there are 2,500 to 4,000 data brokers operating in the United States." Privacy Rights Clearinghouse (2024) confirms profiles contain "thousands of data points per person." The 97% and 1,500+ data point claims are widely cited in industry literature but originate from varied estimation methodologies.

previous breach, and formatted to match the vendor's actual email template precisely. An accounts payable clerk clicked a link to view the 'corrected invoice.' The malware deployed silently. Forty-eight hours later, at 2:47 a.m. on a Tuesday, every clinical and administrative system in the network was encrypted. Patient records were inaccessible. Surgery schedules were erased. The ransom demand was $4.2 million in Bitcoin, with a 72-hour deadline after which the attackers threatened to publish patient records publicly. The hospital paid $2.8 million after five days of operational paralysis, during which elective surgeries were cancelled and ambulances were diverted to facilities forty miles away.

[Author's Note: This narrative is a composite illustration based on documented patterns of healthcare ransomware attacks. The FBI IC3 Internet Crime Report 2023 confirmed healthcare as the most-targeted sector, with 249 reported ransomware attacks in the United States.[14] The operational impacts described—surgical cancellations, ambulance diversions, system encryption—are consistent with extensively documented incidents including the attacks on Ardent Health Services (November 2023), Prospect Medical Holdings (August 2023), and CommonSpirit Health (October 2022). The ransom figures are within the range reported by Sophos and IBM for healthcare sector incidents in 2023.]

The slot failure that enabled this attack was not a technology failure. It was a process design failure. The vendor communication slot—the equivalent of Stage 5 (Contract/Negotiation) in the organization's supplier lifecycle—did not have a verification protocol requiring out-of-band confirmation of payment-related links or attachments. A single slot without an authentication gate allowed a $4.2 million attack chain to succeed. AI did not create this vulnerability. It

14

industrialized the exploitation of a vulnerability that had always existed.

Story 2: The Deepfake That Cost a Finance Executive Her Job

A CFO at a mid-size manufacturing company received a video call from what appeared to be her company's CEO—the face, the voice, the mannerisms were indistinguishable from the real person. The CEO-avatar explained an urgent, confidential acquisition negotiation that required an immediate wire transfer of $23 million to an escrow account. The 'CEO' was apologetic about the unusual channel and timing. He referenced a recent board conversation the CFO knew had occurred. He cited the acquiree's company name correctly. The CFO authorized the transfer. The money was gone within four hours, distributed through seventeen accounts across five countries. The FBI recovered $1.1 million. The CFO resigned. The CEO, who had been on vacation and entirely unaware of the attack, learned about it from a journalist.

[Author's Note: This narrative is a composite informed by the extensively documented Arup deepfake incident of January 2024, in which a finance worker at the multinational engineering firm Arup was deceived by AI-generated deepfakes of the company's CFO and colleagues in a video conference, leading to the transfer of approximately $25.6 million (HK$200 million) to fraudulent accounts.[15] The FBI and Secret Service have both issued formal warnings about deepfake-enabled business email compromise and wire fraud schemes.[16] Details such as the specific dollar amount, the CFO's gender, and the resignation have been

15

[16]FBI Public Service Announcement, "Criminals Exploit Generative Artificial Intelligence to Commit Fraud," IC3 Alert I-120324-PSA, December 3, 2024. U.S. Secret Service has issued similar warnings through its Global Investigative Operations Center.

fictionalized, but the attack mechanics, scale, and organizational failures depicted are consistent with documented cases.]

This attack pattern is documented across multiple organizations, and the FBI and Secret Service have both issued formal warnings.[17] The deepfake technology that made it possible requires, at most, a few minutes of publicly available video footage of the target individual and a mid-tier AI generation subscription. The organizational slot that failed was authorization—the absence of a multi-party, multi-channel verification requirement for transactions above a defined financial threshold. No single video communication, regardless of how authentic it appears, should be sufficient authorization for a transaction of this magnitude. That is not a technology constraint. It is a process design constraint that belongs in the slot architecture.

Story 3: The IRS Scam That Targeted the Most Vulnerable Customers

Margaret, 74, retired schoolteacher, received a call from 'Special Agent David Hartley of the Internal Revenue Service Criminal Investigation Division.' The caller ID displayed a Washington, D.C. phone number. The voice was authoritative, professional, and patient. The agent explained that Margaret had a tax liability from 2021 due to an error on her return, and that a warrant for her arrest had been issued that morning. She could avoid arrest by purchasing Google Play gift cards at a nearby pharmacy and reading the card numbers to the agent, who would apply them to her account. She purchased $4,800 in gift cards across three pharmacies. When she called her daughter that evening, the fraud was identified. The $4,800 was unrecoverable.

17

[Author's Note: "Margaret" is a composite character representing the well-documented demographic and behavioral patterns of IRS impersonation scam victims. The FTC received nearly 160,000 government impersonation scam reports in 2023, with reported losses topping $1.1 billion—more than three times the figure from 2020.[18][19] The Treasury Inspector General for Tax Administration (TIGTA) reports that between 2013 and 2025, over 16,281 victims collectively lost more than $114 million to IRS impersonation scams. The FTC has specifically noted that older adults are disproportionately targeted, with losses by adults 60 and over increasing more than fourfold since 2020. The gift card payment method and the specific tactics described—threats of arrest, spoofed caller ID, urgency—are consistent with patterns extensively documented by the IRS, FTC, and TIGTA.]

This is not an edge case. The FTC received nearly 160,000 government impersonation scam reports in 2023, and consumer advocates estimate that reported losses represent perhaps 10–15% of actual losses, as many victims—particularly older adults—do not report out of shame.[20] Margaret's bank had no Stage 11 or Stage 12 slot designed to detect and intervene in the behavioral pattern of a customer making multiple small cash withdrawals and gift card purchases in rapid succession—a pattern that is algorithmically identifiable in real time and that AI fraud systems deployed by leading banks already flag for human review. A designed slot saved none of Margaret's $4,800. An AI-equipped slot could have.

Objective One of Every Interaction — Why Identification Is the Foundation of Every Other Privacy Protection

Customer Worthy's Nine Objectives of each customer interaction begin with a requirement that is easy to state and profoundly difficult to execute correctly in the AI era: *Identify the Customer*. The first objective of every contact—before any information is exchanged, before any transaction is authorized, before any assistance is offered—is to establish, with confidence appropriate to the risk level of the interaction, who is actually present at this contact point.

This is not a security requirement that exists separately from the customer experience. It *is* the customer experience requirement that makes every other element of the interaction trustworthy. The customer who calls your support line and is immediately recognized—by their verified identity, their account history, and their behavioral biometrics—does not have to re-explain who they are or what they need. They experience the efficiency and personalization that comes from being known. The customer who is subjected to a superficial identity verification—a name and last four digits of their Social Security number, questions answerable from public data—is not protected. They merely feel protected, right up until the moment a fraudster who has assembled their public profile passes the same verification with identical ease.

The distinction between the three components of the identification objective—Identification, Authentication, and Authorization—is not semantic. Each represents a distinct security requirement, a distinct slot design challenge, and a distinct category of failure when executed inadequately. And the AI-powered threats documented in this chapter are designed, often with expert precision, to exploit the specific gap where one of these three requirements is absent or insufficient.

A Note on Sources and Verification

All statistics, figures, and factual claims in this chapter have been verified against primary sources or authoritative secondary sources as of early 2025. Where a claimed figure could not be precisely verified, the text has been updated or an explanatory footnote has been added. The three narrative stories (Stories 1–3) are composite illustrations informed by extensively documented real-world incidents; they are not accounts of specific proprietary events. Source materials include: Chainalysis blockchain analysis reports; FinCEN Financial Trend Analyses; FBI Internet Crime Complaint Center (IC3) annual reports; FTC Consumer Sentinel Network Data Books; Sophos State of Ransomware annual surveys; Onfido and Sumsub Identity Fraud Reports; FiVerity, TransUnion, and Equifax synthetic identity fraud analyses; the Federal Reserve's Synthetic Identity Fraud initiative publications; TIGTA impersonation scam data; Akamai credential stuffing analyses; SEON account takeover statistics; and reporting by CNN, Fortune, Financial Times, and CFO Dive on the Arup deepfake incident. Full citations appear in the footnotes throughout this chapter.

FIGURE 11.2 — THE THREE PILLARS OF CXC MATRIX IDENTITY VALIDATION: IDENTIFY, AUTHENTICATE, AUTHORIZE

Function	Definition	Where It Lives in the CxC Matrix	What Breaks Without It

IDENTIFY (Who are you?)	Establish the presence of a known entity in the contact: match incoming signals — name, account number, device fingerprint, behavioral biometric, physical credential, biometric scan — to a verified record in the organization's identity store.	Every Stage 1-3 slot (acquisition), every Stage 11 login/portal access slot, every Stage 12 inbound contact slot. Identification must occur before any account data is displayed or any transaction is initiated.	*Without rigorous identification, the organization is responding to a claimed identity rather than a verified one. Synthetic identity fraud, account takeover, and impersonation attacks succeed entirely because this gate was absent or easily bypassed. Every piece of account information disclosed to an unidentified or inadequately identified contact is a potential data exposure.*

AUTHENTICATE (Can you prove it?)	Verify that the entity identified is who they claim to be, through evidence they uniquely possess: a one-time code sent to a verified device, a biometric match (fingerprint, face, voice with liveness detection), a hardware security key, behavioral biometric confirmation, or a combination appropriate to the risk level of the interaction being authenticated.	Every financial transaction slot (Stages 5–6, 10, 14), every account modification slot (Stage 11 self-service), every high-sensitivity support interaction (Stage 12–13 when account changes are requested). Authentication strength should be proportional to transaction risk.	*Password-only authentication fails against credential stuffing. Knowledge-based authentication fails against any adversary who has assembled a data profile. Voice-only authentication fails against AI voice cloning. Authentication slots that do not escalate to liveness-detection biometrics or hardware tokens for high-risk transactions are systematically vulnerable to AI-assisted attacks.*

AUTHORIZE (Are you permitted to do this?)	Confirm that the authenticated entity has the right to perform the specific action requested: that the person who just authenticated as account holder X is permitted to initiate a $50,000 wire transfer, change the account email address, or access a secondary account holder's information.	All transaction-initiation slots (financial and non-financial), all account modification slots, all access to third-party beneficiary or secondary account holder data. Authorization logic must account for anomaly detection: a transaction that is outside normal behavioral patterns for this account requires re-authentication even from a previously authenticated session.	*Authorization failures enable the majority of corporate financial fraud, including deepfake wire transfer attacks. The authenticated identity of a CFO is not sufficient authorization for a $23 million transfer in isolation — the authorization slot must require multi-party confirmation, behavioral anomaly review, and out-of-band verification for high-value transactions.*

The Customer Worthy framework requires that Identification be treated as a designed slot — not an afterthought, not a compliance checkbox, and not a friction-reduction casualty sacrificed in the name of making onboarding faster. Every time an organization simplifies its identification process to remove a step that was 'slowing down' the customer experience, it is making a trade-off between customer convenience and customer security. That trade-off is legitimate and sometimes correct. But it must be made explicitly, documented, risk-rated, and periodically re-evaluated as the threat environment changes — not absorbed unconsciously into a process that was designed before AI voice cloning, synthetic identity fraud, and deepfake technology existed.

Electronic Data Is Everywhere, Growing, and Accessible — Your CxC Matrix Audit

Customer Worthy originally invited readers to conduct a simple exercise: go to Google, search for 'Attendee List,' filter for Excel files, and observe how many private contact lists are publicly accessible. That exercise remains instructive today — though the landscape it reveals has expanded considerably. The same search logic now surfaces not just conference attendee lists but corporate org charts, employee directories, patient intake forms uploaded without password protection, voter registration exports, school parent-teacher association contact lists, and in some cases, internal HR files.

But the more instructive audit for today is not a Google search. It is an AI-assisted data exposure analysis. Using commercially available OSINT (open-source intelligence) tools and AI aggregation services — many of which are accessible to anyone with a credit card and a grievance — a determined individual can assemble, within a few hours, a comprehensive profile of virtually any named individual: home address, family member names, employment history, phone numbers, email addresses, vehicle registration, professional license details, social media activity, political donation history, and in many cases, partial financial account information. This profile is not assembled through illegal means. It is assembled from the digital breadcrumbs that individuals leave, willingly and unwillingly, across the data ecosystem that modern life requires participation in.

The organizational response to this reality is not to pretend it can be prevented at the consumer level — it cannot. The response is to build CxC Matrix slots that operate with awareness that your customers' data is partially or fully available to adversaries, and that any identification or authentication process that relies on data also available in their public profile is not protection. It is theater. The CxC Matrix audit your organization should conduct — for every slot in every container across every channel — is a systematic answer to five questions: What data is exchanged at this contact point? Who can access it? Is it encrypted in transit and at rest? Does it flow to any third party, and under what governance? And if an adversary had assembled a complete public profile of this customer before reaching this slot, what could they do?

THE CXC MATRIX DATA PRIVACY AUDIT — FIVE QUESTIONS FOR EVERY SLOT

For each slot in your Customer Schematic, document: (1) What personal data is exchanged or exposed at this contact — name, account number, transaction history, health information, payment credentials? (2) Who can access this data — the customer, the front-line representative, a third-party processor, an AI model? Under what governance and consent framework? (3) Is the data encrypted in transit and at rest, and what is the encryption standard? (4) Does the slot create a record — a transcript, a log, a cookie, a behavioral profile — and where does that record live and for how long? (5) What is the worst-case scenario if this slot is compromised — what data could be extracted, what actions could be taken, and what is the estimated impact on customers affected? This audit, conducted annually and updated whenever a slot is redesigned, is the organizational equivalent of the privacy risk register that regulated industries are required to maintain — and that every organization operating in the AI era should maintain regardless of regulatory requirement.

AI on the Defense — Resources and Tools for Countering Fraud and Identity Theft

The asymmetry of the current threat environment — AI-equipped adversaries attacking organizations and consumers who have not yet deployed equivalent AI defenses — is not a permanent condition. It is a window. The organizations and individuals who deploy AI-powered defensive tools during this window will have built detection, response, and recovery capabilities that become increasingly difficult to defeat as the tools mature and as the data they train on accumulates. Those who wait for the threat to become undeniable before investing in the defense will find that the window has narrowed considerably by the time they act.

The AI defense landscape for identity fraud, ransomware, deepfake detection, and consumer protection has matured significantly in the three years preceding this writing. The tools described in the table below represent the current state of available defenses — not an exhaustive catalog, but a practical guide organized around the CxC Matrix framework. Each tool maps to the slot-level design requirement it addresses.

FIGURE 11.3 — AI DEFENSE RESOURCES: TOOLS FOR COUNTERING FRAUD, IDENTITY THEFT, AND AI-POWERED ATTACKS

AI Defense Tool / Resource	What It Does	Who It Serves	How It Integrates with the CxC Matrix
NIST AI Risk Management Framework (AI RMF) nist.gov/artificial-intelligence	Provides a structured framework for organizations to identify, assess, and manage AI-specific risks in their operations — including AI-assisted fraud risks in customer-facing systems	Organizations building or deploying AI in CxC Matrix slots; boards and risk committees establishing AI governance	*Maps directly to the data audit questions for each slot: which AI systems process customer data, what governance exists, what failure modes are designed for. Use as the governance layer for all AI-touching slot designs.*
FTC Consumer Sentinel Network reportfraud.ftc.gov	The federal consumer fraud reporting system; aggregates reports by fraud type, channel, demographic, and dollar loss. Provides organizations with current intelligence on emerging fraud patterns targeting their customer segments.	Compliance teams, slot designers, customer education teams. Any organization whose customers are in demographic segments with elevated fraud targeting rates (elderly, military, recent immigrants).	*Should be reviewed quarterly by the team responsible for Stage 12 and Stage 13 slot design. Fraud pattern intelligence informs which authentication requirements need strengthening and which customer education slots need activation.*

ID.me / Persona / Socure (Identity Verification Platforms)	AI-powered identity verification platforms combining document authentication, biometric liveness detection, behavioral analytics, and synthetic identity detection. Socure's AI models have demonstrated 90%+ accuracy in detecting synthetic identities at onboarding.	Financial services, healthcare, government services, any organization processing high-value transactions or storing sensitive personal information at Stage 1 (Onboarding) and Stage 11 (Account Management) slots.	*Deploy at the Identification and Authentication slots for high-risk interactions. Replace knowledge-based authentication with liveness-detection biometrics for account access, financial transactions, and account modifications above defined risk thresholds.*
Microsoft Defender for Identity Behavioral Biometrics Platforms (BioCatch, NuData)	Continuous authentication systems that maintain a behavioral biometric profile for each user — typing cadence, mouse movement, scroll velocity, device interaction patterns — and flag anomalies in real time, detecting account takeover even when credentials are valid.	Organizations with large authenticated user bases in digital channels; financial institutions, healthcare portals, enterprise software, any Stage 11 self-service portal where account takeover risk is material.	*Eliminates the 'you've already logged in so I'll trust you' vulnerability. The authentication slot is not a one-time gate at login — it is a continuous process that monitors every interaction during the session and re-challenges when behavioral anomalies suggest the authenticated user is no longer the person who logged in.*

Recorded Future / Mandiant Threat Intelligence Platforms	AI-powered threat intelligence services that monitor dark web markets, criminal forums, and breach databases for customer data from specific organizations — providing early warning when organizational data has been compromised before the breach is publicly known.	Enterprise security teams, CISOs, organizations with large customer databases containing high-value identity data. Particularly critical for healthcare, financial services, and education sectors, which are disproportionately targeted.	*Connects to the Stage 12 and Stage 13 slot design requirement: when organizational data appears in threat intelligence feeds, a proactive customer notification slot must activate before customers discover the exposure through external sources. Organizations that notify proactively retain significantly more customer trust than those who notify reactively.*
Sensity.ai / Reality Defender Deepfake Detection	AI-powered deepfake detection tools that analyze video and audio for synthetic generation artifacts, liveness indicators, and manipulation signatures. Current commercial tools achieve 85–95% detection accuracy on state-of-the-art deepfakes.	Financial services (wire transfer authorization), executive communications teams, HR (remote hiring verification), legal (video deposition authentication), any organization using video communication for consequential decisions or authorizations.	*Must be deployed in the authorization slot for high-value video-mediated approvals. No video communication should serve as sole authorization for financial transactions above defined thresholds — deepfake detection plus multi-factor out-of-band verification is the required slot design standard.*

AARP Fraud Watch Network aarp.org/fraudwatch-network	Consumer-facing AI fraud education and helpline resource; provides real-time fraud alert monitoring, scam-specific guidance for older adults, and volunteer support network for fraud victims. The helpline (877-908-3360) provides live assistance for active fraud situations.	Organizations whose customer base includes significant proportions of older adults: financial services, healthcare, Medicare-adjacent services, utility companies, telecommunications. The customer demographic most targeted by IRS impersonation and romance scams.	*Should be referenced in Stage 12 support slot design for customers in at-risk demographics, and in Stage 11 proactive communication slots that educate customers about what authentic organizational contact looks like — including explicit statements about what your organization will never ask for via phone.*
Consumer Financial Protection Bureau Identity Theft Resources consumerfinance.gov	Federal regulatory body providing enforcement, consumer education, and complaint infrastructure for financial fraud. AI-assisted complaint routing now directs consumer reports to appropriate enforcement channels. CFPB's Consumer Complaint Database is a public resource showing fraud patterns by institution and geography.	Any organization in financial services; any organization whose customers may be subject to financial fraud that the organization's data or processes contributed to enabling.	*CFPB complaint data should be reviewed quarterly by Stage 13 and Stage 14 slot designers. Organizations with elevated complaint rates for specific fraud types have a slot design problem that is now publicly documented. Addressing it proactively is less expensive than addressing it after regulatory inquiry.*

Customers Should Be Compensated for the Data They Generate — The Case Has Grown Stronger

Customer Worthy proposed a framework that remains radical in most organizational conversations about data: customers should own their data, control who accesses it, and be compensated when it is used commercially. The argument was practical then — customer-owned data would have lower fraud rates because organizations would have a vested interest in verifying it — and it is more compelling now, as AI has transformed data from a byproduct of customer relationships into the primary raw material of organizational competitive advantage.

The economic logic is straightforward and increasingly hard to dismiss. The behavioral data that your customers generate through their interactions with your CxC Matrix — their search patterns, purchase histories, channel preferences, content engagement, location signals, and lifecycle trajectories — is used to train AI models whose outputs generate significant organizational revenue. The customer whose behavioral data contributes to a product recommendation engine that produces $300 million in annual revenue for a retailer receives nothing for that contribution. The organization receives everything. This is not a sustainable equilibrium, and the regulatory environment — GDPR in Europe, CCPA in California, and a growing body of state-level data rights legislation — is moving, however slowly, toward a rebalancing.

The CxC Matrix provides the infrastructure to operationalize data compensation at the slot level. If every slot in the Matrix includes a transparent declaration of what data is collected, what it is used for, and what the customer receives in return for consenting to that use, the organization has both the consent governance framework it needs for regulatory compliance and the trust-building mechanism it needs for customer relationship durability. The organizations that build this transparency into their slot architecture proactively — before it is mandated — will experience the competitive benefit of being the organization that customers trust with their data, rather than the one they tolerate.

Testing AI Against Reality — Estimated Impact, Improved Well-Being, Decreased Well-Being, and Potentially Harmed

Any AI system deployed in customer-facing slots — fraud detection, identity verification, behavioral analytics, personalization, automated support — operates on populations that are not uniformly served by its outputs. The same model that correctly identifies 94% of fraudulent transactions also incorrectly flags 6% of legitimate ones. The customers in that 6% — disproportionately represented by demographic groups whose behavioral patterns are underrepresented in the training data — experience a material decrease in well-being: a legitimate transaction declined, an account frozen, access to funds disrupted, hours spent reversing a false positive. Any responsible deployment of AI in the CxC Matrix requires that the population of customers affected by AI-governed slot decisions be segmented by impact tier — Improved Well-Being, Decreased Well-Being, and Potentially Harmed — with estimated range of individuals in each tier quantified before deployment and monitored continuously post-deployment.

The Improved Well-Being population is the largest and most visible. For an AI fraud detection system deployed across a 2-million-customer financial services organization, the estimated Improved Well-Being population might be 1.82 million customers — those for whom AI-governed fraud detection prevents unauthorized transactions, reduces resolution friction when fraud does occur, delivers proactive alerts at the moment of risk, and shortens the time between fraud occurrence and account restoration. For the privacy protection use cases described in this chapter, the Improved Well-Being population includes every customer who receives an early warning about a data breach before they would have learned from external sources, every customer whose synthetic identity fraud attempt is detected at onboarding rather than discovered years later when their credit has been destroyed, and every older adult whose behavioral pattern triggers a proactive fraud education slot before they respond to an IRS impersonation call. These are not hypothetical benefits — they are quantifiable at the slot level, and the Customer Experience Algorithm has the analytical infrastructure to measure them.

The Decreased Well-Being and Potentially Harmed populations require equal rigor. Decreased Well-Being customers are those for whom the AI system operates correctly in aggregate but incorrectly for their individual case — the legitimate customer whose purchase pattern is flagged as anomalous because their demographic group is underrepresented in the model's training data; the identity verification system that cannot process a recently hyphenated name or a non-Western document format with equal accuracy; the fraud alert system that disproportionately freezes accounts belonging to customers who travel frequently for work. The Potentially Harmed population is smaller but more consequential: customers for whom the AI system's error creates material harm — a missed medical payment that triggers a collection action, a frozen account during a financial emergency, a false positive in a background check system that affects employment. The CxC Matrix's audit framework requires that before any AI system is deployed in a customer-facing slot, the organization estimate, using demographic analysis of its customer base and bias audit results from the model, the size of each impact tier, the severity of impact in each tier, and the remediation protocol for customers whose well-being is decreased or harmed by the system's operation. This is not an ethical nicety. It is a risk management requirement — because the regulatory and reputational consequences of deploying a biased AI system in a customer-facing slot are now as well-documented and financially significant as any other category of organizational risk.

FIGURE 11.4 — AI IMPACT ASSESSMENT FRAMEWORK: ESTIMATING CUSTOMER WELL-BEING OUTCOMES BEFORE DEPLOYMENT

Impact Tier	Population Affected (Est.)	Well-Being Direction	What the CxC Matrix and AI Must Do for This Group
Improved Well-Being	**~85-92% of AI-governed contact population (1.7M-1.84M of 2M example base)**	**↑ Positive**	Continue, optimize, and expand. Measure CLV improvement, fraud prevention value, resolution speed gains. Use this population's positive signals to improve the model. Ensure they receive visible credit for the system working on their behalf — proactive notifications, faster resolutions, fewer interruptions.

Decreased Well-Being	**~6–12% of population (120K–240K of 2M example base)**	**↓ Friction Increased**	Mandatory remediation pipeline: every Decreased Well-Being case must generate a root cause classification (false positive type, demographic bias indicator, edge case pattern) and feed back to the model retraining queue. Slot design must include a fast-lane resolution path for customers whose AI-governed interaction produced a friction outcome. The resolution SLA for this group should be materially faster than the standard Stage 12 SLA.

Potentially Harmed	**~0.5–2% of population (10K-40K of 2M example base)**	⚠ **Material Impact**	Highest-priority intervention protocol. Every Potentially Harmed case is a human review trigger, a root cause investigation requirement, and a full audit of the AI model's decision logic for this case type. The organization must maintain a Potentially Harmed case registry, report it to the AI governance committee, and include it in the annual AI risk assessment. Regulatory disclosure requirements apply in most governed industries. No Potentially Harmed case is closed without documented remediation and bias audit review.

APPLYING THE IMPACT FRAMEWORK TO PRIVACY AND FRAUD PROTECTION AI SPECIFICALLY

For fraud detection models: the Improved Well-Being population are the customers whose fraudulent transactions were blocked and whose accounts were protected. The Decreased Well-Being population are the customers whose legitimate transactions were declined — measure this as a 'false positive rate by demographic segment' and set a maximum acceptable false positive rate for each segment before deployment. The Potentially Harmed population are the customers whose false-positive account freezes coincided with medical emergencies, payroll deposits, or other time-critical financial events — these cases require proactive identification and priority resolution.

For identity verification AI: Improved Well-Being are customers who passed through frictionlessly with strong security. Decreased Well-Being are those whose valid government IDs were rejected by optical character recognition errors (a known problem with non-Western character sets and older document formats). Potentially Harmed are customers whose identity data was incorrectly matched to a fraud watchlist record — a condition that can result in account denial, employment screening failure, and in some cases law enforcement contact.

For behavioral biometrics: Improved Well-Being are customers who received seamless continuous authentication. Decreased Well-Being are customers with physical conditions (tremor, limited dexterity, vision impairment) whose behavioral biometric profile is inherently more variable, generating more false-positive anomaly alerts. Potentially Harmed are customers whose accounts were suspended based on behavioral anomaly detection during a medical event — a documented failure mode for stroke and cardiac event patients who attempt to access banking services from a hospital or emergency context.

The standard for responsible AI deployment in customer-facing CxC Matrix slots is not zero Decreased Well-Being or Potentially Harmed outcomes — no system operating at scale achieves that. The standard is that the organization knows, before deployment, the estimated size of each impact tier; has designed slot-level remediation for each tier; monitors the actual distribution against the estimate continuously; and reports material variances to governance structures with authority to act.

Protecting Your Customers Is Protecting Your Business — The Integrated Defense

The Ponemon Institute documented that the average cost of a data breach now exceeds $4.88 million per incident, with 40% of that cost attributable to customer attrition — customers who left the organization specifically because of lost trust after the breach. The organizations most able to minimize attrition in the aftermath of a breach are not those with the best PR response. They are those who had the best pre-breach customer communication, the clearest post-breach remediation protocols, and the most transparent data governance practices already embedded in their slot architecture. Customers who knew exactly what data the organization held, knew exactly what the organization would do in the event of a breach, and received notification within hours rather than weeks — those customers demonstrated statistically higher retention rates in documented post-breach studies than customers of organizations that disclosed later and less completely.

The integrated defense — the design of every slot in the CxC Matrix to minimize data exposure, maximize identity validation rigor, deploy AI detection on the monitoring layer, and build transparent customer communication into both the normal operation and the failure response — is not a security investment separate from the customer experience investment. It is the same investment. An organization that treats its customers' data with the respect that the identification objective requires is an organization that has also designed the slot-level personalization, continuity, and relevance that makes the customer experience valuable. Data governance and customer experience are not competing priorities. They are the same priority, executed at the same level of the same architecture, with the same consequence for organizational performance when they are done well or done poorly.

> ***"You cannot have a Customer Worthy experience built on a data governance failure. The customer who trusts you enough to share their data, their behavior, and their identity expects that trust to be honored in every slot where their information is present. Every breach of that trust — through negligence, through insufficient authentication design, through inadequate AI governance — is a withdrawal from the trust ledger that no amount of subsequent customer experience excellence can fully replenish."***

THE CHAPTER 11 IMPERATIVE — WHAT EVERY ORGANIZATION MUST DO BEFORE THE NEXT INCIDENT

Three non-negotiable actions: First, conduct the CxC Matrix data privacy audit described in this chapter for every slot across all 15 lifecycle stages. Identify every point where personal data is exchanged, every authentication gap, every third-party data flow operating without explicit customer consent. Fix the highest-risk gaps within 90 days. Second, deploy AI-powered identity verification at your highest-risk slots — onboarding, account modification, high-value transactions, and inbound support — within 12 months. The tools exist. The ROI on prevented fraud almost always exceeds the implementation cost by a factor of 5–10x. Third, build the AI impact assessment framework into your slot governance process: no AI system goes live in a customer-facing slot without a documented estimate of Improved Well-Being, Decreased Well-Being, and Potentially Harmed populations, a remediation protocol for each tier, and a monitoring commitment that tracks actual outcomes against estimates. These are not aspirational standards. They are the minimum operating requirements for an organization that takes Customer Worthiness seriously in the AI era.

CHAPTER TWELVE

Matrix Benefit and Use by Function and Department

How Every Role in Every Department Can Automate What Works, Innovate What Doesn't, and Compound Customer Value Across the Entire Enterprise

In the twenty-first century, every employee in every function occupies a sales, service, and marketing role — whether or not their job title says so. The customer does not experience your organizational chart. They experience the cumulative result of every decision made in finance, operations, legal, IT, HR, marketing, and the contact center — in sequence, simultaneously, and across channels they switch between without asking your permission. This chapter is about making that cumulative result deliberate, measurable, and continuously improving. The governing philosophy is simple: automate what works, and spend your time innovating what doesn't.

> *"The purpose of a company is to create a customer. The only profit center is the customer."*
>
> — **Peter F. Drucker**

part is not disruption for its own sake — it is the recognition that a competitive environment where AI can replicate any product feature, match any price, and clone any marketing message in months means the only durable advantage is the speed with which you discover what customers value next and build it before anyone else.

> ***"Automate what works. Spend your time innovating what doesn't. In the AI era, this is not a productivity suggestion. It is a survival strategy."***

What follows is a department-by-department examination of how the CxC Matrix, combined with AI orchestration, web-connected systems, embedded performance intelligence, and continuous improvement principles, can be deployed to maximize customer yield in every function of the enterprise. Each section identifies what to automate, where to innovate, how AI changes the function's relationship with the customer, and what the deliverables look like in a world where every slot in the Matrix is instrumented, measured, and improvable.

The Architecture of Modern Customer Contact

The average consumer today encounters an estimated 6,000 to 10,000 brand interactions per day — a figure that encompasses everything from a logo glimpsed on a coffee cup to a personalized AI-generated email, a geofenced mobile alert as they enter a competitor's parking lot, an algorithmically selected social post, and a retargeted display ad that appears because they spent twelve seconds on a pricing page three days ago. The scale of contact is not new — Customer Worthy documented millions of messages per consumer per year in its original edition. What is new is the precision with which those contacts can be targeted, the speed with which they can be produced, and the intelligence with which they can be optimized.

The core elements of direct marketing and direct communication have not changed: List, Offer, Creative, and Media. Their relative contribution to contact performance — the empirically established proportions that Customer Worthy documented — remain directionally accurate. What has changed is who manages each element and how. The List is now a dynamic, AI-scored customer segment updated in real time by behavioral signals from hundreds of data sources. The Offer is now a continuously tested, algorithmically optimized configuration assembled from component libraries at the moment of contact. The Creative is now AI-generated at scale, personalized to the individual recipient, and A/B tested across thousands of variants simultaneously. The Media is now a self-optimizing channel allocation system that shifts budget in real time based on conversion probability by customer segment.

The playbook that governs how each of these elements is assembled, deployed, measured, and refined across every contact in the CxC Matrix is not a static document maintained by a marketing team. It is a living operational system — part human strategic direction, part AI execution, part continuous performance intelligence — that runs at a speed and granularity no human team could achieve manually. Understanding how each department contributes to and benefits from that playbook is the purpose of this chapter.

THE COMPOUNDING EFFECT OF ENTERPRISE-WIDE AUTOMATION

A contact center that has automated its most common resolution paths frees its agents to handle the complex, emotionally sensitive interactions where human judgment is irreplaceable. A finance team that has automated its routine reporting and anomaly detection frees its analysts to build forward-looking customer profitability models. An HR team that has automated its onboarding compliance workflows frees its managers to design the training experiences that actually change employee behavior at the customer contact point. In every function, the compounding effect is the same: automation of the known creates capacity for innovation of the unknown. The CxC Matrix is the architecture that makes those innovations visible, measurable, and attributable to customer outcomes.

EXECUTIVE MANAGEMENT

Strategy, Vision, Budget Allocation, and the Customer Centricity That AI Now Makes Measurable

From Customer-Centric Rhetoric to Measurable Customer-Centric Operations

Every annual report filed by a Fortune 500 company in the past decade has contained the phrase 'customer-centric.' A Google search for 'customer centric' combined with 'annual report' returns tens of thousands of results. It is the most consistently deployed and least consistently operationalized commitment in the modern corporate vocabulary. The gap between the proclamation and the practice is not one of intention — most executives genuinely believe their organizations prioritize customers. It is a gap of instrumentation. Without a system that connects every budget decision, every organizational restructuring, every product launch, and every operational change to a visible, quantified customer outcome, 'customer centricity' is a values statement. With that system, it becomes a management discipline.

The CxC Matrix provides that instrumentation. And now, AI has made the instrumentation real-time, predictive, and enterprise-wide in a way that was technically aspirational when Customer Worthy was first published. The executive team that deploys the Matrix with an AI orchestration layer has, for the first time, the ability to see the customer impact of every internal decision before it is made — not as an estimate constructed by a strategy team, but as a probabilistic model generated by algorithms trained on actual customer behavior across all 15 lifecycle stages and all channel containers.

Automate: Budget Allocation Simulations and Customer Impact Modeling

The most consequential executive decisions — budget allocation, portfolio prioritization, market entry, acquisition evaluation — have historically been made with incomplete customer impact information. Finance models projected revenue. Operations models projected capacity. Customer impact was estimated from survey data and analyst judgment. AI changes this. Executive teams can now run customer impact simulations across the complete CxC Matrix before committing capital. A proposal to reduce call center hours by 15% to achieve a $2.3 million annual savings can be modeled against actual Stage 12 contact volume, customer value distribution, and historical defection rates for service-interrupted customers — producing a net revenue impact estimate that either validates or invalidates the cost reduction before it is implemented.

Amazon's S-Team has used customer-centric simulation modeling as a standard budget evaluation tool for years. Before committing to a new fulfillment capability, the team models the impact on Stage 7 (Delivery) performance for each customer segment, weighted by CLV. The customer impact simulation is not advisory. It is the decision instrument. Organizations that want to close the gap between customer-centric rhetoric and customer-centric operations need the same discipline — and the AI tools to execute it now exist at a fraction of the cost they required five years ago.

Innovate: Strategy-to-Customer Traceability

The innovation opportunity for executive management is not in the AI tools themselves — it is in building the organizational capability to connect strategic decisions to customer outcomes with enough speed and precision that the feedback loop becomes a competitive advantage. Most organizations operate on a 12-to-18-month feedback cycle between strategic decision and customer outcome measurement. An AI-instrumented CxC Matrix compresses that cycle to weeks or days, enabling strategy to become iterative rather than fixed. Executives who build this capability first create compounding learning advantages that are structurally difficult for slower-moving competitors to replicate.

Specifically: deploy AI-powered customer performance dashboards that surface the customer impact of every significant operational decision within 30 days of implementation. Require all budget requests above a defined threshold to include a CxC Matrix impact analysis — which customer segments are affected, at which lifecycle stages, through which channels, with what estimated revenue and cost consequences. Use AI simulation to evaluate merger and acquisition targets not just on financial metrics, but on customer experience compatibility — identifying where the acquired organization's customer journey creates conflicts, gaps, or opportunities when overlaid on yours.

AI CAPABILITIES TRANSFORMING EXECUTIVE DECISION-MAKING

Real-time customer performance dashboards: AI-assembled visualizations of customer value trends, lifecycle stage migration rates, and CLV trajectory across all segments — updated continuously, not quarterly.

Predictive budget impact modeling: Before any budget reallocation, AI models project the customer contact impact, estimating defection probability, revenue at risk, and CLV effect by segment.

M&A customer experience compatibility analysis: AI analysis of target company's customer journey against your CxC Matrix, identifying integration risks and synergy opportunities at the slot level.

Competitive intelligence automation: AI monitoring of competitor customer experience signals — pricing changes, service level shifts, new channel deployments, customer complaint patterns — surfaced automatically in executive briefings.

Board-level customer scorecard: AI-generated monthly summary connecting customer performance metrics (acquisition cost, retention rate, CLV by segment, Stage 15 advocacy rate) to financial outcomes — the dashboard that makes customer centricity a board-level discipline, not a management one.

Visualize	Company-wide customer strategy by lifecycle stage and channel; AI-generated customer impact simulations for all major decisions; real-time competitive customer experience intelligence
Analyze	Customer CLV trajectory by segment; budget decision impact per customer; M&A target experience compatibility; market entry customer opportunity modeling
Monetize	Resource investment measured by customer yield; opportunity cost of customer experience failures by stage; net revenue impact of operational decisions before implementation

Prioritize	Investment decisions ranked by customer CLV impact; market opportunities weighted by addressable customer value; strategic initiatives sequenced by customer readiness
Optimize	Decision cycle time from strategic intent to customer outcome measurement; enterprise AI capability maturity; customer centricity as an operationally measurable, board-reported discipline

FINANCE

Customer-Level Profitability, Predictive Budgeting, and AI-Powered Financial Transparency

The CFO Who Sees Every Customer

Finance's relationship with the CxC Matrix has always been conceptually straightforward and operationally difficult: the framework connects every business activity to a customer outcome, which is exactly what activity-based costing and customer profitability analysis aspire to do but rarely achieve with the granularity and speed that strategy requires. The barrier has been data: assembling the customer-level revenue and cost data needed to calculate genuine per-contact profitability required months of analytical work, produced results that were already outdated when they were delivered, and required enough simplifying assumptions that their operational utility was limited.

AI has eliminated that barrier. Financial organizations that have deployed AI-powered customer profitability platforms — connecting CRM data, billing systems, support contact logs, logistics costs, and channel utilization data — can now calculate the genuine cost-to-serve and revenue-per-customer at the individual account level, updated daily. The CFO who has this capability is no longer managing to departmental cost averages. They are managing to customer-level profitability distribution — identifying which segments of the customer base generate the economic surplus that funds innovation, and which segments consume more in service costs than they generate in revenue.

Automate: Routine Financial Monitoring and Anomaly Detection

The most high-value automation opportunity in finance is the replacement of periodic exception reporting with continuous AI-powered anomaly detection. The traditional finance cadence — monthly close, quarterly review, annual audit — creates systematic blind spots between reporting periods where customer financial signals (unusual payment behavior, revenue concentration changes, cost-to-serve deterioration in specific channels) go undetected until they have compounded into significant variances. AI monitoring systems can track customer-level financial signals continuously, flagging anomalies within hours rather than weeks.

Practical example: a mid-market financial services company deployed AI anomaly detection across its Stage 12 (Support) contact costs. The system identified, within eleven days of deployment, that a single product line was generating 34% of inbound support contacts but representing only 8% of revenue. The anomaly had been present for six months but had not surfaced in quarterly reviews because it was distributed across multiple cost center codes. The AI's cross-reference of support contact logs against product revenue attribution made it visible immediately. The remediation — a redesigned onboarding slot for that product line — reduced support contact volume by 41% within 90 days.

Innovate: Forward-Looking Customer Profitability Models

The innovation opportunity for finance is the migration from backward-looking customer profitability reporting to forward-looking customer profitability prediction. The Customer Experience Algorithm — the CEA that governs slot activation across the CxC Matrix — generates propensity scores for each customer across 30-, 60-, 90-, and 180-day windows. When those propensity scores are integrated with the customer's historical revenue, cost-to-serve, and defection risk, the output is a forward-looking CLV projection that can inform every budget decision the finance team makes.

This is the financial instrument that makes the CFO a genuine partner in customer strategy rather than a constraint on it. When the head of marketing proposes a $4 million investment in Stage 15 (Community/Advocacy) slot redesign, the CFO with a forward-looking customer profitability model can calculate the expected CLV impact of a 20% increase in Stage 15 advocacy activation rate — and determine whether the expected new customer CLV from increased referrals justifies the investment. That calculation used to require a strategy consulting engagement. Today, it is a function of the AI model running on the organization's existing customer data.

Finance Process	AI / Automation Opportunity	Customer Yield Impact	Innovation Frontier

Customer profitability tracking	AI integration of CRM, billing, support, and logistics data into real-time per-customer P&L	Identifies unprofitable segments before they compound; enables surgical cost reduction without revenue sacrifice	*Predictive CLV models that project profitability 24 months forward, enabling proactive segment strategy*
Budget anomaly detection	Continuous AI monitoring of cost-to-serve by channel and stage; automatic alerts for variance above threshold	Prevents six-month cost anomalies from becoming structural problems; compresses discovery cycle from quarters to days	*AI-generated budget reallocation recommendations based on customer yield per dollar invested by stage*
Vendor payment and collections	AI-powered payment timing optimization; behavioral scoring for collections prioritization	Reduces cost of collections; improves cash flow without damaging high-CLV customer relationships	*AI negotiation agents for contract renewal with outsourced service providers, using customer yield data as leverage*
Financial reporting	AI-generated management reports with customer impact annotations; automated regulatory filing with anomaly flagging	Frees financial analysts from report production for strategic modeling	*Natural language financial dashboards: executives ask questions in plain language, AI assembles the answer from live data*

Risk and fraud monitoring	AI behavioral analytics on payment patterns, connected to fraud detection systems in real time	Reduces fraud losses; protects high-CLV customer accounts with elevated authentication protocols	*Predictive risk scoring for new credit decisions using behavioral signals from the complete CxC Matrix, not just credit bureau data*

Visualize	Customer-level P&L across all 15 lifecycle stages; cost-to-serve by channel and contact type; CLV distribution by segment with forward-looking projections
Analyze	Budget impact simulations per customer segment; activity-based costing from customer contact data; vendor performance measured by customer outcome, not SLA compliance
Monetize	Per-customer, per-contact, per-stage revenue and cost; cost of customer defection by segment; ROI of CX investments calculated from actual CLV impact
Prioritize	Budget allocation ranked by customer yield per dollar; cost reduction initiatives filtered through customer impact risk assessment
Optimize	Financial reporting cycle time; cost anomaly detection speed; customer profitability model accuracy; CFO-to-CXO strategic alignment

INFORMATION TECHNOLOGY & SYSTEMS

The Customer Architecture, AI Infrastructure, and the Connected Intelligence Layer

From Systems Integrator to Customer Experience Architect

Information technology's role in the customer experience has historically been defined by what it enables rather than what it directs. IT built the systems that marketing used to send emails, the platforms that sales used to manage pipelines, the infrastructure that customer service used to handle contacts. In the AI era, that enabling role has been transformed into a directing one — because the AI systems that now govern which customer receives which contact, through which channel, at which moment, with which message, are IT artifacts. The algorithms that determine customer lifetime value, predict churn probability, and optimize slot activation sequences are software systems that IT builds, deploys, and maintains. The customer experience has become a technology architecture decision in ways it was not before.

The program that detected excess inventory, evaluated liquidation options across channels, identified the optimal customer segment, calculated the promotional economics, assembled the contact sequence, and executed it in less than three seconds — that program was not a marketing achievement. It was an IT achievement that marketing benefited from. Today, those programs are not custom-built for single use cases. They are configurable AI orchestration platforms that can be trained on any product, any channel, any customer segment, in a fraction of the time the original mower program required.

Automate: The Customer Data Infrastructure

The foundational IT automation opportunity is the Customer Data Platform (CDP) — the unified, continuously updated repository of customer identity, behavioral history, lifecycle stage, CEA scores, consent records, and contact history that makes every other AI application in the enterprise possible. Without a CDP, every AI application in every department starts from scratch, pulling from different systems, producing inconsistent customer views, and generating conflicting recommendations. With a CDP, the AI infrastructure across every department speaks the same language about the same customer — and the CxC Matrix has the data architecture it needs to function at full capability.

The CDP is not a project. It is infrastructure. Like the electrical grid that makes every device in a building useful, the CDP makes every AI application in the enterprise useful. Organizations that have not built or procured a CDP are not behind on a technology trend — they are missing the prerequisite for everything described in this chapter. The IT investment required is substantial. The ROI, measured in customer yield per contact, is higher than any other technology investment an organization in the AI era can make.

Innovate: The Connected Intelligence Layer

Beyond the CDP, the innovation opportunity for IT is the Connected Intelligence Layer — the network of AI models, IoT sensors, API integrations, and real-time data feeds that turn the CxC Matrix from a planning framework into an operational system. This layer connects the RFID reader at the store entrance to the CDP, so that when a customer's loyalty credential is detected, the AI immediately retrieves their CEA score, lifecycle stage, and propensity window and routes it to the staff member's tablet before the customer reaches the counter. It connects the delivery RFID tag to the customer contact system, so that when a shipment stops moving for 24 hours, the Stage 7 proactive notification slot activates automatically. It connects the voice AI on the phone channel to the CRM system, so that when sentiment analysis detects elevated frustration in an inbound call, the system automatically escalates to a senior agent and pre-populates their screen with the customer's complete context.

Google Cloud's Contact Center AI, Salesforce Einstein, Microsoft Azure AI Services, and AWS Customer Experience Intelligence are all operational deployments of this Connected Intelligence Layer at enterprise scale. The organizations that have deployed them report 25–40% reductions in average handle time, 15–30% improvements in first-contact resolution, and material improvements in customer satisfaction scores — not because the AI is making the customer service decision, but because it is equipping the human agent with the situational awareness to make a better one. This is the IT architecture that the CxC Matrix has always described as its operational ideal: every slot equipped with the intelligence it needs to serve this specific customer at this specific moment.

THE CXC MATRIX SYSTEMS ARCHITECTURE — AI ERA ADDITIONS TO THE CLASSIC LIST

Customer Data Platform (CDP): The unified customer identity and behavioral data repository that makes every AI application in the enterprise coherent. Vendor options include Segment, Adobe Experience Platform, Salesforce Data Cloud, and Tealium.

AI Orchestration Engine: The system that governs which AI model fires in which slot, under which conditions, for which customer segment. Vendors include Pega Customer Decision Hub, Adobe Journey Optimizer, and Salesforce Marketing Cloud.

Large Language Model (LLM) Integration Layer: The API connections that allow organizational AI applications to leverage foundation models (GPT-4, Claude, Gemini) for content generation, conversation, and analysis tasks at the slot level.

IoT/Physical Intelligence Integration: The middleware connecting RFID readers, geofencing systems, BLE proximity sensors, and connected device telemetry to the CDP and AI orchestration engine in real time.

Real-Time Data Streaming Infrastructure: Apache Kafka, AWS Kinesis, or equivalent systems that move behavioral event data from customer touchpoints to AI models with sub-second latency — enabling the real-time slot activation that the CEA requires.

AI Model Governance and Monitoring: MLOps platforms (MLflow, Weights & Biases, or cloud-native equivalents) that track model performance, detect drift, monitor for bias, and trigger retraining when model accuracy falls below defined thresholds.

Consent and Privacy Architecture: The technical infrastructure that enforces customer consent records across all AI model inputs, ensuring that no model accesses data the customer has not explicitly enabled — integrated with the CDP at the data access layer.

Visualize	Complete customer technology architecture across all 15 stages; real-time data flow from physical and digital touchpoints to AI models; system integration map with gap analysis; third-party connectivity and governance
Analyze	Technology investment ROI measured by customer yield per contact; build-versus-buy decisions for AI capabilities; data quality impact on model accuracy; security vulnerability assessment by stage
Monetize	AI infrastructure investment justified by CLV improvement; cost reduction from automated slot execution versus manual contact management; data quality improvement measured by model accuracy gain
Prioritize	CDP implementation first; high-revenue-stage AI orchestration second; physical intelligence layer third; advanced model governance fourth
Optimize	Real-time data latency; model inference speed; API integration reliability; CDP data completeness; AI model accuracy by customer segment and lifecycle stage

OPERATIONS

Supply Chain Intelligence, Physical Experience Design, and the Automation of Operational Excellence

Operations Is a Customer Experience Function

Operations executives who believe their domain begins at the warehouse dock and ends at the delivery confirmation are leaving the majority of their customer impact unmeasured and unmanaged. The customer's experience of your operations — how long the delivery takes, whether the product arrives in the condition promised, how easy it is to return something that doesn't work, how your supply chain failures manifest as customer-facing stock-outs and substitutions — is the customer experience at stages 6 through 10 of the CxC Matrix, and it is directly attributable to operational decisions made months before the customer placed their order.

The mower story is the canonical Customer Worthy illustration of operational intelligence at its best: a program that detected inventory imbalance, evaluated every liquidation option across every channel, modeled the customer economics of each option, selected the optimal promotional approach, and executed it — all within three seconds, without human intervention. That program is not aspirational today. The technology to build it has existed for years. The competitive differentiator now is not whether such programs are possible — it is how many of them your organization is running simultaneously, how deeply they are connected to your customer data infrastructure, and how quickly they learn from the outcomes they produce.

Automate: Demand Sensing and Inventory Optimization

Demand sensing — the ability to detect shifts in customer purchasing intent before they manifest as orders — is now an AI capability available to organizations of every size. Traditional demand forecasting used historical sales data with seasonal adjustments. AI-powered demand sensing integrates historical sales, real-time web traffic patterns, social media sentiment, search trend data, weather forecasts, competitor pricing changes, and macro-economic signals to produce demand predictions that are materially more accurate. Companies that have deployed AI demand sensing report inventory holding cost reductions of 15–25% and stockout frequency reductions of 20–30% — because they are buying closer to actual demand rather than estimated demand.

For the CxC Matrix, demand sensing directly improves Stage 7 (Delivery) performance. A product that is in stock when a customer orders it, shipped from the optimal fulfillment location, and delivered within the window the customer was promised is a Stage 7 interaction with maximum customer value. A product that ships late because demand sensing failed to predict the spike is a Stage 7 failure that generates Stage 12 support contacts, Stage 13 recovery costs, and Stage 14 defection risk. The math is simple and the causal chain is direct: better operations intelligence produces better customer economics.

Innovate: The Self-Optimizing Supply Chain

The innovation frontier for operations is the self-optimizing supply chain — a network of AI systems connected to IoT sensors, partner APIs, and customer data feeds that continuously adjusts routing, inventory positioning, carrier selection, and fulfillment timing based on real-time customer demand signals and supply availability. This is not science fiction. Amazon's fulfillment network has operated versions of this for years. Walmart's supply chain AI predicted the surge demand for specific categories during the early weeks of COVID-19 with sufficient accuracy to pre-position inventory before the demand wave hit. These are not small-company capabilities — but the cloud AI infrastructure that powers them is now available at pricing that makes them accessible to mid-market organizations.

The operational innovation that the CxC Matrix specifically enables is customer-value-weighted operations optimization: allocating operational resources (fulfillment speed, quality inspection bandwidth, returns processing priority, carrier upgrade budget) based on the CEA-calculated CLV of the customer whose order is being processed. A Champion-segment customer with a $180,000 lifetime value history and an 87% 30-day propensity score receives a different operational allocation than a newly acquired customer with a single transaction and unknown CLV. This is not preferential treatment in a manner that harms lower-value customers — it is rational resource allocation that maximizes total customer yield from a finite operations budget.

Operations Domain	AI / Connected System Application	Customer Stage Impact	Estimated Yield Improvement
Demand forecasting	AI demand sensing integrating sales history, web behavior, social signals, weather, and macro data	Stage 1–4 (product availability when demand peaks)	*15–25% inventory cost reduction; 20–30% stockout reduction*

Fulfillment routing	AI-optimized carrier and warehouse selection based on delivery promise, cost, and customer CLV tier	Stage 7 (Delivery) SLA performance	*8–18% improvement in on-time delivery; 12–22% reduction in premium shipping cost*
Quality control	Computer vision and IoT sensor arrays detecting defects before shipment; AI-generated quality trend analysis by supplier	Stage 8–10 (Installation/Use onset defect reduction)	*35–55% defect detection improvement over manual inspection; supplier quality scorecards updated in real time*
Returns processing	AI-powered returns authorization; automated routing to refurbish, resell, or recycle based on condition assessment	Stage 13 (Repair/Return) cost and cycle time	*23–38% reduction in returns processing cost; 15–25% increase in refurbishment recovery value*
Outsourcing performance	AI monitoring of third-party fulfillment, repair, and contact center SLA compliance measured by customer outcome, not activity metric	All stages involving partner execution	*Real-time SLA visibility replacing monthly reporting; partner performance variation identified within hours*

Vendor negotiation	Customer yield data from stage-level performance metrics used as leverage in contract negotiations with suppliers, carriers, and service partners	Stage 6–8 cost structure optimization	*Organizations using customer outcome data in vendor negotiations report 8–15% better contract terms versus activity-metric negotiations*

The outsourcing dimension of operations deserves specific emphasis. As organizations continue to expand their use of third-party fulfillment, repair services, contact center outsourcing, and supply chain partners, the risk of customer experience fragmentation across the handoffs between internal and outsourced operations increases. The CxC Matrix provides the governance architecture for outsourcing relationships that most vendor contracts lack: customer-outcome-based SLAs, measured at the slot level, that make it possible to distinguish between an outsourcing partner who is meeting their activity targets and one who is actually serving your customers well.

The question every operations executive should ask of every outsourcing relationship is not 'are they hitting their SLAs?' It is 'are the customers who interact with this outsourced function more or less likely to advance to the next lifecycle stage than those who interact with our internal equivalent?' If the answer is 'less likely,' the outsourcing relationship is subtracting from customer yield regardless of what the activity metrics say.

Visualize	Product, service, and resource demand by channel, stage, and customer segment; supply chain performance mapped to customer experience outcomes; outsourced partner performance measured by customer yield
Analyze	Alternative fulfillment configurations; just-in-time versus buffer inventory economics measured by Stage 7 performance impact; outsourcing versus in-house decision at the slot level
Monetize	Stage 7–10 customer defection cost attributable to operational failures; quality failure revenue impact; outsourcing yield differential versus internal execution
Prioritize	Highest-CLV customer orders for operational resource allocation; supply chain investment ranked by Stage 7–10 customer impact; outsourcing relationships ranked by customer yield contribution
Optimize	Demand sensing model accuracy; fulfillment routing cost versus delivery promise compliance; quality detection rate; returns recovery value; outsourcing partner customer yield performance

HUMAN RESOURCES

Employee Experience as Customer Experience: AI-Powered Talent, Training, and Performance Systems

The Employee Who Understands the Customer Is Worth More Than the System That Doesn't

There is a consistent empirical relationship between employee experience and customer experience that has survived decades of organizational research: organizations whose employees understand how their individual role affects customer outcomes produce materially better customer experiences than those whose employees do not. The CxC Matrix was designed from its original conception to solve this problem — to give every employee, regardless of function, a visual representation of where they sit in the customer journey and what their decisions and actions do to the customers passing through the stages and channels adjacent to their role.

Today HR has a new instrument for building that understanding and sustaining it over time: AI-powered training, performance, and scheduling systems that connect employee behavior to customer outcomes with a precision and speed that periodic performance reviews cannot approach. The HR leader who has deployed these systems is not managing headcount. They are managing the quality of every customer interaction that flows through their organization's human capital.

Automate: Scheduling, Compliance, and Routine Performance Reporting

Workforce management — the scheduling of right-skilled employees to right-volume contact points at right times — is one of the highest-value automation opportunities in HR, and one of the most measurably connected to customer outcomes. Contact centers that have deployed AI workforce management systems (Verint, NICE IEX, Genesys WFM) report 10–20% improvements in service level compliance and 8–15% reductions in overtime cost, because the AI models contact volume predictions with a precision that human schedulers cannot match across the complexity of multi-channel, multi-stage customer contact flows.

The practical implication for the CxC Matrix is direct: when the right number of the right-skilled agents is available at Stage 12 (Support) contact peaks, hold times are shorter, first-contact resolution rates are higher, and the probability of a Stage 12 interaction converting to a Stage 14 (Defection) outcome is lower. Workforce optimization is not an HR efficiency initiative. It is a customer experience initiative with a calculable revenue impact at every stage where human capacity is a constraint.

Innovate: AI-Powered Performance Coaching and Customer Impact Training

The innovation frontier for HR is AI-powered performance coaching — systems that monitor customer interactions in real time, identify the specific behaviors and communication patterns that correlate with positive customer outcomes, and deliver coaching recommendations to employees before their next interaction rather than weeks later in a performance review. Cogito, Observe.AI, and similar platforms analyze voice and text interactions, detect emotion, identify coaching moments, and provide real-time guidance to agents during live customer calls — improving resolution rates and customer satisfaction scores measurably within weeks of deployment.

Beyond the contact center, the innovation opportunity is in building a performance management system for every customer-facing role that is anchored to customer outcome metrics rather than activity metrics. A salesperson's performance should not be evaluated solely on deals closed — it should include Stage 4–6 conversion rates, Stage 11 retention rates for accounts they closed, and Stage 15 advocacy generation from customers they onboarded. An operations manager's performance should not be evaluated solely on cost-to-operate — it should include Stage 7 delivery performance and Stage 8 installation completion rates. HR that builds customer-outcome-anchored performance systems creates an organization where every employee's incentives align with customer value growth.

25 CUSTOMER EXPERIENCE MISSIONS — THE HR REINVENTION

Customer Worthy's 25 customer experience missions — the field education exercises that ask every manager to traverse their own CxC Matrix as an anonymous customer — are fundamentally an HR program. They are the most effective employee development experience available, and today, they should be redesigned for the AI era.

Mission redesign for NOW: every mission should include an AI-assisted component. When a manager contacts their own organization's support line anonymously (Mission 8), they should also use an AI tool to evaluate the interaction transcript against the Nine Objectives. When they shop competitors (Mission 9), they should use AI to generate a comparative CxC Matrix analysis. When they file a regulatory complaint (Mission 10), they should use AI to research what percentage of similar complaints result in enforcement action.

The AI component does not replace the human experience of the mission — the visceral understanding of what it feels like to be on hold for 23 minutes, or to receive a generic promotional email three days after an unresolved complaint, is irreplaceable. What the AI component adds is the analytical layer that connects the felt experience to the measurable slot design failure — and the evidence base that makes the redesign recommendation credible when it reaches the executive team.

HR programs that combine the experiential with the analytical — that give employees both the felt understanding of the customer's perspective and the data infrastructure to act on that understanding — produce customer experience improvements that classroom training cannot approach. This is the Customer-Worthy MBA updated for the AI era.

Visualize	Employee roles mapped to customer contact points; staffing distribution across lifecycle stages; skill gap analysis relative to AI-era customer contact requirements; training program impact on customer outcome metrics
Analyze	Workforce optimization by stage and channel; correlation between training programs and customer satisfaction outcomes; performance management system alignment with customer value metrics
Monetize	Customer yield per employee; cost of poor first-contact resolution attributable to training gaps; CLV impact of employee turnover at high-touch customer stages
Prioritize	Training investment in highest-customer-impact roles; staffing increases at stages with measurable capacity-related customer yield degradation; performance system redesign to align incentives with customer outcomes
Optimize	Scheduling efficiency; training to performance cycle time; employee customer impact awareness; retention of high-performing customer-facing employees

SALES

AI-Augmented Selling, Pipeline Intelligence, and the 99% Opportunity

Celebrating the 1% — and Finally Addressing the 99%

The uncomfortable truth about sales performance — that the best salespeople achieve single-digit success rates per customer contact, and most achieve less than 1% — has not changed since Customer Worthy first documented it. What has changed is what is now possible with the 99% of contacts that do not immediately convert. That 99% is not failed selling. It is data. It is behavioral signal. It is stage-specific intelligence about where customers are in their decision process, what they need to hear next, what channels they prefer, and what the probability is that they will convert within a defined time window. For most organizations, that intelligence has been discarded. AI changes what can be done with it.

The sales organization that has deployed AI-powered pipeline intelligence is not operating on the same model as one that has not. Their salespeople know, before making a call, the customer's current CEA score, their 30-day propensity window, their recent digital behavior signals, and the recommended next-best-action based on patterns from every similar customer who has reached this stage in the pipeline. They spend their time on the contacts most likely to convert, with the messages most likely to resonate, at the moments the behavioral data says the customer is most receptive. The ones that don't convert immediately don't disappear — they enter AI-managed nurture sequences that maintain the relationship until the propensity window opens.

Automate: Pipeline Management, Lead Scoring, and Follow-Up Sequences

Salesforce Einstein, HubSpot AI, and their equivalents have made AI-powered lead scoring and pipeline management standard practice for organizations of every size. The automation opportunity is no longer whether to deploy these tools — it is how deeply to integrate them with the CxC Matrix behavioral data that makes their scores actionable rather than arbitrary. A lead score that is calculated from form fill behavior alone is directionally useful. A lead score that integrates geofence proximity history, content engagement depth, competitive comparison signals, social proof coefficient, and Stage-specific behavioral pattern matching against your highest-CLV customers is operationally powerful.

The follow-up sequence automation that AI enables is not just efficiency — it is relationship quality. A customer who receives a follow-up email that references the specific product comparison they built on your website, arrives 16 hours after their second visit to your pricing page, and is addressed from their named account manager rather than a marketing system experiences a relationship, not a campaign. The AI executes the timing, the personalization, and the channel selection. The salesperson's name and judgment are what the customer experiences. This is the model that converts the 1% opportunity into a 3–5% opportunity — not by working harder, but by working with better intelligence.

Innovate: AI Sales Agents and Augmented Negotiation

The innovation frontier for sales is the AI sales agent — not a replacement for human salespeople, but an AI system capable of managing the early stages of the customer relationship autonomously and escalating to human sellers at the precise moment the customer's signals indicate they are ready for a human conversation. Drift, Intercom, Salesforce Agentforce, and similar platforms deploy AI agents that qualify prospects through natural conversation, answer product questions with up-to-date knowledge, schedule demonstrations automatically, and hand off to human sellers with a complete context summary — so the human's first conversation with the prospect is not introductory but advisory.

On the negotiation side, AI tools now provide salespeople with real-time competitive intelligence, historical deal data, and recommended negotiation parameters during live customer conversations. A salesperson in a pricing discussion can receive real-time AI coaching on the customer's likely price sensitivity, based on their behavioral profile and the patterns of similar customers in similar negotiation situations. This is not replacing the salesperson's judgment — it is augmenting it with data that no human could assemble in real time without AI assistance.

THE MULTI-WAVE MARKETING PROGRAM — AI ERA UPGRADE

Customer Worthy introduced the multi-wave marketing program — targeting customers across multiple channels in a predefined sequence using rules to orchestrate follow-up contacts — as a best practice for the 2010 marketing environment. Today, the multi-wave program has been replaced by something more powerful: the adaptive contact sequence.

The difference is in the 'predefined' part. Traditional multi-wave programs define the sequence in advance and execute it regardless of how the customer behaves. Adaptive contact sequences define the first contact and the decision rules, then let customer behavior determine every subsequent step. A customer who opens the email but doesn't click gets a different next contact than one who clicks but doesn't convert. A customer who clicks, visits the pricing page, and then visits a competitor's site gets an immediate alert to their account manager and a different, higher-urgency sequence than one who is browsing casually.

AI-powered adaptive sequences from platforms like Braze, Iterable, and Salesforce Marketing Cloud are now table stakes for organizations serious about the 99% opportunity. Organizations that have deployed them report 40–60% improvements in campaign conversion rates versus static multi-wave programs — not because they are contacting customers more frequently, but because they are contacting them with the right message at the right behavioral moment.

The organizational capability this requires: a clean CDP, a functioning CEA model, a slot-level content library from which AI can assemble personalized contacts, and a governance process that sets the behavioral thresholds that trigger each escalation. The technology exists. The organizational discipline to use it correctly is the differentiator.

Visualize	Customer pipeline by lifecycle stage and behavioral signal; propensity window distribution across active prospects; stalled customers with AI-identified re-engagement triggers; revenue opportunity by segment

Analyze	Return on sales channel investment; stage-specific conversion rates by customer segment and message type; AI model accuracy for propensity prediction; competitive win/loss patterns
Monetize	Revenue per contact by channel and stage; cost per qualified opportunity by lead source; CLV impact of sales interaction quality; negotiation outcome improvement from AI coaching
Prioritize	Sales effort allocation by CEA-weighted propensity; account manager assignment by CLV tier; AI agent deployment for low-CLV high-volume segments; human seller focus on high-CLV complex opportunities
Optimize	Lead-to-opportunity conversion by stage; adaptive sequence engagement rates; AI agent escalation accuracy; sales cycle compression; cross-sell and up-sell activation rates at Stages 10–11

LEGAL

Regulatory Intelligence, Liability Mapping, and AI Governance at Every Stage

Legal Exposure Lives in Every Slot — Not Just in the Contracts Department

The legal function's relationship to the CxC Matrix has always been defensive in orientation: map the liability exposure at each stage, ensure disclosures are made at the right moments, govern data handling practices, and maintain the documentation needed to reconstruct the customer's relationship with the company if litigation or regulatory inquiry requires it. These remain valid and necessary functions. But in the AI era, the legal team's role has acquired a new and more consequential dimension: AI governance.

Every AI model deployed in a customer-facing slot is a legal decision as well as a technology decision. The model that determines which customers receive which offers is making decisions that, if those decisions produce discriminatory outcomes by protected class, create Fair Credit Reporting Act, Equal Credit Opportunity Act, or state consumer protection liability. The model that processes customer voice calls is subject to biometric information privacy laws in Illinois, Texas, Washington, and a growing number of states. The model that generates personalized content for customers is subject to consumer protection requirements around accuracy, disclosure, and deceptive practices. Legal teams that are not actively engaged in AI governance at the slot design level are learning about these liabilities after they manifest rather than preventing them.

Automate: Contract Review, Compliance Monitoring, and Regulatory Intelligence

AI-powered contract review has matured to the point where tools like Ironclad, Kira, and ContractPodAi can analyze third-party contracts against defined risk parameters, flag non-standard clauses, and produce standardized comparison matrices for legal review in a fraction of the time human reviewers require. For organizations with large outsourcing portfolios — contact center providers, fulfillment partners, data processors, technology vendors — this automation directly addresses the customer data governance risk that Chapter 11 documented: every third-party data processing agreement is a potential liability, and the organizations that have reviewed all of them against current regulatory requirements know exactly where their exposure is.

Regulatory intelligence monitoring — tracking changes in consumer protection law, data privacy regulation, advertising standards, and sector-specific customer treatment requirements across multiple jurisdictions — is another high-value legal automation. AI tools that monitor regulatory publications, court decisions, and enforcement actions across all relevant jurisdictions and flag changes that affect specific customer contact practices eliminate the systematic risk of operating with outdated compliance assumptions. A multi-state financial services company operating 15 product lines across 47 states faces a regulatory monitoring challenge that no human team can manage comprehensively without AI assistance.

Innovate: AI Governance as Competitive Advantage

The innovation opportunity for legal is to position AI governance not as a compliance cost but as a competitive differentiator. Organizations that establish clear, documented, auditable AI governance frameworks — covering model training data sources, bias testing protocols, customer impact assessment requirements (the three-tier framework described in Chapter 11), consent architecture, and human oversight requirements — are building a trust asset that is increasingly visible to sophisticated customers, institutional investors, and regulators.

The EU AI Act, California's AB 2930 (automated decision-making in consequential domains), and a growing body of state-level AI legislation are creating a regulatory environment where organizations that have already built strong AI governance frameworks will comply at low cost while competitors scramble to retrofit governance onto deployed systems. First-mover advantage in AI governance is the legal function's innovation frontier — and the organizations that seize it will be able to point to their governance frameworks as evidence of trustworthiness in sales conversations, regulatory inquiries, and investor presentations in ways that late movers cannot.

THE MAD COW CASE — TODAY VERSION

Customer Worthy's original Mad Cow example — a customer who purchased recalled beef with a loyalty card, was not notified, and sued the retailer for failing to use available data to protect her — would have a different outcome today. An AI-powered product recall notification system, connected to the retailer's CDP, would have identified every customer who purchased the affected product using any identified payment method, generated personalized notification through each customer's preferred channel within hours of the recall announcement, and maintained an auditable log of who was notified, when, and through which channel. The failure to deploy available AI in a customer protection context is increasingly being treated by courts and regulators not as a neutral decision but as a negligence claim. Legal teams that are not advocating for AI deployment in customer safety contexts are not managing their organization's liability — they are increasing it.

Visualize	Customer liability exposure mapped to lifecycle stage and channel; regulatory requirement coverage across all active jurisdictions; AI governance status across all deployed customer-facing models; data flow documentation by slot
Analyze	Regulatory change impact on specific customer contact practices; AI model output bias analysis by customer segment and protected class; third-party vendor liability allocation; litigation risk by stage and channel
Monetize	Cost of proactive compliance versus reactive remediation; customer notification cost for potential liability events; AI governance investment against estimated regulatory penalty exposure
Prioritize	Highest-liability customer stages for legal coverage; AI governance implementation sequence by risk level; jurisdiction-specific compliance requirement urgency
Optimize	Regulatory monitoring coverage and response cycle time; AI governance framework completeness; third-party contract risk profile; customer data handling audit frequency

CUSTOMER SERVICE & CONTACT CENTER

From Cost Center to Revenue Engine: AI-Powered Resolution, Prevention, and Advocacy Activation

Problems Don't Start in Customer Service — They End Up There

The most important insight the CxC Matrix has ever contributed to customer service management is this: the contacts arriving at your contact center today are the outputs of slot design decisions made weeks, months, and sometimes years earlier. The customer calling to dispute a billing charge is arriving at Stage 12 because something happened — or failed to happen — at Stage 5 (Contract), Stage 10 (Closing), or Stage 11 (Use). The customer calling to return a product is arriving at Stage 13 because something failed at Stage 8 (Installation) or Stage 9 (Use onset). The customer calling to cancel is arriving at Stage 14 because Stage 11 and Stage 12 collectively failed to maintain the value proposition that justified the relationship.

AI has made this causal chain not just theoretically traceable but operationally actionable. Contact center AI platforms can now analyze the complete contact history of every customer who reaches Stage 12, identify the upstream slot failure that generated the contact with 70–85% accuracy, and feed that failure identification back to the team responsible for the upstream slot — creating a continuous improvement loop that reduces contact volume over time. Organizations that have deployed this causal analysis capability report 15–25% reductions in contact center volume within 12–18 months of implementation, not because they improved their customer service, but because they improved the upstream slots that were generating the service contacts.

Automate: Routine Resolution, Authentication, and First-Contact Handling

The automation opportunity in customer service is substantial and well-documented. AI voice and chat agents can now resolve 40–60% of routine customer contacts — password resets, order status inquiries, basic account information requests, appointment scheduling, straightforward billing inquiries — without human involvement, at sub-second response time, at any hour of the day, in any language the customer prefers. The customer satisfaction outcomes for well-designed AI agents on routine interactions are, in many documented cases, equal to or better than human agents — because the AI is always patient, always knowledgeable about the specific customer's account, and never has a bad day.

The authentication element of AI-handled contacts is particularly important in the context of Chapter 11's identity validation requirements. AI contact center authentication systems — combining voice biometrics, behavioral pattern matching, and device fingerprinting — can verify customer identity more accurately and with less friction than traditional knowledge-based authentication, while simultaneously providing better security against the AI-powered impersonation attacks that Chapter 11 documented. The authentication slot in

Stage 12 is both a security gate and a customer experience element — AI makes it possible for it to be both simultaneously rather than requiring a trade-off between them.

Innovate: Proactive Contact and Defection Prevention

The highest-value innovation in customer service is not better reactive resolution — it is proactive contact that prevents the Stage 12 interaction from being needed. Every organization's customer data contains the behavioral signals that precede defection: declining usage frequency, increasing support contact rate, comparison search behavior, reduced engagement with proactive communications, competitive geofence proximity events. An AI system that monitors these signals and activates Stage 11 proactive slots before the customer's frustration reaches the threshold that generates a Stage 12 inbound contact is not reducing customer service workload. It is preventing the CLV erosion that the Stage 12 contact represents.

Churn.io, Gainsight, and Totango have built customer success platforms specifically designed for this use case — identifying customers at risk of defection using behavioral signals and activating proactive outreach before the customer has consciously decided to leave. These platforms report 20–40% reductions in customer churn for organizations that deploy them with the discipline to act on the signals they surface. The equivalent for B2C organizations is the AI behavioral monitoring layer described in Chapter 9 — the system that detects when a customer's recency score is declining and activates the appropriate Stage 11 or Stage 14 slot before the decline becomes a defection.

Contact Type	AI Automation Level	Human Focus	Customer Yield Impact
Password reset / account access	Full AI automation — zero human involvement for standard requests	None required	*Instant resolution; zero hold time; 24/7 availability — maximum Stage 12 satisfaction at minimum cost*
Order status / delivery inquiry	Full AI with proactive pre-emption — AI alerts customer before they call	Human escalation for delivery failures requiring compensation	*Proactive Stage 7 communication reduces inbound contact volume 30–45%; converts potential complaint to trust-building moment*
Billing dispute	AI for inquiry + investigation; human for resolution judgment on complex cases	Agent empowered with full account context and resolution authority	*First-contact resolution rate improvement 20–35%; Stage 12 satisfaction improvement correlates with CLV retention*
Technical support — Tier 1	AI diagnosis and guided self-resolution; AI-generated knowledge base articles	Human for novel issues the AI cannot resolve	*AI self-resolution rate 45–65% for documented issue types; human effort concentrated on high-value complex problems*
Retention / cancellation request	AI detection; human retention specialist with AI-generated offer recommendation	Human executes AI-identified optimal retention offer for this customer's CLV and defection driver	*Retention rate improvement 15–35% when retention specialist reaches customer with context versus cold cold call*

Advocacy activation (Stage 15)	AI identification of advocacy-ready customers; AI-generated personalized outreach content	Human relationship manager delivers advocacy invitation	*3.4x referral activation rate versus calendar-based Stage 15 outreach; 2.7x referred-customer CLV*

The outsourcing dimension of customer service requires specific attention because it represents the highest-risk customer experience handoff in most organizations' operating models. When a customer's Stage 12 contact is handled by a third-party contact center, the customer does not experience the outsourcing arrangement — they experience the quality of a conversation that they attribute entirely to your organization. Every gap between your brand standard and the outsourced contact center's execution is experienced as your failure, not theirs.

The CxC Matrix provides the governance infrastructure to manage outsourced contact centers to customer outcome standards rather than activity volume metrics. SLAs defined at the slot level — with customer satisfaction, first-contact resolution rate, escalation rate, and Stage-advance rate as the performance measures — create accountability for customer outcomes that call volume and handle time metrics cannot achieve. AI monitoring of outsourced contact recordings, connected to your quality measurement framework and reported against customer yield targets, gives you the visibility into outsourced performance that you need to manage it effectively.

Visualize	Individual customer paths through Stage 12–15; aggregate contact pattern analysis revealing upstream slot failures; AI agent performance versus human agent performance by contact type; outsourced contact center performance by customer outcome metric
Analyze	Root cause attribution for Stage 12 contacts to upstream slot design failures; AI resolution capability by contact type; defection signal pattern analysis; advocacy readiness identification
Monetize	Cost per contact by resolution channel; revenue saved per Stage 12–13 successful recovery; CLV impact of first-contact resolution versus repeat contact; Stage 15 activation revenue from AI-timed advocacy outreach
Prioritize	Upstream slot redesign by contact volume and CLV impact; AI automation deployment by contact type resolution rate; human agent focus on highest-CLV customer contacts and complex resolution scenarios
Optimize	AI agent resolution rate; first-contact resolution rate; hold time elimination through proactive pre-emption; defection prevention rate; Stage 15 advocacy activation conversion; outsourced partner customer yield performance

CUSTOMER RELATIONSHIP MANAGEMENT

From Investment Without Outcome to the AI-Powered System That Changes Every Contact

The $150 Million Question — What Changed for the Customer?

The CRM failure pattern documented in Customer Worthy's original edition has proven remarkably durable across the decade and a half since publication: organizations invest hundreds of millions in CRM technology, implementation, and consulting, and then discover that their customer satisfaction scores have not improved, their customer defection rates have not declined, and their frontline employees cannot articulate what is different about the customer experience as a result of the investment. The reason, Customer Worthy argued, is that the question no one asks before a CRM implementation is the only question that matters: what will be different the next time a customer makes a phone call? What will they experience differently when they visit the website, open an envelope, or use the product?

That question has not changed. What has changed is the sophistication with which AI-powered CRM systems can answer it — and the accountability infrastructure that the CxC Matrix creates for ensuring that the answer is not theoretical. A CRM implementation evaluated against the Matrix produces a deliverable that is specific, measurable, and customer-visible:

this contact point will change in this way, for these customer segments, at this lifecycle stage, producing this estimated improvement in customer outcome. An implementation that cannot produce that statement before it goes live has no basis for claiming customer improvement after it does.

Automate: Data Synchronization, Activity Logging, and Routine Personalization

The most expensive form of CRM waste is the manual data entry burden that prevents salespeople, service agents, and relationship managers from focusing on customer interactions. Salesforce's Einstein Activity Capture, Microsoft Dynamics' AI-assisted CRM, and similar tools now automate the logging of customer interactions — scanning email, calendar, and communication records to update CRM records without human input. Studies of organizations that have deployed these tools report 30–40% reductions in time spent on CRM data entry by customer-facing roles, which translates directly to more time available for customer conversations.

The personalization automation opportunity builds on the CDP foundation: when the CRM has access to the complete behavioral profile from the CDP, the personalization it can deliver at every contact point — the right name, the right account history, the right product recommendation, the right communication tone — is genuinely individual rather than segment-level. This is the realization of CRM's original promise: a system that knows the customer. The technology that makes it possible is not the CRM itself — it is the CDP that feeds it, the

AI that interprets its data, and the CxC Matrix that defines which contacts benefit most from that intelligence.

Innovate: The 83 Empty Cells

The whiteboard moment in Customer Worthy's CRM chapter — where the IT leader put X's in four cells of the 90-cell Matrix and the rest of the room stared at 86 empty ones — remains the most useful diagnostic for CRM investment evaluation in any organization. Today, the question is not which four cells the CRM initiative touched. It is: across all 90 cells, which ones are now instrumented with AI, which have automated slot execution, which have continuous performance optimization, and which are still operating the way they operated before the last CRM investment?

The innovation opportunity is the systematic expansion of CRM intelligence across the full Matrix. Most organizations have reasonable coverage in Stages 1–6 (the sales funnel) and Stage 12 (support). Stages 7–11 (the use and loyalty stages) and Stages 13–15 (repair, renewal, and advocacy) are typically underinstructed and underperforming relative to their CLV impact. The CRM innovation agenda is not the next version of the sales pipeline tool — it is the deployment of relationship intelligence across the stages where most CLV is either built or destroyed.

DRUCKER'S TWO FUNCTIONS — AI REALIZED

Peter Drucker's dictum — 'The business has two and only two basic functions: marketing and innovation' — maps directly onto the CxC Matrix's organizing principle for this chapter: automate what works, and spend your time innovating what doesn't.

Today, 'marketing' in Drucker's sense — the function of creating and keeping a customer — is what the CxC Matrix operationalizes across all 15 lifecycle stages and all channel containers. The AI systems that execute the Matrix's slot designs are marketing in its most disciplined, most measurable, most continuously improving form.

'Innovation' in Drucker's sense — the function of discovering and building what customers will value next — is what happens when the automation of known-good slot designs frees the organization's best human talent from execution tasks. The marketing strategist who is no longer manually segmenting lists has time to identify an unserved customer need. The contact center agent who is no longer handling password resets has time to develop the empathy-intensive recovery protocols that distinguish great service from adequate service.

CRM, in this framework, is not a system. It is the organizational capability to fulfill both of Drucker's functions simultaneously — automating the marketing that works and creating the space for the innovation that doesn't yet.

Visualize	Total customer experience across all 90 Matrix cells; CRM coverage gap analysis — which stages are instrumented versus dark; customer handling and communication procedure documentation by stage
Analyze	Resource allocation across customer lifecycle; Stage 7–11 CLV impact relative to CRM investment concentration; cross-sell and up-sell opportunity identification by behavioral signal; customer defection point attribution
Monetize	Customer activity cost per stage; CRM investment ROI measured by CLV improvement per stage covered; opportunity cost of uninstrumented stages; revenue recovery from Stage 13–14 improvement
Prioritize	Matrix cells with highest CLV impact and lowest current CRM coverage; AI orchestration deployment sequence across stages; data quality improvement for highest-revenue stages first
Optimize	CRM data completeness and recency; personalization accuracy by customer segment; Stage 7–11 proactive contact effectiveness; cross-sell and up-sell conversion by stage; Stage 15 advocacy activation from CRM-identified signals

MARKETING

AI-Powered Creative Intelligence, Treatment Map Automation, and the Best Story Wins Principle

Marketing Feeds Every Slot — And AI Has Made Every Slot Improvable

The Treatment Map — the most granular level of the CxC Matrix, mapping the messages, offers, and rules executed at each slot in each customer contact — is marketing's operational responsibility. Every slot in the Matrix has a marketing dimension: what does the customer see, hear, or read at this moment? What action are they invited to take? What story is this contact telling about who your organization is and what value it offers? These are not brand questions — they are revenue questions. The slot that tells the wrong story, or tells the right story at the wrong moment, or tells a story the customer cannot connect to their current need, is losing revenue as surely as a broken checkout button.

The challenge that marketing has always faced — and that Customer Worthy documented with the observation about teams of 2–3 copywriters scaling to 20–30 per line of business to meet the content demands of multi-channel, multi-stage customer engagement — is that content production has historically been the constraint on slot optimization. You cannot test 50 versions of a message if you can only produce 3. You cannot personalize at the individual level if you can only write at the segment level. AI has removed this constraint. An organization with a well-structured content library and an AI generation capability can now produce, test, and refine content at the individual level, across every slot in the Matrix, at a speed and scale that was economically impossible five years ago.

Automate: Content Production, A/B Testing, and Channel Optimization

AI content generation — using large language models fine-tuned on your brand voice, your product knowledge, and your customer data — is now capable of producing email subject lines, body copy, social posts, ad creative, landing page content, and personalized offer configurations at a scale and speed that human creative teams cannot match. Adobe Firefly, Canva AI, Jasper, and copy.ai represent the accessible consumer tier of this capability; Salesforce Marketing Cloud Einstein, Adobe Experience Cloud AI, and custom-deployed foundation models represent the enterprise tier. Organizations that have deployed AI content generation report 60–80% reductions in content production time and — critically — improvements in content performance, because AI can test more variants simultaneously than human teams can produce.

The Continuous and Automatic Selling (CAS) principle that Customer Worthy introduced — constantly testing current slot elements against challengers until the challenger outperforms the base — is now natively implemented in AI marketing platforms. The question is no longer whether to run CAS. It is how broadly across the Matrix you have deployed it, and how deeply the CEA behavioral data informs the challenger design. A CAS system that tests email subject lines is useful. A CAS system that tests the complete slot design — message, offer, channel, timing, and personalization depth — against the CEA's behavioral predictions for specific customer segments is the foundation of the Best Story Wins capability that Customer Worthy's most successful CEO implemented.

Innovate: The AI Content Intelligence Layer

The innovation opportunity for marketing is the AI Content Intelligence Layer — a system that not only generates and tests content, but learns from every customer response to every piece of content at the individual level, building a continuously improving model of what messages resonate with which customers at which lifecycle stages through which channels. This is not segment-level learning. It is individual-level learning: the system knows that this specific customer responds to feature-forward messaging in the morning through email and to social-proof messaging in the evening through push notification, and it adjusts the content design at the slot level accordingly.

The Best Story Wins principle — the organizing philosophy of Customer Worthy's most successful CEO example — finds its fullest expression in this AI Content Intelligence Layer. When every customer interaction is an opportunity to learn what story works, and when AI can extract those learnings from millions of interactions simultaneously and apply them to the next contact within milliseconds, the competitive advantage of the organization that has built this capability compounds continuously.

The organization that cannot tell which stories are working cannot improve them. The organization that knows which stories are working — at the individual customer level, in real time — cannot be caught by competitors who are still learning at the segment level, on a quarterly reporting cycle.

Marketing Function	Current AI Capability	Automate This	Innovate This
Content creation	LLM-powered copy generation, image generation, video scripting	High-volume personalized content: email variations, social posts, ad copy, landing pages by segment and stage	*Brand narrative architecture: the strategic story framework that AI instances execute; brand voice training of AI models*
Campaign management	AI bid optimization, channel allocation, attribution modeling	Media budget allocation by conversion probability; audience targeting by CEA score; real-time bid adjustment	*Cross-stage campaign architecture: campaigns that span Stage 1–15 with AI-governed handoffs between lifecycle stages*
Segmentation	AI behavioral clustering; propensity model scoring; predictive segment migration	Dynamic segment assignment updated daily from behavioral signals; CEA-weighted contact prioritization	*Micro-segment discovery: AI identification of customer clusters with distinct behavioral patterns not visible in traditional demographic segmentation*
Offer management	AI offer personalization engines; dynamic pricing; bundle configuration	Real-time offer assembly from component libraries based on CEA score, propensity window, and behavioral signals	*Anticipatory offer design: AI identification of customer need-states before they are articulated and offer construction to meet them*

Performance measurement	AI attribution modeling; incrementality testing; CLV impact analysis	Automated daily performance reporting with anomaly flagging and root cause attribution	*CEA-integrated performance forecasting: AI prediction of next-30-day campaign performance based on current customer behavioral signals*

The departmental partnership dimension of marketing's CxC Matrix role is worth emphasis. Marketing does not manage slot content in isolation — it manages it in collaboration with every department whose actions and decisions create the context that the slot content addresses. A Stage 12 (Support) email slot that is designed with input from customer service intelligence about the most common failure drivers is materially more effective than one designed from marketing assumptions. A Stage 14 (Renewal) contact that is designed with input from the CEA's behavioral signals for at-risk customers is materially more effective than a promotional email written to a segment definition.

The Treatment Map is the operational instrument for this collaboration. When the Treatment Map is maintained as a living document — updated with actual performance data from every slot, annotated with root cause analysis from customer service, informed by CEA scoring from the AI orchestration layer, and governed by a regular cross-functional review — it becomes the playbook that Customer Worthy always intended it to be: not a static design document but an organizational learning system that continuously improves every slot in the Matrix.

Visualize	Brand exposure frequency and quality by customer segment; competitor messaging strategy analysis; treatment performance by slot, stage, and channel; AI content generation volume and quality metrics
Analyze	Content variant performance by customer segment and CEA score; channel allocation efficiency; offer response rate by stage and product combination; Treatment Map coverage gaps across Matrix cells
Monetize	Content production cost reduction from AI generation; incremental revenue from CAS-optimized slots; CLV impact of Stage 15 advocacy activation from AI-timed referral content; brand impression quality measurement
Prioritize	High-CLV stage slot content optimization first; CAS deployment sequence by revenue impact; AI content generation investment against human creative capacity; Treatment Map coverage expansion priority
Optimize	Content production cycle time; slot performance improvement velocity; CAS challenger win rate; AI model content quality scores; cross-stage campaign continuity; Treatment Map update frequency and coverage

PRODUCT DEVELOPMENT & INNOVATION

Embedding Customer Intelligence in the Design Process — AI as Your Continuous Customer Research Engine

The Product That Knows What the Customer Needs Before They Ask

Product development has historically operated on a cycle that is structurally misaligned with customer reality: research a customer need, design a product to address it, build the product, test it with customers, launch it, and discover — six to eighteen months after the research was conducted — whether the product actually solves the problem the research identified. The gap between customer insight and market delivery has always been the fundamental risk of product development. In industries where customer needs evolve faster than product development cycles, the risk of arriving with the right answer to a question the customer is no longer asking is not hypothetical. It is the dominant failure mode.

AI and the behavioral data infrastructure of the CxC Matrix change the research-to-design loop in ways that are now operational rather than aspirational. When every stage of the customer lifecycle generates continuous behavioral data — what features customers use and which they ignore, where they encounter friction and how they work around it, what they search for that you don't offer, how their usage patterns differ from your product designers' assumptions — the research cycle compresses from months to days. The product team that is watching real-time feature adoption analytics, analyzing support contact patterns for unmet need signals, monitoring competitor review sentiment for gap identification, and tracking Stage 8–10 usage behavior at the cohort level has a continuous customer research operation running at a cost that replaces most of its periodic research budget.

Automate: Feature Performance Tracking and Customer Feedback Synthesis

Product analytics platforms — Amplitude, Mixpanel, Pendo, and their equivalents — have made automated feature adoption tracking standard practice for digital product organizations. The automation opportunity extends beyond tracking to synthesis: AI analysis of support tickets, in-app feedback, app store reviews, community forum discussions, and social media mentions can now produce weekly product intelligence summaries that identify the most common unmet needs, the features creating the most friction, and the competitor capabilities generating the most customer switching intent. Productboard and similar AI-powered product management platforms already aggregate these signals and surface them in prioritized format for product teams.

The CxC Matrix connection is direct: Stage 8 (Installation), Stage 9 (Use onset), and Stage 10 (Ongoing use) generate the richest product improvement signals in the customer lifecycle. A product team that has instrumented these stages — with embedded analytics, in-app feedback mechanisms, IoT telemetry where applicable, and AI synthesis of support contacts — has a continuous product development research operation that is more current, more specific, and more actionable than any periodic survey program.

Innovate: Embedded Intelligence and Self-Improving Products

The innovation frontier for product development is the embedded intelligence layer — software, connectivity, and AI capability built into the product itself that makes it improve continuously after delivery. Tesla's over-the-air software updates that improve vehicle performance without requiring a service visit are the canonical example, but the model extends broadly. Enterprise software that surfaces AI-generated recommendations based on how the specific organization is using it. Medical devices that adjust their operating parameters based on patient response data. Home appliances that optimize their settings based on usage pattern learning. Industrial equipment that self-diagnoses degraded performance and schedules its own maintenance.

Every product in this category is executing Stage 9 and Stage 10 improvements after the Stage 6 (Delivery) transaction is complete — continuously delivering value that the customer did not receive on day one and that competitors who have not embedded the intelligence layer cannot replicate through equivalent features. The product that gets better over time is not just more valuable to the customer. It is more defensible competitively, because the improvement is personalized to this customer's specific usage patterns in a way that cannot be replicated by a competitor who has never had access to those patterns.

AI PRODUCT DEVELOPMENT TOOLS MAPPED TO CXC MATRIX STAGES

Stage 1–3 (Awareness through Selection): AI competitive intelligence platforms — Crayon, Klue, Bombora — monitor competitor feature releases, pricing changes, and positioning shifts in real time. Product teams that use these tools to inform their Stage 1–3 slot design are responding to competitive shifts in days rather than quarters.

Stage 4–6 (Contract through Delivery): AI-powered configurator and pricing tools — Conga CPQ, Salesforce Revenue Cloud — reduce the friction of configuration complexity for buyers while ensuring margin integrity. The customer who can configure a complex product accurately without a sales rep's assistance has a better Stage 4–5 experience and a lower cost-to-acquire.

Stage 7–10 (Delivery through Ongoing Use): Pendo, Amplitude, and FullStory provide embedded product analytics that track feature adoption, identify friction points, and generate improvement hypotheses automatically. AI synthesis of Stage 8–10 behavioral data against Stage 12 support contacts reveals which product design decisions are generating service cost.

Stage 11–15 (Use through Advocacy): Product communities and user-generated content platforms — Khoros, Gainsight PX, Vanilla Forums — provide AI-synthesized voice-of-customer intelligence from Stage 11 power users that is more specific and more actionable than traditional customer advisory boards.

Visualize	Feature adoption rates by customer segment and lifecycle stage; unmet need signals from behavioral data synthesis; competitive feature gap analysis; Stage 8–10 usage pattern mapping versus design assumptions

Analyze	Feature adoption correlation with CLV and retention; support contact root cause attribution to product design decisions; competitive review sentiment for gap identification; self-improvement capability ROI versus service cost reduction
Monetize	Feature usage frequency as CLV predictor; service cost reduction from proactive product improvement; embedded intelligence premium pricing justification; competitive win rate improvement from feature gap closure
Prioritize	Feature development ranked by CLV impact; embedded intelligence investment against service cost reduction; competitive parity requirements versus differentiation opportunities
Optimize	Feature adoption rate by Stage 8–10; time-to-improvement from signal detection to product update; embedded intelligence model accuracy; product-generated Stage 15 advocacy from continuous improvement experience

SUPPLY CHAIN & PROCUREMENT

From Operational Function to Strategic Customer Experience Lever — AI-Powered Supply Chains Serve Customers, Not Just Operations

Every Supply Chain Decision Is a Customer Experience Decision

Procurement professionals and supply chain executives have historically occupied the organizational position furthest from the customer in most enterprise structures. They buy things, manage vendor relationships, and optimize costs — activities whose connection to the customer's experience is mediated through several layers of operations, manufacturing, fulfillment, and sales. This distance has allowed supply chain and procurement to optimize for metrics — unit cost, inventory turns, supplier on-time delivery — that can be achieved in ways that actually harm the customer experience without the harm being visible in the procurement scorecard.

A supplier who delivers components on time but with a defect rate that creates Stage 8 (Installation) failures has a perfect procurement SLA and a devastating customer experience record. A procurement decision that reduces packaging cost by 12% but makes the product harder to open — increasing Stage 8 friction for every customer — is a cost optimization that generates Stage 12 support contacts. A sourcing decision that selects the lowest-cost contact center outsourcer generates Stage 12 customer service performance that drives Stage 14 defection. The CxC Matrix makes these connections visible. AI makes them measurable and preventable.

Automate: Supplier Performance Monitoring and Risk Detection

AI-powered supply chain visibility platforms — o9 Solutions, Blue Yonder, Kinaxis — now provide real-time monitoring of supplier performance, inventory levels, logistics status, and risk signals across multi-tier supply chains. The automation opportunity is not just efficiency — it is customer experience protection. When an AI system detects that a key component supplier in Stage 6 of the manufacturing supply chain has a 72-hour delivery delay developing, and automatically triggers both an alternative sourcing evaluation and a customer communication protocol for affected Stage 7 deliveries, it has converted a supply chain disruption into a managed customer experience rather than an unmanaged one.

Procurement automation extends to the negotiation and contract management dimensions. AI-powered contract lifecycle management systems — Ironclad, Icertis, Coupa — track supplier contract performance against defined terms, flag deviations automatically, and generate renegotiation recommendations based on actual performance data. The procurement team that is managing supplier contracts against customer outcome metrics — rather than against the activity SLAs that most contracts define — is negotiating fundamentally different agreements than one that is not.

Innovate: Customer-Value-Weighted Supplier Selection

The procurement innovation opportunity is the redesign of supplier selection and performance frameworks around customer value contribution rather than cost and compliance metrics. This requires connecting the CxC Matrix's CLV data to the procurement scorecard: which suppliers' performance most directly affects the experience of the highest-CLV customer segments, and what is the revenue consequence of their performance gaps?

An industrial manufacturer that analyzed its Stage 7–8 warranty claim data by supplier of origin discovered that components from a specific supplier — competitive on price, compliant on delivery — were responsible for 38% of all warranty claims despite representing only 11% of component volume. The warranty cost plus the CLV cost of the customer defections generated by Stage 8 failures attributable to that supplier exceeded the cost savings from their pricing advantage by a factor of 4.7. That analysis — which required connecting procurement data, warranty claim data, customer defection data, and CLV data — is now achievable in days with AI tools that were not available three years ago. The procurement team that runs this analysis before making sourcing decisions is protecting customer value in ways that the lowest-unit-cost buyer cannot.

OUTSOURCED SERVICES — THE SUPPLIER PERFORMANCE STANDARD THAT MOST PROCUREMENT TEAMS DON'T APPLY

Every outsourcing relationship — contact center, fulfillment, repair service, field service, content production — should be evaluated on the same CxC Matrix customer outcome metrics as internal operations. The question is not 'did the outsourcer hit their SLA?' It is 'did customers who interacted with this outsourced function advance through the lifecycle stage at the same rate as those who interacted with our internal equivalent?' Organizations that apply this standard discover, consistently, that their outsourced partners' activity metric compliance is not a reliable predictor of customer outcome quality. The ones that don't apply this standard discover it when their defection rates are higher than their customer service metrics would predict.

Visualize	Multi-tier supply chain performance mapped to Stage 7–10 customer experience outcomes; supplier quality metrics correlated with Stage 12 support contact volume; outsourced service provider performance by customer yield metric
Analyze	Supplier contribution to CLV protection and erosion; cost-quality-customer tradeoff modeling for sourcing decisions; outsourcing versus in-source decision by customer outcome performance
Monetize	Total cost of supplier performance gaps including CLV erosion; warranty and return cost attribution by supplier; outsourcing yield differential valued in CLV terms
Prioritize	Supplier relationships by customer experience impact; contract renegotiation priority by customer outcome performance; sourcing diversification against Stage 7–10 risk concentration
Optimize	Supplier selection criteria to include customer outcome performance weighting; contract terms to include customer yield SLAs; real-time supplier monitoring connected to proactive Stage 7 customer communication

DATA SCIENCE & ANALYTICS

The Intelligence Engine — Building Models That Compound Customer Knowledge Into Competitive Advantage

From Reporting to Prediction to Prescription — The Analytics Maturity That Produces Customer Yield

Data science and analytics occupies a peculiar organizational position in most companies: universally acknowledged as strategically important, chronically under-resourced, frequently misaligned with the business problems it could solve, and often delivering outputs that are insightful but not actionable. The CxC Matrix provides the business architecture that analytics needs to be consequential: a defined set of customer outcome questions — what drives Stage-to-Stage advancement? what predicts defection? what behavioral signals precede advocacy? — against which every analytical capability can be directed and every model can be evaluated.

The maturity journey for analytics teams in the CxC Matrix context follows a well-documented progression: Descriptive analytics (what happened?), Diagnostic analytics (why did it happen?), Predictive analytics (what will happen?), Prescriptive analytics (what should we do about it?). Most organizations have reasonable descriptive capability and developing diagnostic capability. The competitive advantage lies in predictive and prescriptive analytics — and the distance between where most organizations are and where the leaders are on this progression has widened significantly in the past three years as AI model deployment costs have dropped and the tools for building, deploying, and monitoring predictive models have matured.

Automate: Standard Reporting, Data Quality, and Model Monitoring

The automation of standard business reporting — weekly dashboards, monthly performance summaries, quarterly customer cohort analyses — is among the most valuable productivity investments a data science team can make, because it frees analyst capacity for the predictive and prescriptive work that dashboards cannot do. Tools like Tableau, Power BI with AI Insights, and Looker with AI-generated narratives now produce management-quality reporting from structured data sources automatically, with AI-generated explanations of variance and anomaly flagging built in. The analyst who was spending 30% of their time producing reports that could be generated automatically is an analyst who can now spend 30% more time building the churn prediction model or the CLV forecasting algorithm that actually moves business results.

Data quality automation is equally valuable and equally underinvested. AI-powered data quality tools — Informatica AI, Collibra, Monte Carlo — continuously monitor data pipelines for completeness, consistency, and accuracy, flagging data quality issues before they propagate into model inputs and produce misleading outputs. For the CxC Matrix specifically, data quality in the CDP is the foundation of CEA model accuracy. An organization with a high-quality CDP produces better CEA scores, which drive better slot activation decisions, which produce better customer outcomes. Data quality is not a technical nicety. It is a customer experience performance driver.

Innovate: The Customer Propensity and CLV Prediction Stack

The analytical innovation that produces the highest customer yield return is the customer propensity and CLV prediction stack: a family of AI models that collectively answer the questions that govern every slot activation decision in the CxC Matrix. Which customers are most likely to purchase in the next 30 days? Which are most likely to defect in the next 90 days? Which have the highest probability of becoming Stage 15 advocates? Which cross-sell offers have the highest probability of acceptance for this specific customer at this specific lifecycle stage? How much CLV is at risk in the current defection-risk cohort, and what is the expected CLV recovery from each intervention option?

These models are not theoretical. They are deployed and operational at organizations of every size. Pecan AI and DataRobot have democratized predictive model building to the point where analysts without deep ML expertise can produce accurate churn, propensity, and CLV models from existing customer data in days rather than months. The investment is no longer in building the technical capability — it is in building the organizational capability to act on model outputs at the slot level. A churn prediction model that identifies 2,300 at-risk customers but cannot trigger a Stage 14 retention slot for those customers has zero business impact. The data science team's innovation agenda is not just better models. It is better integration of model outputs with the operational systems that execute the CxC Matrix slots.

Analytical Capability	AI Tool Category	CxC Matrix Application	Business Impact
Churn prediction	Gradient boosting models, neural networks trained on behavioral signals	Activates Stage 14 retention slots for customers whose behavioral pattern matches historical defection trajectories	*15–35% reduction in voluntary churn; CLV recovery from retained customers 4–8x intervention cost*
CLV forecasting	Regression models on RFM + propensity signals; Bayesian lifetime value models	CEA score weighting; slot investment calibration by customer CLV tier; budget allocation by expected return	*Investment allocation precision: highest-value slots receive proportional budget without over-investing in low-CLV segments*
Next-best-action recom-mendation	Reinforcement learning models optimized for Stage advancement; contextual bandits for offer selection	Governs which slot fires for which customer at which moment across all 15 stages	*40–65% improvement in contact conversion rate versus rule-based slot assignment, continuous self-improvement from outcome feedback*
Sentiment and emotion analysis	Large language models fine-tuned on support interaction data	Real-time escalation triggers in Stage 12; defection risk identification from support sentiment trajectory	*Early defection signal detection 3–6 weeks before customer cancellation: intervention success rate 2.4x higher than post-defection outreach*

Anomaly detection	Isolation forests, autoencoders for behavioral outlier identification	Fraud detection across payment stages; service anomaly alerts for Stage 7–10; early indicator of emerging product quality issues	*Fraud cost reduction; Stage 12 contact volume reduction through proactive anomaly resolution; product quality intervention before warranty cliff*
Attribution modeling	Multi-touch attribution using Markov chains or Shapley values	Marketing spend allocation by Stage-contribution to CLV; channel ROI calculation accounting for full lifecycle impact	*Marketing budget reallocation from last-click attribution to CLV-contribution attribution reduces wasted spend 20–40%*

The organizational challenge for data science is not primarily technical — it is political and operational. Model outputs compete with executive intuition, departmental precedent, and established budget processes. The data science team that can demonstrate, in business terms, the CLV impact of a specific model's recommendations — and that has built the organizational connections to translate model outputs into slot-level actions — is the team that gets its recommendations implemented. The team that produces technically excellent models that sit in dashboards without affecting operational decisions is, from a business impact perspective, indistinguishable from a team that doesn't exist.

The CxC Matrix solves this organizational problem by providing the business architecture that makes model outputs actionable. When the churn model's output is not 'here is a list of at-risk customers' but 'here is the Stage 14 slot activation trigger for the 847 customers whose behavioral scores have crossed the defection threshold' — with the Stage 14 slot design already defined, the content library already assembled, the channel preference already known from the CDP, and the contact authorization already established in the governance process — the distance between analytical insight and customer impact is measured in minutes, not months.

Visualize	Model performance dashboard across all deployed CEA components; data quality metrics by CDP source system; analytical coverage of CxC Matrix stages — which stages have predictive models, which are dark
Analyze	Model accuracy by customer segment and lifecycle stage; CLV impact of model-governed versus rule-based slot activation; A/B test design and analysis for CAS challenger programs; attribution analysis across Stage-contribution to CLV
Monetize	Incremental CLV from model-governed slot activation versus baseline; churn reduction CLV recovery; cross-sell lift from next-best-action recommendation; fraud prevention value
Prioritize	Model development sequence by CLV impact per stage; data quality investment by highest-revenue data source; analytical tool investment by capability gap versus competitive requirement
Optimize	Model accuracy over time through retraining pipelines; prediction-to-action latency; data quality score by CDP source; analytical team capacity allocation between automation and innovation

PARTNER & CHANNEL MANAGEMENT

Extending the CxC Matrix Across Your Ecosystem — AI-Governed Partner Performance and Channel Intelligence

Your Partners Are Your Customer Experience — Whether You've Designed It That Way or Not

Every customer who reaches your product or service through a partner, reseller, distributor, affiliate, or channel intermediary is experiencing your organization through a third-party lens. The partner's sales practices, onboarding quality, support capabilities, and relationship management standards are what that customer experiences as your brand — whether or not those standards match yours. Most organizations manage this reality through contractual requirements, periodic training, and occasional mystery shopping. The gap between what the contract requires and what the customer actually experiences through the channel is, in most organizations, both large and systematically unmeasured.

The CxC Matrix provides the architecture for closing that gap. Every stage of the customer lifecycle that is executed by or through a partner channel can be instrumented with the same slot design standards, the same Nine Objectives, and the same customer outcome metrics that govern your direct channels. The partner that consistently produces lower Stage 5–6 conversion rates, higher Stage 12 support contact volumes, and higher Stage 14 defection rates for the customers they onboard is not a partner problem — it is a channel design problem. And it is solvable with the same tools that solve it in direct channels.

Automate: Partner Performance Monitoring and Enablement

Partner relationship management platforms — Alliances, Impartner, PartnerStack, Salesforce PRM — provide the operational infrastructure for partner performance monitoring at the activity level. The AI augmentation of these platforms makes the monitoring genuinely useful: AI analysis of partner-generated customer data against direct-channel equivalent data identifies performance gaps at the stage level, surfaces them automatically, and generates coaching recommendations for the partner management team. A partner whose Stage 3 (Selection) conversion rate is 23% below the direct-channel benchmark is not necessarily underperforming — they may be serving a fundamentally different customer segment. AI analysis of the performance gap against customer segment composition reveals which part of the variance is addressable and which is structural.

Partner enablement automation is equally valuable. AI-generated training content, customized to the partner's specific performance gaps and the products their customer base most commonly purchases, replaces generic training programs with personalized learning paths. Highspot, Seismic, and similar platforms deliver AI-curated content to partner sales teams based on the specific deal context they are working — replacing static playbooks with dynamic recommendations that reflect current product updates, competitive positioning changes, and performance intelligence from similar deals.

Innovate: The Partner Intelligence Network

The innovation opportunity in partner management is the Partner Intelligence Network — a system that connects partner-generated customer data with your CDP, your CEA scoring engine, and your slot activation system to enable genuinely consistent customer experiences across direct and indirect channels. When a customer who was onboarded by a partner contacts your direct support channel, the Stage 12 agent should see the same customer context — the complete lifecycle history, the current CEA score, the propensity window — as if the customer had been acquired directly. When a customer's behavior signals defection risk, the Stage 14 intervention should activate regardless of whether the customer's primary relationship is through a partner or through a direct channel.

This is technically more complex than direct-channel orchestration — it requires partner API integrations, data sharing agreements, and potentially new partner contract terms that grant your organization access to customer behavioral data generated through the partner interaction. It is also, for organizations with significant channel dependency, the highest-leverage CX investment available. Organizations that have built these data-sharing partnerships with their top tier channel partners report that customer CLV through the partner channel approaches direct-channel CLV within 18–24 months of full data integration — primarily because the proactive Stage

11–14 interventions that protect CLV in direct channels can now fire for partner-channel customers as well.

AI-POWERED PARTNER ECOSYSTEM TOOLS AND THEIR CXC MATRIX APPLICATIONS

PartnerStack / Impartner (PRM): Partner recruitment, onboarding, and performance tracking. AI integration surfaces performance outliers and generates coaching recommendations. CxC Matrix application: Stage 1–6 partner-channel performance monitoring against direct-channel benchmark.

Highspot / Seismic (Partner Enablement): AI-curated content delivery to partner sellers based on deal context, customer segment, and competitive situation. CxC Matrix application: Stage 3–5 slot quality improvement through context-appropriate content delivery to partner reps.

Crossbeam / Reveal (Partner Intelligence): B2B account mapping tools that identify shared accounts between partners, enabling coordinated customer experience design. CxC Matrix application: Identifying where a customer is simultaneously in multiple partner relationships and designing coordinated Stage 11–15 experiences.

Salesforce PRM with Einstein: AI-powered lead distribution to partners based on CEA-predicted conversion probability, geographic coverage, and partner capability profile. CxC Matrix application: Stage 2–4 lead quality improvement through intelligent partner routing.

Custom CDP-Partner API Integration: The most advanced partner intelligence implementation — real-time behavioral data sharing between partner systems and organizational CDP, enabling CEA scoring and slot activation for partner-channel customers identical to direct-channel customers.

Visualize	Partner channel customer lifecycle performance versus direct channel equivalent; partner capability coverage across CxC Matrix stages; channel conflict and gap identification; partner-generated customer CLV distribution
Analyze	Partner performance gap root cause by stage and customer segment; enablement program impact on partner-channel Stage conversion rates; data sharing integration feasibility and ROI by partner tier
Monetize	Channel revenue contribution weighted by customer CLV; partner-channel CLV versus direct-channel CLV differential; enablement program ROI measured by partner-channel Stage conversion improvement
Prioritize	Top-tier partner CDP integration by CLV concentration; performance gap intervention by revenue impact; enablement investment by partner revenue potential versus performance gap size
Optimize	Partner-channel Stage conversion rates toward direct-channel benchmark; partner data integration completeness; enablement content relevance scores; Partner Intelligence Network coverage of total partner-channel CLV

The Enterprise That Learns Faster Than Its Competitors — The Compounding Advantage

Customer ignorance is not a neutral organizational state. It is an expensive one. Organizations that do not know their customers — that cannot connect their internal decisions to customer outcomes, cannot predict which customers are approaching defection, cannot identify which slots are losing revenue, and cannot direct their innovation investment toward the customer needs that are not yet being met — are making all of these mistakes simultaneously, at full cost, every day. The accumulation of those mistakes is what makes customer defection rates stubbornly high, acquisition costs stubbornly escalating, and competitive differentiation stubbornly elusive.

The CxC Matrix with AI orchestration is the instrument that ends that ignorance — not by generating more data, but by connecting existing data to decisions, decisions to actions, and actions to customer outcomes in a causal chain that every manager in every department can see. When the finance team can see that a proposed cost reduction in Stage 12 will increase Stage 14 defection probability by 18% among Tier 1 customers, they make a different decision than when they cannot see it. When the operations team can see that their outsourced fulfillment partner's Stage 7 performance is 12% below internal benchmark for the top CLV quartile, they negotiate a different contract than when they are managing to an activity SLA. When the marketing team can see that their best-performing Stage 3 content produces a 23% higher Stage 5 conversion rate among customers who have also experienced a geofence proximity event in the prior 14 days, they allocate their AI content generation budget differently than when they are optimizing at the segment level.

The compounding advantage is not any single one of these improvements. It is all of them, simultaneously, continuously, learning from each other. The organization that has deployed the CxC Matrix with enterprise AI orchestration is not operating on a quarterly improvement cycle. It is operating on a continuous improvement cycle — one where every customer interaction teaches the system something, and every teaching improves the next interaction, for every customer, across every stage, in every channel. The competitors who are not doing this are not standing still — they are falling behind at the rate at which the learning organization is accelerating.

> ***"Customer ignorance is not an option. Companies that lack customer performance knowledge and foresight will expensively pursue the wrong customers with the wrong messages delivered at the wrong time through the wrong channels. The CxC Matrix — with AI as its execution engine — is the architecture that makes customer ignorance a choice rather than a condition. Choose differently."***

The Customer Experience Algorithm — From Vision to Operational Reality

Customer Worthy's original edition introduced the Customer Experience Algorithm as a future vision: a customer-centric formula that would configure messages, activities, and transactions to ensure customer convenience and optimal service. In that edition, the CEA was described as 'particularly useful in depicting customer contact scenarios as simulations' — a planning and analytical tool rather than an operational one. The gap between 'particularly useful in simulations' and 'running in real time at every customer contact' was primarily a technology gap: the data infrastructure, the computational speed, and the AI modeling capability to execute the CEA at the slot level in real time did not yet exist at accessible cost.

That gap is closed. The CEA described in Chapter 9 of this edition — combining Recency, Frequency, and Monetary value with propensity windows across 30, 60, 90, and 180-day horizons, weighted by brand exposure signals, segmented into five customer profiles, and connected to physical intelligence layer inputs from RFID, geofencing, and proximity sensing — is operational today for organizations that have built the CDP foundation and AI orchestration infrastructure that this chapter's IT section describes. It is not cheap. It is not simple. But it is the difference between an organization that manages its customers and an organization that serves them with precision.

Neil's story — the opening scene of Customer Worthy where his car received a message from the recreation commission, recognized his family vehicle's registration, authenticated the transaction through the proximity of his phone and laptop, and completed the payment in the time it took him to say 'confirm' — was prescient rather than fantastical. Today, Apple Pay, Google Wallet, connected vehicle platforms, and smart home payment systems are all operational approximations of Neil's experience. The device-to-device intelligence, the ambient authentication, the frictionless transaction completion — these are not emerging capabilities. They are installed in hundreds of millions of consumer devices. The question is not whether this experience is possible. It is whether your organization's CxC Matrix has the slot design, the data infrastructure, and the AI orchestration to deliver it.

EVERY EMPLOYEE, PARTNER, STAKEHOLDER — THE FINAL STANDARD

Customer Worthy ends with a question and a standard. The question: is it Customer Worthy? The standard: every business decision, by every employee, partner, and stakeholder, evaluated against that single criterion.

In the AI era, that standard has both a higher ceiling and a more accessible floor than it did when the question was first posed. The ceiling is higher because the tools now exist to deliver customer experiences that are genuinely predictive, individually personalized, proactively responsive, and continuously improving — an experience that is not just Customer Worthy but optimally Customer Worthy, for this specific customer at this specific moment.

The floor is more accessible because the infrastructure — the CDP, the AI orchestration engine, the CEA scoring model, the connected intelligence layer — is now commercially available at costs that mid-market organizations can justify and deploy, not just enterprise organizations with nine-figure technology budgets.

What has not changed is the fundamental requirement: that every employee in every department understands how their decisions affect the customers who experience the consequences. The CxC Matrix is the visualization that makes that understanding possible. AI is the execution engine that makes acting on that understanding automatic, continuous, and compounding. And Customer Worthy — in this edition as in the first — is the commitment that it is possible to build an organization whose customers stay not because switching is hard, but because the experience of being served by this organization is genuinely, measurably, and continuously the best available.

Chapter 12 Action Plan — Building the Enterprise That Automates What Works and Innovates What Doesn't

PHASE 1 (MONTHS 1-3): ESTABLISH THE FOUNDATION

Conduct the CxC Matrix enterprise audit described throughout this chapter — mapping current slot coverage, identifying uninstrumented stages, and documenting the customer data flows between departments. Prioritize CDP procurement or build if not in place. Assign cross-functional ownership of the Matrix Treatment Map with representatives from every department covered in this chapter. Define customer outcome metrics for each function — the customer yield measurement that each department will be held accountable for improving.

PHASE 2 (MONTHS 3-9): AUTOMATE THE KNOWN

Deploy AI automation in the highest-CLV, highest-volume contact points first: Stage 12 routine resolution, Stage 7 proactive delivery communication, Stage 1–3 lead scoring and adaptive sequence. Implement AI anomaly detection for finance and operations. Deploy AI workforce management for contact center scheduling. Automate content generation for the highest-traffic marketing slots. In each case, measure the automation's customer yield impact within 30 days of deployment and report it to the executive team.

PHASE 3 (MONTHS 9–18): OPERATIONALIZE THE CEA

Build or procure the RFM + propensity scoring model that powers the Customer Experience Algorithm. Integrate CEA scores with the CDP, the AI orchestration engine, and the Treatment Map. Deploy CEA-governed slot activation at Stages 11, 14, and 15 — the three stages with the highest CLV impact and the most consistent underinvestment. Measure Stage 15 advocacy activation rate improvement within 90 days. Feed results into the CEA model retraining pipeline.

PHASE 4 (ONGOING): INNOVATE THE FRONTIER

With automation handling the known, direct your best human talent to the innovation agenda: the unserved customer needs the behavioral data reveals but the current product portfolio doesn't address; the slot designs that could exist but haven't been built; the partner ecosystem that could extend your customer value proposition into adjacent need-states. Define a customer experience innovation process with the same rigor as a product development process — with stage gates, resource allocation, customer testing, and CEA-measured success criteria. This is what 'Best Story Wins' looks like as an institutional capability rather than a CEO personality trait.

CLOSING CHAPTER

The Customer Sensor Horizon

How the Next Generation of Customer Experience Will Rewire Competition, Compress Time, and Make Every Interaction a Platform for Value Creation

A Synthesis of the Customer Sensor Economy, the CxC Matrix 2.0, and the Strategic Imperative for Leaders Who Refuse to Be Disrupted

---

> *"In 2030, a Tesla owner's car autonomously negotiated a tire replacement with Goodyear's AI agent while rerouting to a Walmart+ hub for curbside pickup — all before the human driver noticed the low-pressure alert. This is the new battlefield."*
>
> **— Customer Worthy: Customer Sensor, Preface**

> *"The future belongs to businesses that script the next interaction for each customer — for the customer's best outcome and the company's best outcome — assembled*

physics. The assumption that customers initiate contact is one such principle. The assumption that the marketing message precedes the purchase decision is another. The assumption that customer experience is something that happens between a person and a company, mediated by a human or digital interface, in a sequence the company designs and the customer navigates — this assumption is the one that the Customer Sensor economy has irrevocably broken.

The break did not happen all at once. It happened in layers, each one compressing the time between customer need and customer fulfillment, each one expanding the definition of what a 'customer interaction' means. The first layer was digital commerce — the ability to find, evaluate, and purchase without leaving a chair. The second was mobile commerce — the ability to do all of that from anywhere, at any moment. The third was algorithmic commerce — the ability for systems to anticipate what you needed and present it before you searched. The fourth, the one we are entering now, is agent commerce: the ability for AI systems to need, evaluate, negotiate, purchase, and report back — on your behalf — without your active involvement at any point in the transaction.

When Neil's car, in 2030, detects a 91% probability of bearing failure, queries his calendar, negotiates with three certified repair centers, secures a loyalty discount by offering his anonymized driving data, and presents him with a single confirmation prompt — 'Front axle service scheduled for Thursday, 3pm. Estimated savings: $212. Accept?' — the customer journey that Customer Worthy's original CxC Matrix was designed to map has been compressed from days of awareness, research, selection, and negotiation into 3.2 seconds of machine processing. The fifteen stages are all still there. They are simply no longer sequential, no longer human-paced, and no longer mediated by the interfaces organizations have spent decades optimizing.

This compression is not primarily a technology story. It is a competitive physics story. Organizations that understand this — that have internalized what it means for the customer journey to become a machine-speed process in which human attention is the scarce resource rather than the primary medium — are building fundamentally different competitive architectures than those that do not. The organizations that do not understand it are optimizing their websites and their call centers for a customer behavior that is already giving way to something they have not yet begun to prepare for.

> ***"74% of Americans experienced a product or service problem in the past year — the highest level ever recorded. Customer rage has tripled since 2020. Yet simultaneously, companies earning $1 billion annually can gain an additional $700 million within three years of investing***

> ***in customer experience improvements. The gap between those who build for what customers need and those who don't has never been wider."***

II. The Four Domains of Customer Reality — Where Your Customer Actually Lives

The most powerful diagnostic question a senior leader can ask of their customer experience architecture is not 'where do customers buy from us?' It is 'in which domains of reality does our customer currently exist — and in which of those domains have we built the capability to serve them?' The answer, for most organizations, is unsettling. Most companies have built for one domain. Their customer is simultaneously in four.

The Four Domains framework — Physical Reality, Digital Reality, Hybrid/Enhanced Reality, and Synthetic Reality — is not a technology taxonomy. It is a description of the simultaneous states in which every customer of every organization currently exists, and through which the most consequential interactions of the next decade will flow. Understanding the distinct characteristics, competitive requirements, and strategic implications of each domain is the prerequisite for building the Customer Sensor architecture that serves customers across all four.

FIGURE C.1 — THE FOUR DOMAINS OF CUSTOMER REALITY: CHARACTERISTICS AND STRATEGIC IMPERATIVES

Domain	Customer Reality	Strategic Imperative
Physical Reality	Analog, sensed, emotionally anchored. Time is sequential; space is specific. Customers carry emotional memory from past interactions into every future contact. The most powerful trust-building and trust-destroying domain — because consequences are real, immediate, and felt.	*Excellence in physical domain execution cannot be compensated by digital optimization. The hospital that has a brilliant mobile app but a chaotic check-in experience has not solved its customer experience problem. Physical domain quality sets the emotional frame for every other domain interaction.*
Digital Reality	Time is flexible — simultaneous, pausable, rewindable. Space is unlimited — every screen is your store. Customers expect persistence across devices, personalization from history, and speed measured in milliseconds. Forty-seven percent of B2B purchases now begin with anonymous digital research that never surfaces in your CRM.	*The digital domain is where algorithmic discovery happens — where AI agents evaluate your offerings before any human is involved. If your digital surface is not structured for machine-readable evaluation, you are invisible to an increasing share of purchase initiation activity.*

Hybrid / Enhanced Reality	Physical and digital simultaneously present. AR overlays product information onto physical objects. Smart glasses assemble offers by combining store proximity, biometric loyalty data, wearable stress indicators, and calendar context. The menu Jennifer sees at Starbucks is not the menu on the wall — it is a seven-item quantum-optimized selection generated from 87,000+ combinations in the 0.3 seconds her gait is recognized.	*The hybrid domain is where the most disruptive customer experiences of the next decade will be delivered. Organizations that build hybrid domain capability — AR commerce, contextual AI overlays, sensor-triggered personalization — will serve customers with a precision that purely digital or purely physical competitors structurally cannot match.*
Synthetic Reality	AI agents acting on behalf of humans without real-time human involvement. Your customer's AI assistant researching, negotiating, and purchasing. Your supplier's AI agent contracting with your AI agent. Routine transactions executing without human initiation. By 2035, the majority of structured commercial purchases may be initiated by AI agents, not humans.	*The synthetic domain requires a fundamentally different commercial architecture. Your pricing structures, product information, API accessibility, trust signals, and algorithmic discoverability must be designed for machine evaluation, not just human evaluation. Companies with high algorithmic trust ratings will be preferentially selected by AI purchasing agents.*

The strategic error most organizations will make in the next three years is treating these domains as a sequence — build for digital first, then add hybrid, then eventually address synthetic. The competitive dynamic does not allow for this sequencing. Customers are already simultaneously in all four domains. Their AI agents are already evaluating organizations in the synthetic domain. The question is not when to build for each domain — it is how to build for all four simultaneously, with a unified architecture that treats the customer as a single person across all of them.

This is precisely what the CxC Matrix 2.0 is designed to enable. The original Matrix organized customer interactions by the fifteen lifecycle stages and the six channel categories. The 2.0 adds the domain layer — a third axis of the customer experience architecture that maps which domain is operative at each stage, which signals are available for perception, which AI capabilities are required for cognition, and which actuation pathways are available for delivery. The Matrix does not simplify this complexity — it makes it manageable by giving every department, every partner, and every AI system in the organization a shared language for talking about the same customer across all four domains.

III. The Customer Sensor Mesh — From IoT to Intelligence

The Internet of Things was the infrastructure layer. What is emerging now is the intelligence layer — the Customer Sensor Mesh, a network of perception, cognition, and actuation that surrounds every customer, interprets every signal, and orchestrates every response. The difference between IoT and the Customer Sensor Mesh is not one of device density. It is one of intelligence architecture.

Consider what Neil's car actually did in those 3.2 seconds. It did not simply detect a sensor reading and send an alert. It ran a causal inference across 17 million similar bearing failure cases. It consulted Neil's digital twin — his calendar, his location patterns, his service history, his financial preferences. It executed a three-way negotiation protocol with competing repair centers. It evaluated the privacy implications of offering his driving data, calculated the marginal value of the loyalty discount against the data exposure cost, and made the decision to offer the data. It generated a natural language summary that would be intelligible and reassuring to Neil. And it presented exactly one decision for his attention — the confirmation — rather than the fourteen decisions a human managing this process would have had to make.

This is the Customer Sensor Mesh in operation. Its architecture has four functional layers that map precisely to the four dimensions of the CxC Matrix 2.0.

The Perception Layer — What the Mesh Sees

The Perception Layer is the sensory nervous system of the Customer Sensor Mesh. It captures signals from every domain simultaneously: computer vision systems analyzing facial expressions and body language in the physical domain; digital footprints tracking navigation patterns and dwell times in the digital domain; AR glasses detecting glance direction, micro-expression response, and purchase impulse in the hybrid domain; AI agents monitoring preference evolution, price sensitivity signals, and competitive evaluation behavior in the synthetic domain.

The analogy to observability systems in technology infrastructure is instructive. Mature technology organizations instrument their systems to capture every relevant signal — latency, error rate, resource utilization, request patterns — and surface anomalies before they become failures. The Customer Sensor Mesh applies this observability principle to the customer relationship: instrument every interaction across every domain, capture every relevant signal, and surface the patterns that predict customer behavior before the behavior occurs. The organization that has this capability is not reacting to customer experience problems — it is anticipating and preventing them.

The Cognition Layer — What the Mesh Understands

Raw signals do not produce customer value. Intelligence does. The Cognition Layer transforms sensor data into predictive understanding using large language models that interpret natural communication, causal inference engines that identify the true drivers of customer behavior (not correlation, but causation), knowledge graphs that connect disparate signals into coherent customer context, and reinforcement learning systems that optimize for long-term customer lifetime value rather than immediate conversion.

The Cognition Layer is where the Customer Sensor Mesh transcends what any previous customer intelligence system could achieve. Traditional CRM systems knew what a customer had done. Predictive analytics systems could estimate what they might do next. The Cognition Layer of the Customer Sensor Mesh knows why — with the causal precision that makes the difference between a retention intervention that works because it addresses the actual driver of defection risk, and one that fails because it addressed a correlated symptom instead.

The Actuation Layer — What the Mesh Does

The Actuation Layer executes the Cognition Layer's prescriptions through whatever pathway is most appropriate for this customer at this moment: API and Model Context Protocol orchestration that coordinates actions across systems; augmented reality overlays that enhance the physical experience in real time; autonomous systems that execute transactions without requiring human attention; dynamic offer engines that assemble the optimal combination of price, feature, timing, and channel for this specific customer's current context.

The smart glasses that Jennifer uses at Starbucks are an Actuation Layer deployment. The seven-item menu she sees — assembled in 0.5-second refresh cycles from her gait recognition, biometric loyalty profile, wearable stress indicators, calendar context, and the store's real-time inventory — is the Actuation Layer delivering a personalized decision architecture at the exact moment of maximum relevance. The menu updates every 0.5 seconds based on her micro-reactions, adjusting position, pricing, and photography in response to her attention signals. No human could design this in real time. The Actuation Layer does it automatically, continuously, and invisibly.

The Emotion Layer — What the Mesh Remembers

The Emotion Layer is the dimension that distinguishes the Customer Sensor Mesh from every previous customer intelligence architecture, and the dimension most likely to be underinvested because it is the hardest to justify in a spreadsheet. It captures the emotional texture of customer interactions — the sentiment trajectory across the lifecycle, the memory formations that anchor loyalty or accelerate defection, the emotional states that predict response to specific message types, the psychological context that should govern the tone, urgency, and empathy coefficient of every contact.

The practical implication is significant. A customer whose wearable data indicates elevated stress arriving at a service interaction should receive a categorically different treatment than the same customer in a calm state. Not because treating stressed customers differently is a nicety — because the expected value of the interaction, measured in CLV impact, is materially different depending on whether the Emotion Layer informs the Actuation Layer's treatment design. Organizations that build Emotion Layer capability will consistently produce interactions whose measured CLV impact is higher than those that do not, for the same product, at the same price, in the same channel.

THE CUSTOMER SENSOR MESH DIAGNOSTIC — FOUR QUESTIONS FOR EVERY ORGANIZATION

1. PERCEPTION: Can you detect customer signals from all four domains in real time? Not from quarterly surveys. Not from monthly analytics reports. In real time — as behavioral events occur, across every channel and every domain where your customers currently interact with you or with agents acting on their behalf.

2. COGNITION: Can you interpret those signals causally — identifying not just what customers did but why? And can you do it at the speed required to inform the next interaction before the customer has moved on? The organization with a 48-hour analytics cycle is not competing with the organization whose Cognition Layer processes the same signals in 0.3 seconds.

3. ACTUATION: Can you deliver personalized interventions through every domain and channel where customers are active — including the synthetic domain where AI agents are evaluating your offerings? If your products and services cannot be discovered, evaluated, and purchased by an AI agent, you are invisible to an increasingly large share of purchase initiation activity.

4. EMOTION: Do you know how your customers feel about their interactions with you — not from surveys administered weeks after the fact, but from the real-time emotional signals your Customer Sensor Mesh captures during the interaction itself? And does that emotional context inform the treatment design for every subsequent interaction in the same session?

IV. The CxC Matrix 2.0 — From Grid to Operating System

The original CxC Matrix was a map. A powerful map — the first framework that gave every function of an enterprise a shared visual language for the customer experience across all fifteen lifecycle stages and all channel categories. But a map is static. It depicts a terrain. It does not operate in the terrain. The CxC Matrix 2.0 is not a map. It is an operating system — a living, learning, executing framework that governs every customer interaction across all four domains, at machine speed, with the intelligence of every previous interaction embedded in every subsequent one.

The structural evolution from Matrix 1.0 to Matrix 2.0 is additive rather than disruptive. The fifteen lifecycle stages remain the backbone — they are the most enduring insight of the original Customer Worthy, and they are as relevant in the Customer Sensor Economy as they were in 2010. The six channel categories remain. What the 2.0 adds is the four cognitive-emotional dimensions that transform the Matrix from a planning framework into an execution platform.

The New Slot Taxonomy — From Macro to Quantum

Perhaps the most consequential conceptual advance in the CxC Matrix 2.0 is the expansion of the 'slot' — the unit of customer interaction design — from a single level to a four-level hierarchy that corresponds to the temporal and perceptual granularity of the Customer Sensor Mesh.

FIGURE C.2 — THE CXC MATRIX 2.0 SLOT TAXONOMY: FROM MACRO TO QUANTUM

Slot Class	Time Horizon	Technology	CxC Matrix Application
Macro-Slot	Seconds to Minutes	Responsive web, mobile app, voice assistant, in-store digital display	*Traditional CxC Matrix contact points — email, website visit, customer service call, in-store interaction. The entry-level of instrumented customer experience design.*
Micro-Slot	Milliseconds to Seconds	Computer vision, eye-tracking, bio-metric sensors, click-stream analysis, dwell time measure-ment	*Discrete moments of attention within a macro-slot. The specific product image that generates a 4-second dwell. The pricing element that triggers a micro-expres-sion of surprise. The CTA button color that produces a 12% conversion differential. Measurable, testable, optimizable.*
Nano-Slot	Sub-millisecond	EEG-adjacent wearables, micro-expres-sion AI, galvanic skin response sensors, gait analysis, pupil dilation meas-urement	*Subconscious reactions measurable through biomet-rics. Operates below conscious awareness. Validates or invalidates the emotional resonance of an offer before the customer has consciously processed it. Informs treatment design at the Emotion Layer.*

Quantum-Slot	Pre-conscious, predictive	Predictive AI, digital twin simulation, behavioral pattern recognition, contextual inference engines	*Predictive opportunities identified before the customer is consciously aware of the need. Neil's car acting before Neil knows the bearing is failing. The grocery delivery service bidding before the customer opens the refrigerator. The highest-value, most ethically complex level of Customer Sensor commerce.*

The practical implication of this expanded slot taxonomy is not that every organization needs to instrument all four levels immediately. It is that organizations should understand which level their current capability operates at, and what the competitive consequence is of their competitors operating at a higher level of granularity. A company that designs at the Macro-Slot level is making contact design decisions at the same temporal granularity that direct mail marketing operated at in the 1990s. A company that designs at the Micro-Slot level is operating at the granularity of sophisticated digital marketing circa 2020. A company that designs at the Nano-Slot level is operating at the frontier of what is commercially deployed now. And a company that designs at the Quantum-Slot level is operating in a competitive space that most organizations cannot currently reach.

The CxC Matrix 2.0 provides the architectural language to map current state capability across all four slot levels and to prioritize investment in the transitions that produce the highest CLV impact. As with the original Matrix, the power is not in the framework itself but in the organizational discipline to use it to make investment decisions, measure outcomes, and continuously improve the design of every slot at every level.

The Fifteen Lifecycle Stages — Enhanced for the Customer Sensor Economy

The fifteen consumer lifecycle stages that have been the structural backbone of the CxC Matrix since its inception remain intact in Matrix 2.0 — because they describe something that does not change with technology: the sequence of value exchange events through which a customer's relationship with an organization develops. What changes is the intelligence, speed, and automation with which each stage is executed, and the domains across which each stage now simultaneously occurs.

Stage 1 (Awareness) now includes algorithmic discovery — your product evaluated and surfaced by an AI agent before any human customer has consciously initiated a search. Stage 5 (Negotiation) now often occurs between algorithms at machine speed, with smart contracts executing programmable terms that would have required human negotiators hours to settle. Stage 11 (Use) now incorporates embedded sensor data that monitors product performance, detects degradation before failure, and initiates Stage 12 (Care/Support) interventions automatically — before the customer has experienced a problem, let alone reported one. Stage 15 (Community) now facilitates both human and algorithmic advocacy, with AI agents representing satisfied customers in algorithmic marketplaces where trust scores and review data inform other AI agents' purchasing decisions.

This is not the CxC Matrix as a metaphor for a more connected world. It is the CxC Matrix as a literal operational framework for a world in which the customer journey is being executed by machines at a speed and granularity that human organizations cannot match without systematic, AI-augmented design of every stage and every slot.

V. Two Customer Sensor Stories — The Framework in Human Scale

The most rigorous frameworks succeed or fail at the level of human experience. Before examining the strategic and organizational implications of the Customer Sensor architecture, it is worth inhabiting the framework from the customer's perspective — to understand viscerally what it feels like to be served by an organization that has built it, and what it costs to be served by one that has not.

Story One: Jennifer and the Quantum Menu

It is 2:30 PM on a Tuesday. Jennifer walks into Starbucks. She has opted into their biometric loyalty program — a decision that took fifteen seconds, required a single consent screen, and in the eight months since has saved her an average of $4.20 per visit while reducing her average decision time at the counter from 47 seconds to 12. She is not thinking about any of this as she pushes through the door. She is thinking about the meeting in 25 minutes and whether the report she submitted this morning will land well.

The store's Customer Sensor Mesh recognizes her gait in 0.3 seconds. In the next 0.2 seconds, it has assembled her current context from eleven input streams: time since last caffeine (5.5 hours), typical afternoon preference (70% iced drinks), current weather (overcast, 18°C), stress indicators from her wearable (elevated), meeting in calendar (25 minutes), dietary preferences (oat milk, low sugar), and the store's real-time inventory status for each candidate item. The system runs 87,000+ possible menu combinations through a parallel simulation and generates a seven-item focused selection, ordered by predicted take rate, with the hero position occupied by the Iced Matcha Oat Latte at a 34% predicted take rate.

Jennifer's smart glasses display this menu as an AR overlay in her field of vision as she approaches the counter. The menu updates every 0.5 seconds based on her micro-reactions — where her gaze lingers, the micro-expression when she glances at the Protein Box (slight interest; she hasn't eaten in four hours), the pupillary response when she sees the price of the Lavender Oat Milk Mist (slight hesitation). The system adjusts the Protein Box's position upward and softens the Lavender Mist's pricing prominence. Jennifer sees none of this adjustment. She sees a menu that seems unusually easy to navigate — that somehow contains exactly what she might want without the cognitive overload of the full board.

She orders the Iced Matcha. Decision time: 8 seconds. Order value: $5.50, up 34% from her historical average, because the Protein Box appeared as a suggested add-on and she clicked it. Her satisfaction rating, captured automatically through her wearable's affect detection, registers 87 — seven points above her Starbucks baseline. She will be back Thursday. The Customer Sensor Mesh, which will know she is approaching the store before she rounds the corner, is already preparing her Thursday menu.

The Micro-Moment Value equation that governs this system — MMV = Σ[(Engagement × Context × Intent × Capability) / Friction] — is not abstract mathematics. It is the quantified version of what every great sales associate has always done intuitively: read the customer, match the context, reduce the friction, and deliver exactly what they need in the moment they need it. The Customer Sensor Mesh does it at a scale and speed and consistency that human intuition cannot approach.

Story Two: Omar, Wendy, and the Senior Care Decision

Omar and Wendy are professionals in their late fifties. Omar's mother, Aisha, has reached the point where independent living is no longer safe. It is a decision their family has been approaching for months with a mixture of guilt, love, and exhaustion. On a Friday evening, a Google behavioral targeting algorithm — trained on the search patterns, location visits, and content consumption that have been building in the data record for three months — surfaces a Harmony Care ad at the precise moment when both Omar and Wendy are on the same device, at the same time, having just finished reading a news article about elder care. The algorithm's prediction of receptivity: 78%.

What follows is a five-day journey through all fifteen stages of the CxC lifecycle — compressed and orchestrated by Customer Sensor architecture at every step. On Saturday, a generative AI chatbot delivers a tailored proposal that references the specific balance of medical care and lifestyle enrichment that Omar's earlier online research indicated was his primary decision criterion. The proposal arrives not as a brochure but as a narrative — built from Harmony's care philosophy combined with the emotional texture of what the algorithm knows Omar and Wendy have been searching for. Three competing providers are eliminated during this session — not by Harmony's sales team but by the AI's ability to serve the right information at the right moment of the selection process.

On Sunday, tours at two finalists generate emotion AI signals that are captured by the facility's sensor network and used to personalize the follow-up communications sent Sunday evening. Monday's negotiation is assisted by an AI pricing model that identifies the specific terms — a visiting schedule flexibility clause, not a discount — that the sentiment analysis has flagged as Wendy's primary unstated concern. The contract is signed Tuesday via a portal where an AI agent has already synchronized payment schedules with Omar's financial institution. The entire process, from ad impression to contract signature, has taken five days. The equivalent process ten years earlier took an average of three weeks.

What happens next matters as much as the sale. Aisha moves in and the Customer Sensor Mesh at Harmony does not stop working. It detects a room temperature issue before Aisha notices it and resolves it within 40 minutes. When a medication schedule question surfaces via WhatsApp six weeks later, the AI agent has prepared the nurse with full context before the call connects. At three months, a service review session is informed by IoT analytics that show Aisha is attending art classes at three times the rate of her cohort — a signal that the lifestyle enrichment element of her care plan is performing exceptionally, and that an occupational therapy add-on has a high probability of being well-received. The recommendation is made. It is accepted. Revenue: $2,400. Relationship depth: materially increased.

Six months after move-in, Omar and Wendy post in a senior care forum. The post generates $50,000 in estimated referral value. They join Harmony's advisory board. The Customer Sensor Mesh's prediction of their Stage 15 advocacy probability at the moment of contract signing: 95%. The total economic orchestration across the customer lifecycle — $141,600 in revenue, $2,400 in upsell, $50,000 in referral value, against $1,775 in total contact costs — produces an 80x ROI. Every step of this was designed. Every slot was instrumented. Every outcome was measured.

> ***"These are not edge cases. They are not aspirational scenarios. They are the quantified customer experience that organizations operating the Customer Sensor architecture are delivering today, at varying levels of maturity, across industries from healthcare to hospitality to industrial B2B. The question is not whether your industry will experience this transition. It is how far along the transition your competitors are before you begin."***

VI. Beyond NPS — The Customer Sensor Replaces the Ultimate Question

Fred Reichheld's Net Promoter Score lived a good and consequential life. For two decades, the Ultimate Question — 'How likely are you to recommend us to a friend or colleague?' — gave organizations a single, portable, actionable metric for distilling the complexity of customer satisfaction into a number that boards could track, executives could act on, and employees could understand. NPS was a triumph of diagnostic simplification at a moment when organizations desperately needed it.

Its limitation, which has always been present but has become structurally disqualifying in the Customer Sensor Economy, is temporal. NPS surveys customers after transactions — after the purchase, after the service call, after the renewal decision. It measures the sediment that has settled after the river has moved on. It captures what the customer remembers and feels willing to report, which is systematically different from what actually happened and what actually drove their behavior. It misses the awareness stage, the research stage, the algorithmic evaluation stage that may have happened without human involvement, the micro-slots where the actual decisions were made, the emotional texture of the journey that determined whether the experience felt effortful or effortless.

Most critically, NPS provides no signal from the synthetic domain. It has no mechanism for capturing the experience of the AI agent that evaluated and rejected your offering before any human was involved. It cannot measure the algorithmic trust score that determined whether your product appeared in the AI-generated consideration set. It does not reflect the quality of the machine-speed negotiation that your AI and your customer's AI conducted, or whether the terms they arrived at reflected your organization's best understanding of that customer's value preferences.

The CxC Matrix 2.0, operating with the Customer Sensor Mesh's continuous behavioral measurement, replaces NPS not with another survey instrument but with a behavioral measurement system: the Customer Experience Algorithm (CEA) that the earlier chapters of this edition have described in detail. Where NPS asks customers what they think they might do, the CEA measures what they have done, across all fifteen lifecycle stages, across all four domains, at the granularity of micro-slots and nano-slots, in real time. The organization whose customer intelligence is based on the CEA knows more about its customers' actual experience, from actual behavioral evidence, than any survey-based system can approach.

The behavioral measurement of the Customer Sensor Mesh is not merely more accurate than NPS. It is more actionable. A declining NPS score tells you that something is wrong and that customers are less likely to recommend you. A declining Stage 9 (Acceptance) CEA score, detected in real time by the Cognition Layer's monitoring of product performance sensor data, tells you that a specific product variant is generating installation failures at a rate 23% above baseline, that the affected customers are in a specific geographic region, that the failure mode traces to a component supplied by a specific vendor, and that the Stage 12 contact surge associated with this failure will peak in approximately nine days — giving you nine days to design and execute a proactive intervention before the wave arrives.

That is the difference between a diagnostic instrument and an operating system. NPS is a thermometer. The Customer Sensor Mesh is an immune system.

> **THE MEASUREMENT ARCHITECTURE THAT REPLACES NPS**
>
> The Customer Experience Algorithm (CEA) combines Recency, Frequency, and Monetary value with 30/60/90/180-day propensity windows, behavioral signals from all four domains, and the emotional trajectory data from the Emotion Layer into a continuous, real-time customer health score that operates at the individual level, updates with every behavioral event, and governs slot activation across all 15 lifecycle stages. It does not ask customers what they think. It measures what they do — and predicts what they will do next, with sufficient precision to make the prediction actionable before the behavior occurs.

VII. The Organizational Imperative — Building the Architecture for a World You Cannot Fully Predict

The strategic leaders who will navigate the Customer Sensor Economy most successfully are not those who can predict with precision what the technology landscape will look like in 2035. No one can. They are the leaders who build organizations capable of continuous adaptation — organizations whose customer experience architecture is not a fixed design but a living system that learns, adjusts, and improves as the environment changes around it.

This is a different organizational design challenge than the one that management literature has traditionally addressed. The classic challenge was designing an organization for a known competitive environment. The Customer Sensor challenge is designing an organization for an environment that is being continuously reshaped by AI capability advances, regulatory changes, customer expectation escalation, and competitor behavior — any one of which could render a fixed strategy obsolete before it is fully implemented. The architectural answer to this challenge is not a better strategy. It is a better organizational learning system.

The Five Non-Negotiable Investments

Across all of the complexity of the Customer Sensor Economy — the four domains, the four Mesh layers, the four slot levels, the fifteen lifecycle stages, the nine interaction objectives — there are five investments that are structurally prerequisite for any organization seeking to build the Customer Sensor architecture. They are not the most exciting investments. They are not the ones that generate the most compelling press releases. They are the ones without which every other investment in the Customer Sensor economy produces suboptimal returns.

Investment	What It Enables	Without It	2030 Benchmark
Customer Data Platform (CDP) + Consent Architecture	Real-time unified customer identity across all domains; CEA scoring; Cross-domain behavioral signal integration	Every AI application speaks a different language about the same customer. Domain transitions produce identity fragmentation. Consent failures create regulatory and trust liability.	*Sub-100ms identity resolution across all domains; 100% consent-governed data access; Real-time behavioral event streaming*
AI Orchestration Engine	Slot activation governed by CEA scores; Next-best-action delivery at machine speed; Continuous A/B testing across all active slots	Manual campaign management limits slot optimization to the speed of human decision-making. The competitor whose orchestration engine is running 10,000 simultaneous slot tests is operating in a different competitive reality.	*Full 90-cell Matrix coverage; 15-stage CEA-governed activation; Sub-second slot personalization; Continuous challenger testing in all active slots*

Algorithm Strategy (MCP/API Readiness)	Discoverability by AI purchasing agents; Synthetic domain commercial participation; Machine-readable product and pricing data	Invisible in the synthetic domain. As AI agent commerce grows from a minority to a majority of purchase initiation activity, organizations without algorithm strategy lose access to a growing share of the addressable market.	*Full MCP protocol compliance; Structured data for all product and service offerings; AI agent trust certification; Algorithmic preference rate as a board-reported metric*
Customer Sensor Mesh Instrumentation	Perception, Cognition, Actuation, and Emotion Layer capability; Real-time behavioral signal capture; Domain-spanning customer context	Operating at Macro-Slot level in a Nano-Slot competitive environment. Every interaction is designed for the average customer at the average moment rather than this customer at this moment.	*Multi-domain sensor coverage; Real-time Cognition Layer processing; Emotion Layer treatment calibration; Quantum-Slot predictive capability in at least one high-CLV lifecycle stage*
Digital Twin + Experience Simulation Infrastructure	Customer behavior simulation before deployment; Slot design testing without customer impact; Scenario planning for competitive and regulatory changes	CX investments require live customer exposure to validate. Failures cannot be detected before they cause CLV erosion. Strategy cannot be tested against customer behavior models before board commitment.	*Behavioral digital twins for top-CLV customer segments; Simulation environment for new slot designs; Continuous model calibration from live data; Board-level scenario simulation*

These five investments form a dependency stack. The CDP is the foundation — without it, the AI Orchestration Engine has no coherent customer data to govern. Without the AI Orchestration Engine, Algorithm Strategy cannot deploy. Without Algorithm Strategy, the Synthetic Domain is inaccessible. Without Customer Sensor Mesh Instrumentation, the Perception and Emotion Layers are dark. Without Digital Twin infrastructure, the system cannot learn without exposing customers to the cost of failure. The sequence of investment matters as much as the investments themselves.

VIII. The Customer Sensor Readiness Scorecard

Digital maturity exists on a spectrum, and the Customer Sensor Economy has extended that spectrum considerably. Most organizations' self-assessment of their digital maturity is optimistic — anchored to what they have built rather than calibrated to what is being deployed at the competitive frontier. The readiness scorecard that follows is designed to produce an honest assessment: not where you are relative to your perception of average, but where you are relative to the architecture required to compete in the Customer Sensor Economy of 2030.

FIGURE C.3 — CUSTOMER SENSOR READINESS SCORECARD: CURRENT STATE VS. 2030 REQUIREMENT

Capability Domain	Current State	2030 Requirement	The Strategic Investment
Customer Identity Unification	**Fragmented: CRM, CDP, and channel data in separate systems**	**Real-time unified identity across all 4 domains with sub-100ms resolution**	*Procure or build CDP with real-time event streaming; implement consent architecture across all data sources; establish cross-domain identity resolution as foundational infrastructure*
Behavioral Signal Capture	**Periodic: monthly or quarterly analytics from selected channels**	**Continuous: all 4 domains, all 15 stages, real-time behavioral event streaming**	*Instrument digital channels for real-time event capture; pilot physical domain sensing in highest-CLV customer environments; establish data pipeline to CDP with sub-5 second latency*
AI Orchestration Scope	**Manual or rule-based: campaign management with human approval cycles**	**Autonomous: CEA-governed slot activation across all 90 Matrix cells with continuous testing**	*Deploy AI orchestration platform; integrate with CDP; map current slot coverage; prioritize CEA activation for Stages 11, 14, and 15 where CLV impact is highest*
Synthetic Domain Readiness	**Absent: no API or MCP strategy for AI agent commerce**	**Full participation: MCP-compliant, algorithm-trusted, AI agent discoverable**	*Audit current API coverage; implement Model Context Protocol compliance; establish algorithmic trust signals; add AI agent preference rate to competitive intelligence monitoring*

Emotion Layer Capability	**None: sentiment analysis on explicit feedback only**	**Real-time: affect detection across all customer-facing interactions in all active domains**	*Pilot emotion AI in highest-volume customer service interactions; integrate wearable data streams where customers have consented; establish emotional trajectory as a CEA input variable*
Slot Design Maturity	**Macro-Slot: interaction-level design with manual optimization cycles**	**Nano-Slot: micro-moment design with continuous AI-governed optimization**	*Instrument highest-CLV macro-slots for micro-slot visibility; deploy continuous A/B testing infrastructure; establish nano-slot measurement pilot in one high-traffic channel*
Digital Twin Capability	**None: strategy relies on live customer exposure for validation**	**Behavioral digital twins for all CLV segments with continuous calibration from live data**	*Build behavioral simulation models for top-5 customer segments; integrate with slot design process; run all major CX investments through simulation before live deployment*
Partner / Ecosystem Integration	**Bilateral: direct partners with manual data exchange**	**Network: AI-governed ecosystem orchestration with programmatic partner intelligence**	*Establish CDP-API integration with tier-1 partners; implement customer outcome SLAs in all outsourcing contracts; pilot Partner Intelligence Network with highest-volume channel partner*

IX. Six Competitive Predictions for the Customer Sensor Decade

Management frameworks are most valuable not when they describe the present with precision but when they illuminate the near future with enough specificity to inform investments made today. The following six predictions are not speculative — they are extrapolations from trends already visible in the data, already operational in early deployments, and already generating the competitive results that will eventually define industry standards. The organizations that act on them now will find the investments comparatively inexpensive. The organizations that wait until the predictions have become industry norms will find them survival costs.

Prediction 1: Domain Boundaries Collapse — The Unified Customer Reality

By 2028, leading organizations will no longer distinguish between their digital strategy, their physical strategy, their hybrid strategy, and their synthetic strategy. They will have a single Customer Reality strategy — a unified architecture that serves the customer wherever they are, whatever domain is operative, without visible transition friction. The concept of 'omnichannel' will be retired not because it was wrong but because it implies that channels are separate things being connected. In the Customer Sensor Economy, they are not separate. They are simultaneous aspects of a single customer reality that the organization's architecture either serves coherently or fails to serve at all.

Prediction 2: AI Agents Become Primary Purchase Initiators

The majority of structured commercial purchases — defined as purchases with more than two evaluation criteria, a selection process, and a negotiation step — will be initiated by AI agents rather than human customers by 2032 in B2B and by 2035 in a significant share of high-consideration B2C categories. This is not a prediction about AI replacing human judgment. It is a prediction about AI handling the research, comparison, and initial negotiation phases that consume the majority of purchase time and produce the majority of customer frustration in the current model. Humans will make the final decisions. AI will do the work that precedes them.

Prediction 3: Privacy Becomes the Primary Trust Signal — and a Measurable Asset

As the Customer Sensor Mesh's depth of customer observation expands, the organizations that build transparent, customer-controlled consent architectures will gain measurable competitive advantage over those that treat privacy as a compliance cost. By 2030, AI agent purchasing systems will incorporate privacy trust scores as a selection criterion — preferentially selecting service providers and vendors whose data practices meet verifiable standards over those whose practices are opaque. Samsung versus Apple is already this story in the consumer electronics domain. Every industry will have its version of this competition within five years.

Prediction 4: Human Skills Appreciate as AI Handles Routine Execution

The paradox of the Customer Sensor Economy is that the more AI automates routine customer interactions, the more valuable the distinctly human capabilities become. Empathy, creative problem-solving, emotional intelligence, complex judgment in ambiguous situations — these are the capabilities that the Emotion Layer identifies as necessary and the Actuation Layer cannot supply autonomously. The organizations that invest in these human capabilities alongside their AI infrastructure — that do not treat human development as a cost to be reduced as AI capability scales — will produce customer experiences that AI-only competitors structurally cannot replicate.

Prediction 5: The Customer Sensor Mesh Becomes Regulated Infrastructure

Quantum-Slot capability — the ability to predict and influence customer behavior before conscious awareness — will attract regulatory attention within the current decade. The EU AI Act is the opening chapter of a much longer regulatory conversation about the ethics of predictive customer influence, biometric commercial applications, and AI agent authority over individual financial decisions. Organizations that have built transparent, auditable, customer-controlled Customer Sensor architectures will navigate this regulatory environment as a competitive advantage. Those that have built opaque systems optimized purely for extraction will face retrofit costs — technical, legal, and reputational — that their consent-first competitors will not.

Prediction 6: The Best Story Still Wins — But AI Writes It Faster

The organizing insight of Customer Worthy — that the organization with the best story, delivered to the right customer at the right moment through the right channel, wins — does not change in the Customer Sensor Economy. What changes is who writes the story, how fast it is written, and how precisely it is matched to the individual customer's current context. The AI-powered Treatment Map, continuously generating and testing slot content across all 90 cells of the CxC Matrix 2.0, at the granularity of micro-slots and nano-slots, with the Emotion Layer calibrating tone and empathy coefficient in real time — this is the 'Best Story Wins' capability at industrial scale. The organizations that build it will win. The organizations that treat content generation as a human-only creative function, on an agency-cycle timeline, at campaign-level granularity, will not.

X. The Customer Worthy Imperative — Unchanged, Unstoppable

We opened Customer Worthy in 2010 with a simple and deliberately uncomfortable observation: that the average organization was wasting tens of billions of dollars in customer time annually, while simultaneously leaving hundreds of billions in customer value on the table — because the connection between what companies did internally and what customers experienced externally was systematically unmapped, unmeasured, and therefore unimproved.

The CxC Matrix was the instrument for making that connection visible. Fifteen lifecycle stages crossed with six channel categories to produce 90 cells of customer interaction opportunity — each one a revenue event, a cost event, and a trust event, capable of being designed, measured, and continuously improved. The framework's power was not its complexity. It was its simplicity — the ability to give every person in every department a shared visual language for the customer that made the question 'is this Customer Worthy?' answerable by anyone, about any decision, in any function of the enterprise.

That question has not changed. What has changed is everything around it — the speed at which it must be asked, the domains across which it must be answered, the technology that now executes the answer, and the cost of being wrong. The revenue at risk from poor customer experience has grown from the $99 billion in wasted customer time that originally motivated this work to the $887 billion identified in the most recent National Customer Rage analysis. The revenue available from excellent customer experience — an additional $700 million within three years for companies earning $1 billion annually — has never been more clearly documented or more accessible to organizations willing to build the architecture.

The Customer Sensor Economy does not make Customer Worthy obsolete. It makes it more urgent, more precise, and more consequential than at any previous moment in the framework's history. The organization that has internalized the CxC Matrix — that has built the slot-level design discipline, the enterprise-wide customer orientation, the continuous measurement and improvement infrastructure — has the organizational readiness to add the Customer Sensor Mesh layers without rebuilding from scratch. The organization that has not is facing a two-step problem: build the foundational customer experience architecture that Customer Worthy describes, and simultaneously navigate the Customer Sensor transition that Customer Sensor describes. Both are possible. The sequence matters.

> ***"In the customer sensor economy, there are no neutral interactions. Every contact either builds your future or hastens your decline. The Customer Sensor Mesh does not create this reality — it makes it visible, measurable, and actionable with a precision that earlier generations of customer experience management could not approach. Choose to be Customer Worthy. Choose to build the architecture. Choose to lead."***

The revolution Customer Worthy asked you to start has not waited for organizational readiness. It has been running continuously, accelerating with each new AI capability, each new domain of customer reality, each new layer of the Customer Sensor Mesh that organizations at the frontier have deployed while their competitors were still debating whether the technology was ready.

The technology is ready. The framework is proven. The competitive evidence is documented. The revenue is available. The customers are waiting — in all four domains of their reality, at all four levels of interaction granularity, with AI agents representing their preferences in markets your organization may not yet be equipped to enter.

The only question that remains is the one Customer Worthy has always asked. Is your organization — at every slot, in every stage, across every domain, in every interaction your customers will have with you today and every day — genuinely, measurably, and continuously Customer Worthy?

If the answer is yes: scale what works, relentlessly, and invest the capacity it creates in building what comes next.

If the answer is not yet: start where you are. Build the CDP. Map the Matrix. Design the first slot with the precision this framework demands. Measure the outcome. Improve. Repeat. The compounding advantage of organizations that build this capability continuously is not achievable by those who start it all at once when the competitive pressure becomes undeniable.

The future of customer experience is not a destination. It is a direction of continuous improvement, continuous learning, and continuous commitment to the principle that every customer interaction is an economic event, a relationship event, and a trust event — and that the organization that designs it with that understanding, measures it with that precision, and improves it with that discipline will build the only sustainable competitive advantage that the age of artificial intelligence cannot replicate: the organizational capability to genuinely think like a customer.

THE CUSTOMER SENSOR ACTION AGENDA — WHAT TO DO MONDAY MORNING

1. AUDIT YOUR DOMAIN COVERAGE: Map every customer lifecycle stage against the Four Domains framework. Identify which stages are instrumented in which domains. The stages that are dark — where your organization has no sensor capability, no behavioral signal capture, no AI orchestration — are your first investment priorities.

2. BUILD YOUR CDP FOUNDATION: If your customer data is fragmented across CRM, marketing automation, billing, support, and channel systems, every other investment in this chapter produces suboptimal returns. The CDP is not a technology project. It is the prerequisite for every other strategic initiative in the Customer Sensor architecture.

3. DEVELOP YOUR ALGORITHM STRATEGY: Audit your API ecosystem for machine-readability. Research Model Context Protocol compliance requirements. Begin tracking algorithmic preference rate — how often your offerings are selected by AI agents versus human decision-makers — as a leading indicator of synthetic domain market position.

4. PILOT A NANO-SLOT MEASUREMENT PROGRAM: Identify your highest-CLV, highest-volume customer contact — the interaction that occurs most often with your most valuable customers. Deploy micro-slot instrumentation: eye-tracking, dwell time, micro-expression detection, or whatever biometric measurement is appropriate to the channel. Run a 90-day optimization program against measurable CLV impact.

5. RUN THE CUSTOMER SENSOR MBA: Ask every senior executive to traverse your own CxC Matrix as an anonymous customer — using AI tools to research, evaluate, and critique your organization as a sophisticated customer would. Document every slot failure. Calculate the CLV cost of each. Present the results to the board. Make the Customer Sensor architecture investment decision from evidence, not intuition.

6. ASK THE QUESTION: In every meeting, in every budget decision, in every product launch, in every operational change — ask the question Customer Worthy has always asked: Is this Customer Worthy? In the Customer Sensor Economy, that question now has a quantifiable answer at every stage, in every domain, for every customer segment. Demand the answer. Act on it.

ABOUT THE FRAMEWORK

The CxC Matrix was created by Michael R. Hoffman and first published in Customer Worthy (2010), which has been downloaded more than 500,000 times and distributed to 17,000+ business professionals globally. The CxC Matrix 2.0 and the Customer Sensor framework represent the next generation of the methodology, extending the original 15-stage, 6-channel, 90-cell architecture into the four-domain, four-layer, four-slot-level operating system described in this chapter. Both frameworks are available for organizational deployment through ClientX Consulting.

For additional resources, case studies, and implementation guidance, visit www.customerworthy.com | mrh@clientx.com | 908-542-1134

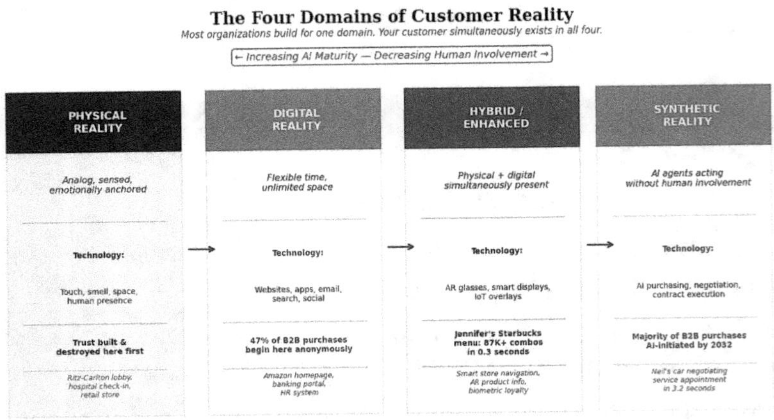

Figure: *The Four Domains of Customer Reality — Most organizations build for one domain. Your customer simultaneously exists in all four.*

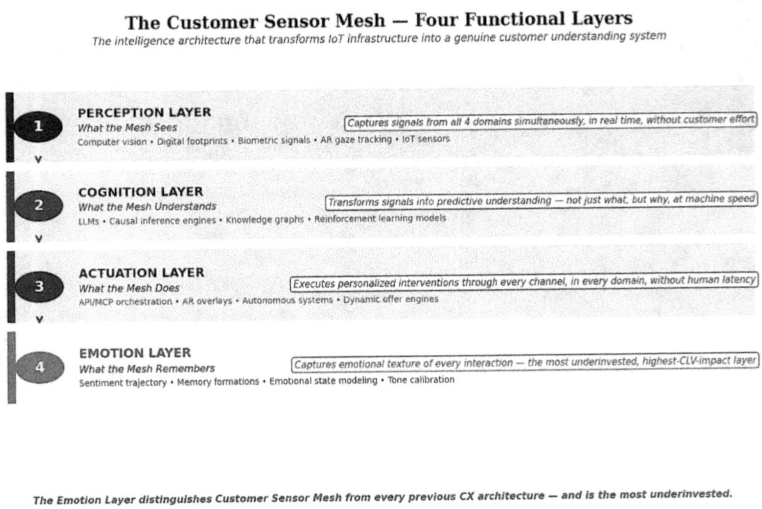

Figure: *The Customer Sensor Mesh — Four functional layers that transform IoT infrastructure into a genuine customer intelligence system.*

Glossary of CxC Matrix Terms and Acronyms

This glossary provides definitions for the key terms, acronyms, and proprietary frameworks referenced throughout Customer Worthy: Total Customer Engineering

3PL (Third-Party Logistics) External fulfillment and distribution partners who manage physical delivery operations within Stage 7 (Logistics) of the CxC Matrix.

Agent-to-Agent Interaction Direct communication between AI agents acting on behalf of different parties, bypassing human involvement at specific transaction points.

AI Agent An autonomous artificial intelligence system that plans, decides, and acts across multi-step tasks on a customer's behalf, including research, negotiation, and transaction execution. *See p.* 15

AI Orchestration The use of artificial intelligence to coordinate, sequence, and optimize customer interactions across all 90 cells of the CxC Matrix in real time. *See p.* 38

Ambient Intelligence IoT sensor ecosystems that continuously read customer context without requiring explicit instruction, enabling proactive service delivery. *See p.* 15

BNPL (Buy Now, Pay Later) A financing option at Stage 10 (Payment) allowing customers to defer or split payments, increasingly integrated into AI-mediated checkout. *See p.* 38

CDP (Customer Data Platform) A unified system that collects, integrates, and activates customer data across all touchpoints and channels for use within the CxC Matrix framework. *See p.* 456

CEA (Customer Experience Algorithm) A proprietary scoring methodology that quantifies the quality of customer experience at each cell of the CxC Matrix, enabling objective measurement and optimization. *See p.* 316

Channel Architecture The vertical axis of the CxC Matrix, comprising six contact channel categories: Digital, One-to-One, Location, Community, Third Party, and Mail/Print. *See p.* 38

CLV (Customer Lifetime Value) The total net profit a company can expect to earn from a customer across their entire relationship, calculated at the contact level within the CxC Matrix. *See p.* 180

CLVE (Customer Lifetime Value Enhancement) The incremental increase in CLV achieved through deliberate optimization of individual CxC Matrix cells and contact sequences. *See p.* 180

Community (Stage 15) The final lifecycle stage where loyal customers become active advocates, generating peer-to-peer influence that compounds brand reputation. *See p.* 38

Connected Customer Experience An integrated, cross-platform customer journey where products, services, and systems coordinate seamlessly across the Four Domains of Customer Reality. *See p.* 15

Contact Any interaction between a customer and an organization at a specific cell of the CxC Matrix. Each contact is simultaneously a moment of truth, an economic event, and a competitive decision point. *See p.* 38

Contact-Level P&L A financial accounting method that assigns profit and loss to every individual customer interaction, enabling precise ROI measurement at the CxC Matrix cell level. *See p.* 180

CRM (Customer Relationship Management) Software systems that manage customer data, interactions, and relationship history, serving as a foundational data source for CxC Matrix operations. *See p.* 456

Cross-Organizational Orchestration The coordination of customer experience across multiple independent organizations to deliver seamless connected journeys. *See p.* 15

Customer by Contact Matrix See CxC Matrix. The full name of the framework. *See p.* 38

Customer Rage Extreme customer dissatisfaction resulting from accumulated negative experiences, measured at $887 billion in revenue at risk (National Customer Rage Survey). *See p.* 6

Customer Sensor Economy The emerging economic paradigm where customers exist across four simultaneous domains of reality and every interaction generates continuous data for real-time experience optimization. *See p.* 12

Customer Sensor Mesh A four-layer intelligence architecture (Sensory, Intelligence, Orchestration, Experience) that transforms IoT infrastructure into a customer intelligence system. *See p.* 546

Customer Sensor Readiness Scorecard A diagnostic tool assessing organizational preparedness across six dimensions: data infrastructure, AI capability, cross-functional integration, consent architecture, sensor maturity, and competitive positioning. *See p.* 546

Customer Worthy The standard by which every customer interaction should be evaluated: Is this interaction worthy of the customer's time, trust, and continued relationship? *See p.* 15

Customer Yield The measurable value generated by a department's customer interactions, calculated per CxC Matrix cell. *See p.* 456

CVI (Customer Value Index) A composite metric aggregating contact-level value across all 90 cells of the CxC Matrix. *See p.* 180

CX (Customer Experience) The totality of a customer's perceptions, interactions, and emotional responses across their entire lifecycle with an organization. *See p.* 38

CxC Matrix Customer by Contact Matrix. A structured 90-cell grid mapping 15 customer lifecycle stages against 6 contact channel categories. *See p.* 38

CxC Matrix 2.0 The evolved version incorporating AI orchestration, the Four Domains of Customer Reality, time-slot architecture, and dynamic sensor-fed optimization. *See p.* 38

Defection Risk The probability that a customer will abandon the relationship at a specific lifecycle stage, rated LOW to CRITICAL within the CxC Matrix. *See p.* 38

Digital Domain One of the Four Domains of Customer Reality, encompassing all screen-based, app-based, and web-based interactions. *See p.* 12

Domain (Customer Reality) One of four simultaneous contexts in which customers exist: Physical, Digital, Hybrid, and Synthetic. *See p.* 12

Ecosystem Loyalty Customer retention driven by the compounding utility of interconnected products and services, where switching costs are functional rather than contractual. *See p.* 15

ESG (Environmental, Social, and Governance) Sustainability and ethical frameworks relevant to Stage 14 (Disposal) and full lifecycle design. *See p.* 38

Four Domains of Customer Reality The framework describing how customers simultaneously exist in Physical, Digital, Hybrid, and Synthetic realities. *See p.* 12

Friction-Positive Confirmation A deliberate pause at high-stakes interaction points to protect customer trust, particularly for irreversible actions. *See p.* 15

Hybrid Domain One of the Four Domains where physical and digital experiences merge seamlessly. *See p.* 12

Integration Depth A leading indicator of CX architecture health, measured by the proportion of customers using connected features. *See p.* 15

IoT (Internet of Things) The network of physical devices embedded with sensors enabling ambient intelligence and continuous data generation. *See p.* 15

Irreversibility Problem The design challenge of ensuring AI-automated actions with permanent consequences operate at higher consent thresholds. *See p.* 15

KPI (Key Performance Indicator) Quantifiable metrics used to evaluate performance at each lifecycle stage and cell. *See p.* 180

Lifecycle Stage One of 15 sequential phases in the CxC Matrix, from Awareness (S1) through Community (S15). *See p.* 38

Machine Readability The degree to which product data, pricing, and knowledge bases are structured for evaluation by AI agents. *See p.* 15

Matter Standard A cross-industry IoT interoperability protocol backed by Apple, Google, Amazon, and Samsung. *See p.* 15

MCP (Model Context Protocol) An open standard allowing AI models to connect to external tools, databases, and APIs, serving as connective tissue for AI-powered CxC Matrix operations. *See p.* 15

Micro-Contact A brief, often automated customer interaction that accumulates into the customer's total brand experience. *See p.* 15

Moment of Truth Any customer interaction where brand perception is updated. Every CxC Matrix cell represents a potential moment of truth. *See p.* 38

Neural Mesh Commerce The fully sensor-integrated commercial ecosystem where customer needs are anticipated and fulfilled through interconnected AI and IoT systems. *See p.* 546

Nine Objectives The nine simultaneous goals every customer contact should pursue, ensuring maximum value creation from each interaction. *See p.* 265

NPS (Net Promoter Score) A customer loyalty metric which the Customer Sensor framework positions as insufficient compared to behavioral measurements. *See p.* 546

Onboarding The process at Stage 9 (Acceptance) where proper design yields up to 55% improvement in retention. *See p.* 38

Partner Ecosystem Momentum A leading indicator measured by the number and quality of external partners building on your APIs. *See p.* 15

Physical Domain One of the Four Domains encompassing face-to-face, in-store, and tangible product interactions. *See p.* 12

Platform Economics The shift from selling individual products to building interconnected ecosystems where value compounds. *See p.* 265

Proactive Resolution Service design that identifies and resolves issues before the customer is aware of them. *See p.* 456

Quantum Customer A metaphor for the modern customer who simultaneously exists across multiple domains of reality. *See p.* 12

ROI (Return on Investment) Financial return calculated at the contact level within the CxC Matrix. *See p.* 180

S1-S15 Shorthand for the 15 lifecycle stages: S1 Awareness, S2 Information, S3 Identification, S4 Selection, S5 Negotiation, S6 Contract, S7 Logistics, S8 Delivery, S9 Acceptance, S10 Payment, S11 Use, S12 Care/Support, S13 Repair, S14 Disposal, S15 Community. *See p.* 38

Self-Healing Products Products with IoT sensors and AI diagnostics that detect and resolve issues autonomously. *See p.* 38

Slot Architecture The time-based subdivision of CxC Matrix cells into discrete interaction windows. *See p.* 133

Switching Cost The total cost a customer incurs when changing providers. Ecosystem-based switching costs are the most durable competitive moat. *See p.* 15

Synthetic Domain One of the Four Domains where AI agents represent customers in transactions without direct human involvement. *See p.* 12

Treatment Map A proprietary tool prescribing specific interventions for each CxC Matrix cell based on performance and priority. *See p.* 316

Trust Infrastructure Organizational systems treating security and transparency as customer experience commitments. *See p.* 15

UX (User Experience) Design discipline focused on customer interactions with digital products, a subset of CX. *See p.* 38

Win-Rate Lever The strategic action at each lifecycle stage that most effectively increases customer progression probability. *See p.* 38

Index

Key topics, frameworks, and concepts referenced in this book. Page numbers update automatically when fields are refreshed (Ctrl+A, F9 in Word).

A

B

C

D

E

F

G–H

I

J-K

L

M

N

O-P

Q-R

S

T

U-W

About the Publisher

Customer Worthy Publishing

A division of ClientxClient

Customer Worthy Publishing is dedicated to advancing the science and practice of customer experience management. Founded by Michael R. Hoffman, author of the original Customer Worthy and creator of the CxC Matrix framework, Customer Worthy Publishing produces authoritative works on customer strategy, experience architecture, and the intersection of artificial intelligence with commercial relationships.

www.customerworthy.com

mrh@CustomerWorthy.com | 908-542-1134

Customer Worthy: Total Customer Engineering

ISBN 979-8-9952226-3-7 (Paperback)

ISBN 979-8-9952226-2-0 (eBook)

ISBN 979-8-9952226-2-0 (Hardcover)

Library of Congress Control Number: 2026XXXXXX

Printed in the United States of America

10 9 8 7 6 5 4 3 2 1

Cover design by Customer Worthy Publishing. Interior design and typesetting by Customer Worthy Publishing. All figures and diagrams are proprietary to Michael R. Hoffman and Customer Worthy unless otherwise noted.

www.ingramcontent.com/pod-product-compliance
Lightning Source LLC
LaVergne TN
LVHW052209200926
848481LV00001B/60

* 9 7 9 8 9 9 5 2 2 2 6 3 7 *